AMERICAN TOMBOYS,

1850–1915

D1602811

A VOLUME IN THE SERIES
Childhoods: Interdisciplinary Perspectives on Children and Youth

Edited by

KAREN SÁNCHEZ-EPPLER
RACHEL CONRAD
LAURA L. LOVETT
ALICE HEARST

AMERICAN TOMBOYS, 1850–1915

Renée M. Sentilles

University of Massachusetts Press
Amherst and Boston

ISBN 978-1-62534-320-8 (paper); 319-2 (hardcover)

Designed by Sally Nichols
Set in Adobe Garamond Pro
Printed and bound by Maple Press, Inc.

Cover design by Sally Nichols
Cover art by John George Brown, *Three Girls on a Swing*, 1868. Courtesy The Athenaeum.

Library of Congress Cataloging-in-Publication Data

Names: Sentilles, Renée M., author.
Title: American tomboys : 1850–1915 / Renée M. Sentilles.
Description: Amherst & Boston : University of Massachusetts Press, [2018] |
Includes bibliographical references and index.
Identifiers: LCCN 2017037665 | ISBN 9781625343208 (pbk.) | ISBN 9781625343192
(hardcover)
Subjects: LCSH: Tomboys—United States—History—19th century. |
Tomboys—United States—History—20th century.
Classification: LCC HQ798 .S4444 2018 | DDC 305.23082/0973—dc23
LC record available at https://lccn.loc.gov/2017037665

British Library Cataloguing-in-Publication Data
A catalog record for this book is available from the British Library.

For Isaac Sentilles Rosenberg
And Claire, Francie, and George Sentilles

Contents

Preface

I grew up in books. Technically speaking, I was walking around and growing up in central Missouri in the 1970s and '80s, when women's liberation and then its backlash were reshaping the cultural landscape. But I was a bookworm, romantic by nature, and tacitly recognized as "not gifted" in sports. So I read. A lot. I learned my clues to being a girl less through current entertainment than by growing up alongside Laura Ingalls, Caddie Woodlawn, Jo March, Scout Finch, Meg Murry, and Katie John.[1] My girl culture spanned a century. All of these awkward, smart, oddball girls with tempers and ambitious self-reliance expressed the weight of not exhibiting the femininity expected by society. Most of them had no known label, but four of them did: Laura Ingalls, Caddie Woodlawn, Scout Finch, and Jo March were clearly tomboys. I needed a self-definition. I decided to go with that one. In the process of writing this book, I have learned that I was not alone in this decision.

"Tomboy" worked for me, internally, because it confirmed my sense of being at odds with girl identity: I did not see myself as a "real" girl. Also, torn blue jeans and raggedy t-shirts (actually quite fashionable in the hippie culture of the 1970s) gave me confidence. In asserting my disdain for femininity, I became powerful. Running along the paths in the woods surrounding our house, swinging on life-threatening vines, reveling in my swagger, I was joy itself. In my head I called myself a tomboy—not because I wanted to be a boy, but because I wanted to be that girl who gets called a tomboy: strong, fearless, undaunted.

Years later my father confirmed my fears: "You? A tomboy? You were never a tomboy. You were too feminine."

I knew what he meant: my outside did not match my inside. Much
to my annoyance, I looked dainty even covered in mud and pond slime.
I was a good fisherman, but was too tenderhearted to keep the fish. My
lack of coordination was a mystery to my family of athletes. But I wore
pants, had lots of male friends, climbed to the top of sky-scraping trees,
was daring, determined, and fiercely independent—didn't that put me in
tomboy territory?

"No. Now your Nan Nan," he added, speaking of his aunt, "she was
a tomboy." Nan Nan's overt female masculinity, to use gender scholar
Judith/Jack Halberstam's term, identified her as a tomboy no matter how
she dressed. She came as close to being a man as a woman could, given her
time and place. She was born butch, as far as I can tell, and when she and
her sisters referred to her as the "man of the family" they meant it in the
most straightforward way: she played that role. After their father died one
Christmas morning, seven-year-old Nan Nan took on the authority to run
interference with the outside world on behalf of the rest of them. Because
of her they were not a family without a male; they had Nan Nan.

As a girl growing up along a rural Louisiana bayou in a devout Catholic
family, Nan Nan did not have much scope for exploring definitions of her
sexuality—if she let herself even contemplate having a sexuality. No one in
the family seems to have given a second thought to the fact that, although
her friends were boys, she had zero interest in boys as romantic partners
and openly dismissed marriage as a possibility. Indeed, she desperately
wanted to become a Catholic sister and pursue a life of scholarship and
devotion, but would not abandon her mother.

So, given my father's confident assertion: Is "tomboy" often seen as
simply a youthful term for a girl who is butch? Who takes pride her in
masculine role? Within the late twentieth and early twenty-first centuries,
butch affect is reflexively interpreted as a sign of lesbian identity, but has it
long been suggestive of attraction to other girls? Is it possible to uncouple
gender and sexuality in this culture?

My nieces once thought so, but then, sexuality was not yet on their
radar. "I'm a girl-girl," five-year-old Claire explained, before pointing to
her three-year-old sister: "Francie's a boy-girl." Francie, dressed as Spi-
derman, nodded happily. "Have you ever heard of the term 'tomboy'?"
I asked. No, and Claire was cheerfully emphatic that tomboy made no
sense at all compared to her rational nomenclature: "A boy-girl is a girl

who acts like a boy, and a girl-girl acts like a girl. Francie likes boy things like superheroes, and I like pretty things." They chose these terms not out of confusion about their bodies or as a reaction to pressure from society, but rather because of their own tastes. And they took pride in in finding terms to self-identify in ways that they both saw to be true.

And in fact, what my nieces suggested was also true in the late nineteenth century: onlookers did not instinctively move from gender to sexual identity based on affect. Tomboys were not envisioned as indicative of sexuality at all—indeed, they were consistently described in short stories, novels, articles, songs, and poetry as intrinsically absent of sexual self-awareness. Tomboyism was not tied to sexual categories until well into the twentieth century. Within a century that coupling, too, has broken down as the process of defining and redefining sexuality and gender in a postmodern world has led to a bewildering (and liberating) array of categories.

My book has taken over a decade to produce, and now Claire and Francie are young women enacting a mixture of gender signifiers, seemingly wed to none of them. They excel at sports and math, devour novels, and move easily from athletic wear to cocktail dresses. They want to be doctors. And mothers. "Tomboy" is more a marketing style than an identity in their world: tomboy looks, tomboy jeans, tomboy swagger.

After I give talks about my project in the United States, or describe it over a friendly academic cocktail, I am often inundated with colorful stories of marvelous grandmothers, daughters, aunts, great-aunts, and nieces who were or are the "family tomboy." They each come with a series of stories, repeated with relish: She rode her horse to the library! She wore pants to a formal dance! She beat all the boys in basketball! I hear all sorts of funny, interesting stories about girls or women who did things that other girls and women "just didn't do in those days." The tellers are from a variety of backgrounds: Asian, African American, elderly, Jewish, rural, blue-collar, inner-city—every shape and size and color of girls and women.

Now that transgender issues have become a common topic in popular culture, many of the conversations contain a not-so-subtle subtext if the tomboy in question is approaching puberty. The person might finally ask, "Will she stay like that?" Sometimes they will ask about connections between tomboys and same-sex attraction. But if speaking of the antics of a tomboy now long past, the tone tends to be only of delight. Wasn't she wonderful? Wasn't she different?

Our culture is hard on those who are different, and yet as far as I can tell everyone is convinced that he or she is different. Teenagers often express the conviction that they are "flawed" or "out of sync" in terms of gender performance. "Tomboy" gives girls a name to apply to the feeling of being a misfit. Tomboys are easily signified yet hard to define, which is why one finds authors from the mid-nineteenth century to the present listing characteristics that indicate a girl is a tomboy. The ambiguity of what defines a tomboy is why the term is used more than ever, despite articles since the 1890s claiming that progressive politics have rendered it obsolete. The ambiguity of the word allows misfit identity to be explained as gender rebellion, allowing people to use it in a variety of ways—to indicate queer identity, to describe an aunt who took on the male family role, for little girls explaining playtime preferences, or to explain an innate resistance to imperatives of convention. And at the same time, "tomboy" remains limiting, because employing the description suggests that all of these behaviors and convictions are stolen from the box labeled "boy."

The following exploration of the emergence of the tomboy in American culture is without doubt the product of my own subjectivities. I came into this project wondering how girls saw themselves represented in the world of print, and how they used print culture to reshape their own girl culture. I write about tomboys not because I personally identify with them as athletes, lesbians, or gender warriors, but because the tomboy became the cultural figure through which girls could celebrate their sense of feeling different, or out of sync with the culture—even as the culture itself was supposedly progressing to meet them halfway.

I am also a product of white, middle-class, heteronormative culture, and came to the project believing that writers assumed tomboys were white, just as they assumed "girl" meant white, out of the hegemonic blindness that continues to dominate into the twenty-first century. But it did not take much exploration of the print culture of the period between the Civil War and World War I to realize that the racial dynamics of tomboy imagery were as important as the gender play. I did not expect that, because "tomboy" is no longer a racially defined term. But "tomboy" meant white for the first few decades when it came into popular usage. I began to see it as not so much a tool of liberation, but a sneaky, conniving term that suggested social inequities were being revised when, in terms of race and ethnicity, they were being strengthened. It was gender freedom allowed by a show of Anglo-Saxon solidarity—not because there was an explicit conspiracy, but because the characteristics of the tomboy that made her worth celebrating were unobtainable for girls outside of the dominant category. Indeed, acting like a tomboy was about the last thing a black girl seeking to improve her life would want to do. For urban immigrant girls and women of color, the class dimensions of their struggle put a premium on public behavior, equating Victorian manners with self-respect and racial advance.[2]

Coming to understand why, when, and how the term became popular has allowed me to see the turn of the twentieth century not as a period simply including dramatic, racially motivated violations of human rights, such as lynching, but as one completely saturated in fears about the weakening of white dominance. White and male were implicitly synonymous with human, and whiteness was peddled through even the most innocuous sources, including didactic children's literature, child-rearing guides, and even beloved figures of feminist resistance. This is what we mean when we speak of "white privilege"—not that whiteness means that all white people are fortunate, wealthy, and free, but that whiteness itself is a privilege made invisible by a discourse that erases all others' existence except as a foil.

Understanding how, why, and when the tomboy went from a negative label to something admirable is central to understanding how gender functioned for girls in this period of dramatic change in adult female status.

Acknowledgments

I want to thank the many interlocking villages of people that helped to raise this text. Their support is what got me through.

Having taken fourteen years to research and write, this book has benefited from the constructive criticism and unshakable support of five editors. I am grateful to Sian Hunter, with whom I originally worked, whose support and interest sustained me through some truly difficult early years of this process. After Hunter left University of North Carolina Press, I elected to work with Clark Dougan of University of Massachusetts Press, and it was his insistence that I stop revising and send him my dreadful first draft that finally got the ball rolling. Of course, I still took too long, and Clark retired to enjoy grandparenthood, which has led to me working with the lovely Mary Dougherty, whose support and enthusiasm have brought this book to its final iteration. Laura Portwood-Stacer, a consulting editor, also provided significant insight on how to reorganize chapters and strengthen frameworks. And, finally, Mary Bellino took the final draft apart line by line and note by note, catching a shameful number of mistakes and oversights. It would be a much weaker (or nonexistent!) text without the efforts of these five generous people.

Every day I recognize my great fortune to be part of the community that makes up the Department of History at Case Western Reserve University. I am thankful to be the colleague of people whose exceptional scholarship is matched by their humanity, to support them and be supported by them. That said, several colleagues gave generously of their time to read chapter drafts and grant applications, and to counsel me through rough patches: Gillian Weiss, Jonathan Sadowsky, Dan A. Cohen, Peter Shulman,

xvi   A C K N O W L E D G M E N T S

Ken Ledford, and Alan J. Rocke, in particular. And then there are the superlative office administrators who helped in myriad ways over the years, particularly Bess Weiss, Emily Sparks, and Kalli Vimr. William Claspy, the librarian for the History Department, was an invaluable ally in the endless search for materials.

Beyond my department at CWRU, I want to thank sociologist Susan Hinze, bioethicist/anthropologist Eileen Anderson-Fye, and my beloved cohabitants of "Writing House," anthropologist Vanessa Hildebrand and musician Robert Walters. My sanity could not have survived the writing of this book without these four people. Fellow author Eliza Cabana helped at the beginning with brainstorming sessions over coffee, and Susan Friemark of the Flora Stone Mather Center for Women coached me through the earliest stage. Lyz Bly played a critical role in laying down that first terrible draft by listening, pitching ideas, and reading materials. And then Ann Warren gave me the tough love I needed by taking apart that first draft while somehow convincing me that I was nevertheless on track.

I am grateful to several extraordinary scholars outside of the Cleveland community who gave generously of their time and wisdom. Joy Kasson and Faye Dudden never once wavered in their faith and support. Helen Horowitz gave detailed, constructive criticism when I needed it most. Laura Lovett, Corinne T. Fields, Allison Miller, Barbara Sicherman, Emily Mieras, Michael Kimmel, and Einav Rabinovitch-Fox gave feedback that surely strengthened the resulting text.

Robert A. Gross gets a special mention not only for serving as my mentor for over twenty years now, but also for steering me into this project in the first place. One day on a walk to lunch from the American Antiquarian Society, I was waxing on about a new project on girlhood when Bob, in his typical way of cutting to the heart of things, asked, "When did it become okay for a girl to behave like a boy?" I erroneously thought that would be an easy question to answer! I could not be more grateful for his friendship.

I feel privileged to work with students who consistently teach me as much as I teach them. I have to single out the amazing Laura Ansley, whose undergraduate work at CWRU shows up in the third chapter of this book. Laura also traveled as my research assistant and in the process became a dear friend. I also want to thank Beth Salem and Katie Callahan, who contributed significantly to the book through archival research and their own sparkling ways of thinking. In the midst of a crushing semester, Meghan

Schill and Sherri Bolcevic made time to search for the illustrations for this book. Their joy in the goofiness of historical pop culture was wonderfully contagious. And then there have been my beleaguered research assistants over the years, charged with typing up and organizing endless notes: Cory Hazlett, Katie Schaub, Eric Miller, Michael Metsner, and Daniel Subwick. I constantly want to apologize and thank them at the same time.

I am grateful for fellowships from the American Antiquarian Society, the New England Regional Fellowship Consortium, and the Sallie Bingham Collection at Duke University. The Flora Stone Mather Center for Women and the History Associates at Case have provided me with ample opportunities to speak, and two fellowships from the alums of Flora Stone Mather College gave me writing time and flexibility when I needed it most.

My family has expressed infinite patience and support. And by family, I mean my divorced family of Daniel Rosenberg and our son, Isaac, and also my birth family. Dan has been supportive every step of the way with this project, always respecting the work I needed to do and helping me find the time in our busy co-parenting schedules. I cannot imagine having done it without him. My mother, Claire Zeringue Tassin, who is ever my rock, cheered me on even when she really just wanted it to be done so I could "have a life." My father—the person whom I think of as opening the world for me—began all of this long ago when he gave me the *Little House* books for my ninth birthday. My beloved older brother, Shawn, was enormously important in shaping my early understandings of gender—or rather allowing me to assume that the patriarchal attitude of our parents' world would not be our own. We both thought the other was capable of anything and completely hilarious. I could not be more fortunate in the family that I have gained with my sister-in-law, Katie, and her parents, George and Ann Cowan, who express unstinting belief and interest in my work. I am incredibly grateful for my in-laws, Steve and Sue Maynard. Sue, historian for Canterbury Shaker Village in New Hampshire, lead me to important sources and talked me through trouble spots.

I want to also thank the people who sustained me in many other ways through the difficulties of working full-time, raising a child, and toiling over a book every single day for far too long: Eran Shiloh, Susan Foster Garton, Susan Berman, Elisabetta Superchi, Hope Schultz (and the women of Pilates), the faculty parent group at Case Western Reserve University, and my ever-supportive and inspiring Mount Holyoke College friends from classes '85–'89. I am also grateful to Jim Raden for bringing fun back into my life in the midst of all the deadlines. It takes multiple levels and kinds of support to write a historical monograph in the teaspoons of spare time left over from a demanding professional and domestic life.

I am grateful for the children who changed my perspective on the past: my nieces Claire and Francie, nephew, George, and son, Isaac. We were still using film cameras when Shawn and Katie made me an aunt of girls, and Katie began sending photographs every few months. I could not possibly throw any one of them away, and began taping them to the walls when there was no more room on the desk. Their fearlessly open faces changed the questions that I brought to women's history and became the reason for this book.

Finally, I want to thank Isaac, the heart of my heart, and my fiercest champion. I am as happy as he is to send this little book into the world, so that we may embark on new adventures.

AMERICAN
TOMBOYS,
1850–1915

Introduction

In May 1911, New Yorkers reading the *Daily People* found a short paragraph headed "Long Live the Tomboy," extolling the virtues of a "tom-boy period" and summarizing what had become almost a mantra by that point: a true tomboy is a natural girl.

> Do not teach our young girls that they must not pass through a tom-boy period. There is a time in which the clean boy and girl live and enjoy in the manner and after the nature of sexless animals. During the period in Nature's own way, there come to the fore, principles that will be utilized to advantage at a later date when more clearly understood.[1]

The tomboy by this reckoning embodies an Edenic period when gender does not exist because sexual knowledge is absent. At the appropriate time, the tomboy's innocent exuberance will lead her into a better kind of womanhood, without the artificial notions created by genteel and fashionable girlhood. The reference to sexlessness was critical (even though one would be hard pressed to actually find a "sexless animal"), because it stressed that the tomboy's antics had nothing to do with usurping male roles or agitating to leave the domestic space. Tomboys—girls who behave like boys—were simply full of youthful joy and therefore had no connection with the meddlesome women activists of temperance, suffrage, and dress reform. Emerging in northeastern print culture, tomboys had become an essential means of articulating a rebellious, fun, and feisty new girlhood. The term sanctioned girls behaving like boys while still separating them by gender, granting girls freedom to temporarily own a boyish identity while denying that same freedom to girlish boys.

This book explores how the tomboy emerged from popular culture of the Civil War period to become the archetypal American girl by the end of the Progressive Era—which is to say, to also become representative of American mythologies in a nationalistic era shaped by white supremacy. Therefore it is as much about the culture that created the tomboy as it is about the figure herself. I argue that a boy-girl allowed Americans to envision a way for white girls to remain tethered to domesticity while also embracing the greater public presence allowed modern women, soon identified as the "New Woman." The tomboy also served to signify a girlhood rooted in white, middle-class conventions of gender and sexuality, making it impossible for many other girls to claim. Thus, although the tomboy was widely understood to embody female liberation, she also rendered her freedoms as white privilege.

In the mid-nineteenth-century United States, "tomboy" became the common term for "a girl who behaves like a boy."[2] The figure became ubiquitous with the advent of the juvenile fiction market, with tomboy heroines offering readers imaginative space in which to enjoy the freedom, adventure, independence, and physical mobility accorded to their male peers. She became all-American through her prominence in print culture. In response to changes in economics and education at the end of the century, middle-class young women began to entertain public ambitions, and the adolescent tomboy became popular as a prescriptive as well as a heroine. Thus, although marketed and largely regarded as a wholly "American" character, the tomboy figure was a product of white, middle-class, northeastern culture to which girls outside of that demographic could aspire but rarely reach. Prominent women began to reminisce about the importance of their tomboy girlhoods, and (slowly) girls began to identify with (rather than bristle at) the term. This book closes with the ending of that era, when increased social attention to sexuality along with the explosion of consumer culture—particularly the output of motion pictures and magazines targeted at youth—took the tomboy in multiple directions and changed her symbolic role in complex ways that are already being explored by scholars such as Jack/Judith Halberstam, Michelle Ann Abate, Allison Miller, and Kristen Proehl.

I depart from this other scholarship on tomboys in particular ways: the tomboy is my subject but also the vehicle I use to explore the culture that shaped her. Unlike most other tomboy studies that are based on fictional texts, I also use newspaper and personal sources, such as letters, diaries, and memoirs, to consider how the literary tomboy connected with the tomboys of prescription, experience, and memory. And while I am interested in how the culture chooses to signify the tomboy, whether by whistling (Civil War era), bicycling (Progressive), or dressing like a guy (present), I focus less on those details than on her cultural service as a figure of ambiguity and transition. Again and again, my research suggests that "tomboy" serves as a category for girls who do not yet have an operating category. This is also why the term, though called outdated since the 1890s, continues to gain usage up to the present day.[3]

Given my approach, it is not surprising that my work draws far less on that of other tomboy scholars than on work in fields such as girl history, masculinity, eugenics, education, and print culture, which have expanded in significant and exciting ways since the late 1990s. Nor would this study be possible without the digitizing of newspapers and magazines by institutions such as the American Antiquarian Society. If tomboys have not been studied in quite the way I undertake here, that has a lot to do with changes in research technology as well as path-breaking work by creative scholars.

I begin with the Civil War era because that is when "tomboy," a very old term, suddenly gained a new and distinctly American meaning. Given the instability of race, class, and gender during this period, the timing of the tomboy's emergence is entirely fitting. In many places, women were running the economy and fighting in the war, some as soldiers, business owners, or planters, and others as pioneers in nursing, office work, and fundraising. These were also the years when secondary public schooling began to spread, which in turn sparked new meanings of girlhood and boyhood (shaped by adults), as well as girl culture and boy culture (shaped by youth themselves). Finally, this is the age in which adult women agitated for full rights as citizens, and experimented with not only new ways to participate in public life but also how to raise daughters with greater awareness of themselves as agents of culture.

After the war and Reconstruction, tomboys became ubiquitous across American culture as a new type of girl. Some references were scathing, but more often authors now held up tomboys as ideals of health and girlish spunk. This was the age of industrialization and urbanization, as more Americans began living in cities for the first time in the nation's history. Immigrants came in droves for low-wage jobs, changing the composition of the citizenry both east and west in ways that alarmed nativist whites. Fears of being overtaken by Chinese, Jews, and Italians, among many other groups, combined with evolutionary theories to create pro-white concepts such as Social Darwinism. Anglo-American girls gained new importance as the mothers of tomorrow, and the tomboy was touted as the best way to grow women strong and self-reliant enough to further develop the race.

Meanwhile, just as the Native American nations were taking their last stands against white invaders (and losing), African Americans in the South were being returned to a different version of slavery and oppression through Jim Crow laws, convict-lease programs, and sharecropping. The black middle class in turn fought valiantly for racial uplift by claiming Victorian mores, just as the Victorians were going out of fashion among middle-class whites.[4] Woman suffrage became a major campaign not only for women to get the vote, but for white women to create a bulwark against perceived usurpation of power by immigrants and people of color—groups the same activists had previously championed. Americans held forth the New Woman, who was truly just a slightly older tomboy, as the new ideal. With a new girlhood shaped by the popular press and youth organizing, behaviors that had formerly marked a girl as a tomboy slowly became the hallmarks of the all-American girl. So the tomboy changed again, this time appearing in newspapers as an athlete, a starlet, or a debutante—in other words, as a young adult no longer resisting maturity so much as reshaping it. Or the tomboy was a preadolescent girl but akin to the tomboy of former times, tearing her frocks and instigating pranks.

A few important (and surprising) details need clarifying at the beginning of this study. "Girl" was also changing definition in this period. Although young females have always existed, and the term "girl" had long been used for servants and adult women of color as well as prepubescent white girls, it gained a significantly different meaning in this period. In print culture, "girl" meant an Anglo-Saxon young female growing up in a middle-class home. This late nineteenth-century version of the girl was often indicated with the modifiers "new" or "modern," much the way the term "new woman" came into vogue beginning in the 1880s. Along with the new articulation of girl came "girlhood": a protected period of youth that extended all the way into marriage or a girl's mid-twenties. And the tomboy came into being as a subset of these two new concepts.

Of course, "white" and "middle-class" were also going through significant changes; whiteness was in the midst of being stretched to include European Americans previously excluded, such as the Irish.[5] The middle class, a significant but still somewhat small social class that had emerged with industrialism in northeastern cities and quickly took control of print culture, now expanded exponentially as industrialism and urbanization became major engines of change in the second half of the nineteenth century. The people who called themselves middle-class in 1890 were far more heterogeneous than those of the 1830s. Many of them were more accurately of what LaKisha Simmons calls the "striving class": "people who attempted to reach middle-class status, not necessarily through higher incomes and 'better' jobs but through the adoption of a specific set of mores."[6] From the beginning, the female tomboy served as a device of modern or "new" girlhood, helping young females (and their parents) transition into a world of opportunities that were changing how gender would need to function.

The sudden and lasting popularity of the tomboy in this period also challenges the notion that Victorians of the postbellum period settled easily into the separate spheres of early middle-class ideology. The high-spirited adventures of tomboys in fiction and journalism highlight the discontent of young women with a gender system simultaneously polarizing in terms of gender identity and blurring in terms of social presence. Many adult women, it appears, did not conform to social conventions without a struggle. They longed for the freedoms allowed their girlhood selves and created tomboy mythologies to support their memories. The tomboy of this period was neither a triumph over conservative ideals nor a suppression of modern liberation, yet she was frequently posited as both of those things. Ambiguity was central to her appeal and acceptable because it was rooted in a youth that would inevitably pass.

Tellingly, in the sixteenth century, when the term "tomboy" first appeared in writing, it was more frequently used for labeling rowdy boys and promiscuous women than boyish girls. According to the *Oxford English Dictionary*, the earliest known use of "tomboy" dates to 1556: "Is all your delite and ioy In whiskyng and ramping abroade like a Tom boy?" In other words, "Don't you have better things to do than act like a common boy?" The term also indicated promiscuity, such as in 1579 when a minister warned that women "must not be tomboyes, to be shorte, they must not bee unchaste." This makes sense: "tom" has connotations of restive sexuality.[7] The fact that the term "tomboy" shifted so dramatically in nineteenth-century America to mean *only* gender-resistant, chaste girls illustrates the cultural wake that followed the romantic period's conflation of childhood and innocence. Society continued to view women who adopted male freedoms as sexually suspect, if not deviant, but now a boyish girl embodied a lack of sexual awareness supposedly innate to children and white youth.

Entertainment played a big role in promoting the tomboy as a stock character. The endearing-though-willful quality of the tomboy may have been influenced by an immensely popular musical, *The Romp,* which played up and down the eastern seaboard for several decades beginning around 1790. The protagonist, Priscilla Tomboy, is a headstrong young woman who pretends her own ruin so that she can marry the man she loves. Clearly more of a coquette than a rebel, Priscilla is not recognizable by later tomboy standards, but she was *named* Tomboy.[8]

In this period "romp" was used much like "tomboy"—except that it applied to boys as well as girls, and was more about violating bourgeois convention than maintaining a particular identity.[9] The *Boston Daily Evening Transcript* in 1835 suggested that a girl's propensity for mindless fun earned her the label: "A romp is generally a good natured sort of a girl, with little mind and far less taste. She does not understand wit or fancy, for to these she makes no pretension. When she is the merriest, she generally jumps the highest; when she is grave, she is a fool, because romps have little intellect."[10] "Hoyden" was a similar favorite, but carried overtones of sexual awareness absent in tomboys and romps. All three terms—romp, hoyden, and tomboy—were used alternatively to rebuke or praise. But as early as the 1830s, tomboy heroines began to appear in American periodical fiction. They were also popular enough in British print culture that in 1876 a best-selling author, Charlotte M. Yonge, defined "tomboyism" as "a wholesome delight in rushing about at full speed, playing at active games, climbing trees, rowing boats, making dirt-pies, and the like."[11] And yet, according to the literary scholar Gillian Avery, late nineteenth-century British authors tended to treat tomboys as products of the American frontier, and a "tomboy" was typically a visiting American.[12]

Americans seemed to agree with that equation of tomboy and American. In 1858 a widely published article called "Our Daughters—Tom-boys" marks the point at which social reformers and cultural critics began to promote tomboys as intrinsically American by nature. Tomboys were depicted as authentic, independent, spirited, and forthright—all traits celebrated as particularly American and male. And tomboys, who resisted aging as a means of resisting the impositions of white femininity, also became a means of working out the parameters of female adolescence. Both then and now, the age of the tomboy is what makes her adorable if she is under twelve, interesting in early adolescence, problematic in late adolescence, and downright dangerous in adulthood (especially if she remains unmarried). Now writers, educators, and cultural critics focused their attention on the tomboy of mid-adolescence—the point at which a girl could (and if she was a real girl, would) connect with her femininity through an innate drive to marry and mother. Although caricatures and fears of "mannish women" abound in this period of women's rights activism, tomboys of print are rarely depicted as truly masculine—outside of the rare article on figures such as the "tomboy murderer" Lillie Duer in 1879.[13] Writers instead tend to exaggerate the beauty and grace of tomboys alongside their boyish behavior, as if their innate femininity undermines their conscious swagger.

By the century's end, prescriptive literature regularly trumpeted the virtue of raising girls as tomboys, which was a major shift in *how* the term was used, but did not signal a new challenge to gender convention per se so much as how gender began to intersect new understandings of age. The United States has a long history of women resisting gender convention. Indeed, the "cult of True Womanhood" that set the tone for industrial-age gender norms at the same time produced a strong countermovement, which Frances Cogan calls the "cult of Real Womanhood."[14] But the Real Woman movement was about adults. Tomboys were about girlish freedoms, and therefore suggested that many constrictions of femininity could be put off until adulthood. Dress reformers, concerned with female physical health in an age of sartorial constriction, were particularly enamored with tomboys. Indeed, the woeful state of a tomboy's dress is usually the first marker of her identity in nineteenth-century tomboy tales (she is also, typically, up a tree or whistling).

In the early nineteenth century, domesticity arose as a feminine corollary to male independence. Domesticity meant that a woman could be the master of her home and children in all but name, even in the most patriarchal of households—because she had become the pillar of the family, the heart of the home. As the century waned, however, the subordination and femininity held in reverence by the earlier middle class was passing out of fashion, even as it continued to provide the counterweight in binary gender roles. The New Woman (a figure of self-cultivation) was elbowing aside the older True Woman (a figure of self-subordination). It was a rough contest, waged over decades, and girls paid attention to changing social cues. Tomboys suggested that healthy girls *should* enjoy the same rights and characteristics as boys.

Despite the lip service given to domesticity and motherhood, the social value of masculinity is made obvious in the social tolerance for girls wanting to be like a boy. Society needed someone to play the subordinate role to the independent one, but when in a female's lifetime did that shift become necessary? American mythologies of independence and self-reliance had been implicitly white and male from the nation's beginning. Could they extend to females for the finite stretch of girlhood?

Perhaps for white girls, for only they could behave like boys and retain their femininity and innocence. Thus the tomboy served to solidify racial assumptions even as she worked to defy gender assumptions. In that sense, the tomboy was an ideal figure for celebrating the unique qualities conferred by whiteness in these racially malevolent times. Race does not simply exist alongside gender, class, and sexuality—it is articulated through them, and vice versa.[15] Through the tomboy, white girls had the opportunity to temporarily assert male privilege, in ways that no child or youth of color could. She was celebrated as an authentic American rebel because of what she signified about gender, yet the race privilege she carried was, as always, no less stifling for its invisibility.

The backdrop of this middle-class reconfiguring of childhood and girlhood was also about creating divisions of "us" and "them," and racial sorting was paramount. "Us" were the white folks, the ones in charge of print culture and large cultural institutions. Whiteness, as many historians have detailed, was actually quite colorful, especially at the end of the nineteenth century when immigration from eastern and southern parts of Europe brought more diversity to Euro-American ancestry. But the "other" was equally complicated: the Native American, Mexican, Asian, and African American peoples who were seen as sharing a space in American society only because they were not of European extraction. When white culture created concepts of "girls" and "girlhood" it did so against a backdrop of intense racial sorting. In 1848, with the end of the Mexican-American War, over fifty thousand Mexicans became US citizens. Most of them would live in Jim Crow–style segregation in the Southwest, where they were tacitly seen by white Americans as a "cut above" the indigenous peoples because of their European blood roots.[16] The Civil War ended the enslavement of African Americans, but other racial atrocities continued under the cover of war. When the cash-strapped Union side stopped paying promised annuities to the now starving Santee Sioux, they "rose up" and killed the

Minnesotans among the rye fields, sparking a war with the United States that continued until their catastrophic defeat in the 1890s. Meanwhile, riots in mining towns, such as the infamous 1885 massacre in Rock Springs, Wyoming, meant that Chinese immigrants, despite having built the transcontinental railroad and manned much of the early extractive economy of the Trans-Mississippi West, would face continued discrimination and the 1882 Chinese Exclusion Act would be extended until 1943.

For those in the Northeast, producing most of the textual materials read nationwide, "race" meant black, but for the nation as a whole, the "them" as well as the "us" of racial sorting was wide and diverse. Because of the centrality of African Americans to the creation of the nation—economically, culturally, socially—whites largely constructed blackness as the foil to whiteness. But the fact that the long-standing "black codes" tended to apply to local nonwhites suggests that "blackness" was itself of many colors.[17] And even in the most seemingly innocuous places, such as child-rearing guides, attitudes toward "us" and "them" underwrote social change.

White, middle-class girls of this era were experiencing more years in school, greater parental oversight, and more public access than their mothers before them. Did they see a conflict between their schoolgirl ambitions and older conventions of female privacy? How did Americans encourage girls to be assertive as girls while discouraging assertiveness in women? How did they understand female gender performance in a culture that stressed feminine modesty at the same time that it touted "modern" self-assertion? How did gender transgression intersect with racial identity? When and why did it become a *good* thing for a girl to behave like a boy? And why did certain activities remain the territory of boys if girls were actively engaging in them as well?

Whiteness was articulated through the tomboy's version of gender. Both the white and black populations of urban areas were moving toward modernity, hoping to secure opportunities for successive generations of girls as well as boys. In the postbellum period, girls of all kinds began to embrace higher education, athletics, and worldly ambitions. But they began from very different starting points. White girls pushed against assumptions of femininity in order to find momentum; within popular culture, they had long been depicted as sweet, gentle, and kind. Girls of color faced intense pressure from their communities to perform respectability in a world that denied them basic human identity and such rights as self-defense and sexual autonomy. White girls could be tomboys—uncouth, ambitious, physical—because such behavior was understood as atypical. Mainstream society read their tomboy antics as a means of claiming boyish male freedoms—and what healthy girl wouldn't long to be an American boy? His freedom was the envy of the world. But for black girls to be uncouth, physical, and ambitious was to confirm a supposedly innate lack of femininity. White girls could afford to pooh-pooh respectability, because it came to them with birth; black girls had to work hard to be seen as respectable, because their birthright in the larger white world was dehumanization. Black girls literally *could not* be tomboys in the positive sense of the term, in the eyes of society—black or white.

In her 2008 study *Tomboys: A Literary and Cultural History,* Michelle Ann Abate notes the white privilege embedded in the acceptance of tomboys but pushes that aspect aside to focus on what she calls the "racialization" of the tomboy, noting that the emergence of tomboys coincides with minstrelsy.[18] She has a point: tomboys of literature were often depicted with tanned skin, dark hair, and "snapping" dark eyes, and they tend to be figures of fun or trickery. Yet focusing on tomboyism as a form of blackface means missing a larger consequence: the celebration of white middle-class tomboys strengthened the whiteness of girlhood, because such behavior was perceived as "tomboy" only in girls with white bodies. And as tomboyism became increasingly central to expressing "American girlhood," girlhood itself became, in an unintentional way, another aspect of the culture of white supremacy that dominated American culture. Tomboyism did push boundaries, and perhaps particular tomboy characters did so in ways that alluded to the trickster figure of African American culture and the subversive qualities of minstrelsy (and burlesque), but because they were white, their mischief was seen as merely youthful.

The connection between tomboys and darkened features also appears to have more to do with images of Native Americans than of African Americans. In the hegemonic popular culture of the time, these populations were interlinked but also presented as distinctly different problems to solve. In the South was a large, recently freed, impoverished population of African Americans eager to pursue a better life. To the west was a Native American population pushed to the brink by white dispossession and crippling governmental policies. Tanned skin, unbound dark hair, and dark eyes tend to appear in tomboy characters coming out of "untamed" mountain or forest life, or girls raised by widowed fathers or elderly grandparents in rural settings. They comment more on a tie between nature and tomboy behavior than the tomboy as a racial outlier within white culture. More importantly for this study, the connection between tomboys and whiteness must not be passed over in search of blackness; whiteness is what enables girls to violate gender boundaries in the years before they awaken to sexual eroticism.

Girls of color could be tomboys in the negative sense—at least by the early twentieth century. The African American press, such as the *Chicago Defender,* the *Baltimore Afro-American,* and *The Crisis,* celebrated the scholastic and athletic achievements of girls of color but did not call them tomboys. That term was reserved for girls with blotchy or dark skin, and no sense of decorum. It was not until 1921 that a black educator, Ruth Arnett of the YWCA, argued that girls raised to be physically healthy make for better wives and mothers.[19] Despite her efforts, "tomboy" did not catch on as a positive label within the black community until roughly the 1950s, with the national celebration of exceptional black female athletes.[20]

Tomboys in the era I discuss were a white, northeastern, middle-class trope; their impact depended on that identity. Middle-class and upper-class white girls faced vastly different realities than girls who did not fall into those categories. Many black middle-class girls of the era experienced similar girlhoods, but the black middle class was still quite limited and located in major southern cities, like Charleston and New Orleans, or in northern states where the statistical presence of African Americans remained small until the Great Migrations of the early twentieth century. Although there were a few papers, such as the *Defender,* addressing middle- and aspiring-class black readers, and novels such as *Iola Leroy* (1892) by Frances E. W. Harper and *The Conjure Woman* (1899) by Charles Chesnutt, for the most part the world of print culture presented girls as white and either relatively privileged or, often in the case of poor girls, able to gain privilege.

My point here is not to erase the existence of girls of color but to highlight the ways the construction of girls and girlhood shut out girls of color. Indeed, recent histories of black girlhood by LaKisha Simmons, Nazera Sadiq Wright, and Marcia Chatelain make it clear that the parents of African American girls, regardless of region, strove tirelessly to carve out a space between childhood and adulthood for their daughters. The challenge was to approximate a prolonged sexually unawakened period when most African American girls were forced to become what the self-emancipated slave Harriet Jacobs called "prematurely knowing." She notes that by the age of fifteen, black girls were forced by circumstance to recognize impending victimization and develop means of self-protection.[21] Print culture, produced by whites for whites, suggests that tomboys played a central role creating a girlhood that hinged on the sexual innocence long denied to girls of color.

The interlinking roles of reading and writing in this process cannot be underestimated. Concepts of age and gender were often marked and worked out on printed pages, and pulled girls away from their own social realities. Through reading and imagining themselves in different social positions, girls could be anyone. Between 1880 and 1940 the United States became a "culture of print," with readers relying on written wisdom to inform their life choices.[22] Magazines for young women proliferated alongside juvenile novels, including the newly popular series novels designed to feed a growing "girl culture." Thus many young women began to imitate what they found in the print world and to absorb and reflect it as reality— even when it bore no resemblance to their own life experiences. Girls were bombarded with prescriptive advice that bemoaned a loss of civility, but when left to their own devices they often chose the more adventurous literature. This holds true for middle-class diarists, second-generation immigrants, and daughters of the black middle class.[23]

Fictional tomboys might express frustration with cumbersome female clothing, but wearing pants required crossing a bright gender line. Nineteenth-century tomboys rarely wore trousers in books or plays, so images of tomboys from this period often depict disheveled white girls with slightly messy hair. Nineteenth-century tomboys did not *dress* like boys (the sign of a twentieth-century tomboy) but rather expressed discomfort with the bother of female dress, suggesting an unconventional spirit more than a deviant one.

Of course, most girls did not enjoy the luxury of choice expressed in the popular press, but changing their expectations (if not their realities) had an impact. The United States was still an overwhelmingly rural country, and over a third of the population under the age of twenty lived in the southern states, where urban centers remained rare, immigrants still more exotic, and education a luxury. Poor children, both white and black, in these areas did not experience the protected childhoods depicted in the popular press. By age nine or ten most African American girls were leaving home for

FIGURE 1: The 1873 painting *The Tomboy,* by John George Brown, illustrates the significance of small details in dividing the nineteenth-century tomboy from her more feminine peers. Clearly under twelve, she enjoys the motion of an open, swinging gate while she focuses her attention forward, intent on catching anything interesting coming down the road. Her clothing, with the exception of one straying strap, is tidy, with a fullness of fabric and detail suggesting a family of means. Courtesy The Athenaeum.

field or domestic labor. One woman from North Carolina recalled: "Your training was early and hard . . . no play ever for a girl. That's just how [women were] on girls. Work, work, work. No play, 'cause they told you, 'Life was to be hardest on you—always.'"[24] On the whole, rural white girls may have experienced more protection because their labor more often remained within the family, but few expected a life any different from that of their female elders. It was a life that, despite the romantic pastoralizing in domestic literature sold to urban audiences, girls themselves knew to be hard and monotonous: marriage, constant childbearing, and years of brutally hard work that might result, if one survived, in veneration as a grandmother. The New Woman was surely an image as far off as the moon for girls residing on farms and prairies, along bayous and rivers, counting their days off in bags of cotton on the Gulf Coast and cleaning fish from the rivers of the Northwest.

But once girls could read, and technology made books both cheap and easily transported, modern girlhood appeared even where it could not flourish off the page, and tomboys proved to be sympathetic heroines. While it is true that the tomboy of literature was always white and nearly always middle-class enough to have ambitions of independence (which she willingly later forsook in favor of love), she also came into the story lovably flawed, so that the inevitable loss brought by maturity could reshape and polish her without disturbing her spirit. Her inevitable triumph appeared attainable in real life.

Yet even as the tomboy became more favored, she was too ambiguous to be a "safe" girl. These were not safe times. By the century's end, she skated near the fault lines of sexuality and gender inversion at a time when scientists such as Herbert Spencer, Havelock Ellis, and G. Stanley Hall were struggling to codify male and female bodies and psyches, and various behaviors, as "normal" or "deviant." Contained within the innocence of childhood and early adolescence, the tomboy embodied a powerful narrative of cultural resistance, fluidity, and change. As Mary Elliott asserts, "Young girls—tomboys—who possess no social or economic power acquire that power by functioning as disobedient, athletic, heroic, entrepreneurial, eccentric, or masculine 'bad girls.'"[25] Without insulting or patronizing other females, tomboy heroines shine a distinctly humorous light on the strange behaviors required to prove femininity. Indeed, the literary scholar Alfred Habegger argues that tomboys, because they poke fun at the assumptions of gender convention, are the only humorous female characters in American literature until the twentieth century.[26]

In the Progressive Era (1880s–1920), tomboy-themed hit songs, celebrities, and glamorous athletes proved the term had more staying power than ever. Tomboys had come to serve as a happy middle ground in the fierce ongoing debate over female gender roles. Trendy urban girls wore "tomboy combinations"—a sort of skirt-and-bloomer set—and both boys and girls nationwide wore "tomboy shoes"—a gender-neutral style of play shoe, built to withstand hard use.[27]

Like most useful and lasting archetypes, tomboys shifted shape to suit their times. As R. W. Connell reminds us, "Rather than attempting to define masculinity as an object (a natural character type, a behavioural average, a norm), we need to focus on the processes and relationships through which men and women conduct gendered lives."[28] In the nineteenth century the tomboy whistled, in the twentieth she wore dungarees, in the twenty-first she plays video games; the markers of masculinity change according to time and place, but they are the primary ways by which the tomboy declares her resistance to conventionality.

Yet, surprisingly, the markers of femininity have changed little over the past two centuries despite unprecedented changes in lifestyles. Recent research suggests that understanding of what it means to be "feminine" remains eerily similar to definitions in the early industrial age, with adolescent girls and women repeating the same words and concepts—that to be "feminine" is to be nice, attractive, modest, domestic, maternal, sexually faithful, and romantic.[29] Although certain nineteenth-century feminine traits of obedience and passivity have largely dropped away, women are still expected to act quietly, politely, and modestly, and to sacrifice themselves for the good of others. Then as now, the feminine female demonstrates deliberative self-care; in the nineteenth century she used bonnets, gloves, and sometimes veils to preserve the whiteness of her skin, now replaced by retinol and omega-3 oil. In other words, femininity is a concept resistant to modernizing.

Tellingly, "good" is often seen as part of the performance of femininity, but the two qualities are not interchangeable, and the slippage between them makes a space for the tomboy to enter. Martha Saxton notes that the virtues women were taught in early American British culture were largely personal, with sympathy and empathy as demonstrative of femininity as chastity, obedience, and passivity, and they became central to indicating middle-class family identity in later decades.[30] But the middle class, however genteel their pretensions, were not aristocrats, merely fortunate players in the capitalist system. Even at the height of domesticity, in the 1830s, the novelist Catharine Sedgwick stated that in such a volatile economy a pampered girl might find herself suddenly in need of life-keeping skills, and that it was vital to train daughters that femininity and self-reliance must not be mutually exclusive.[31] But in the postbellum era the formula for middle-class femininity had to shift to accommodate opportunities, education, and the real need to earn wages, regardless of gender. The question was how much the image could move without trespassing on masculinity. Much of the attention given to the modern girl in the press was essentially verbal hand-wringing over how to promote the more assertive girl who must make her way in the rapidly changing world—how to support the "good" while letting go of the "passive." Tomboys became a practical means of addressing the conundrum.

As figures of gender and age ambiguity, tomboys are intrinsically queer, regardless of how that tomboyism is expressed or repressed. In *Female Masculinity*, Judith (now Jack) Halberstam highlights the complex braiding of age and gender concepts in this figure that render her both a celebration of boyish girls and a means of consigning female masculinity to immaturity. Tomboyism, Halberstam clarifies, is normalized as an "extended period of female masculinity" common for many girls (and therefore normative) and "associated with a 'natural' desire for the greater freedoms and mobilities enjoyed by boys." But at the same time, it is a masculinity tolerated only up to puberty, suggesting that gender-bending in females is no more tolerated than in males.[32] In *The Queer Child, or Growing Sideways in the Twentieth Century*, Kathryn Bond Stockton builds on this concept: "If you scratch a child, you will find a queer, in the sense of someone 'gay' or just plain strange." Within that framework, the child identity of the tomboy is what normalizes her: age normalizes queerness. The central heroine of the typical tomboy tale is in mid-adolescence, brought by age into the doorway between normal and deviant. If the convention is that the tomboy must grow *up*, Stockton questions, what happens if she refuses and instead grows "sideways"? In other words, expanding outward, exploring the dimensions of herself as she is now—in girlhood—as opposed to where society says she must go: womanhood.[33] The female masculinity of older tomboys becomes problematic not because female masculinity is abnormal per se, but because it must be contained by age.

Tomboys find encouragement in their claim to boyhood freedoms because many of the changes being wrought to girlhood were in fact already owned and promoted within boyhood. They had a model, and as their lives became increasingly similar to those of their brothers, they turned to that model for self-expression. The tomboy of mainstream culture was able to claim these privileges because she was white—whiteness, indeed, was intrinsic to the boyish masculinity promoted at the same time that tomboys and bad boys became idealized into heroines and heroes of American juvenile fiction.

One of the most important of these "American" concepts was individualism, and in her heart the tomboy saw herself as singular. Looking at reminiscences of early twentieth-century self-described tomboys, Allison Miller points out a continuing theme: "a collective sense of tomboy identity" did not cohere for young women. For most tomboys, "tomboyism was almost always a matter of individual predilection, even a rejection of anything resembling girl-identification."[34] In other words, tomboys enact their "boyishness" individually—set apart from both girls and boys. Young girls did not bond together as tomboys. And yet their very individualism— their identities as loners—made the tomboy image more applicable to girls outside of the mainstream.

Changes in the family, education, and print culture eventually led to the creation of a young female character bent on resisting age and gender conventions. This book begins by examining the "proto-tomboys" (tomboys in behavior, not name) who emerged from print culture just as modern girlhood itself was finding form. This new girlhood—a creation of elders and print culture, rather than coming from girls themselves—was one of self-cultivation through education and written self-reflection. Real girls influenced by mainstream girlhood found a new sense of comradeship with other girls in their age group. Allowed to be funny and engage in innocent but careless behavior, the proto-tomboys helped girls and their parents navigate the gender tensions fostered by a society transforming from an agricultural to industrial economy. For nineteenth-century audiences, tomboy characters suggested that girls could embrace social freedoms temporarily, but also revealed the deep conflict between self and society girls faced long before they became women.

In chapter 2 I examine how the tomboy character developed into the darling of a new domestic fiction directed specifically at adolescent girls. Louisa May Alcott's *Little Women* is unquestionably the most influential text of the period for girls, and it was followed by several other novels that authors and publishers hoped would prove as successful. This chapter investigates the imaging of youthful tomboy heroines in juvenile novels and series of the 1860s and '70s, such as *Gypsy Breynton, What Katy Did, Hila Dart, Running to Waste,* and *Tattered Tom,* as well as their ubiquity in periodical fiction. It considers conflicting messages of the novels and why reading girls may have found the heroines so attractive for interpreting their own place in society.

Chapter 3 looks at Wild West formula fiction, written for boys and young men, and containing more tomboy-like characters than in any other genre. The characters, whom I call girl sports, behave like ramped-up tomboys—which is to say that they act like their male peers except that the reader is bombarded with innuendos about their sexual attractions. Only in the presence of the hero does the girl sport move firmly into the feminine end of the gender spectrum, much like her domestic tomboy parallel. Otherwise, she rides, shoots, and cusses as much as the men around her. Within this fictional frontier, the girl sport transgresses gender norms in service of white triumph. This is important because, although these novels were designed as lowbrow entertainment, they nonetheless played an important role in the evolving narrative of the Far West as a place of white male dominance, where civilization was depicted as both a desirable outcome and a tragic conclusion.

Chapter 4 explores how the New Woman who emerged in the 1880s was a "tomboy grown up." In the last two decades of the nineteenth century, prescriptive literature and fiction alike praised the tomboy as the new ideal girl for a variety of reasons, including her lack of consumer interest, physical health, and prolonged sexual innocence. The rise of the so-called New Woman—a young woman who began enacting particular freedoms outside of the home, such as going to college, choosing a profession, earning wages, and expressing her sexuality and her physicality—both terrified and electrified the general public. She portended the end of Victorian (or as they saw it, civilized) culture, but also that of conventional family life. Both figures spoke to the growing recognition among females that they had both an interior, sexless self and the self with roles and outlook determined by sex. The tomboy grew away from devotion to her inner self at the expense of social duty, while the New Woman insisted she could have both domesticity and life outside of it. College and the advent of women's sports and physical pastimes—most notably basketball and bicycling—expanded the age of the tomboy into womanhood and blurred the line between them.

Part of the definition of "tomboy" is "boy," and chapter 5 explores how Progressive Era youth organizers, writers, and educators conflated depictions of boyhood with national mythology. The work of G. Stanley Hall emphasizing the importance of adolescence in the growth of white boys, alongside the words of figures such as Teddy Roosevelt and the many self-proclaimed "boyologists," helped to create a new kind of boyhood that put a premium on youthful savagery. But boys were not the only ones listening to the national conversation conflating American identity and masculinity, and girls took many of the messages to heart. They discovered they could enjoy elements of boyhood in the name of youth and American identity. The Camp Fire Girls and the Girl Scouts were part of a movement to give girls organizations akin to those of their brothers, putting them into wilderness and teaching them survival skills, supposedly to encourage their innately domestic spirit. Girls could act like boys, they discovered, if they claimed those freedoms in the name of America and youth.

In chapter 6 I argue that by the turn of the century, earlier positive portrayals of the tomboy merged with and eventually became the American Girl—at the very time when the American Girl became symbolic of the nation itself. Their efforts were helped along by the creation of girls' series novels such as the *Outdoor Girls, Camp Fire Girls,* and *Motor Girls.* By the 1920s, the old version of the tomboy was largely absorbed into the imagery of the all-American girl, and "tomboy" as can be seen in advertising campaigns such as the one launched by Kodak in the first decade of the twentieth century. But the American girl was not a figure of resistance like the tomboy, and she did not fear growing up but rather reveled in her youth.

In the final chapter I suggest that society's reoccurring need to declare "tomboy" outdated is connected with the way girls and women claim or deny the term themselves. Here the tomboy as "queer child" emerges most

clearly. Stockton's assertion of projected Freudian latency on personal histories of gay adults is also true of tomboys: "Since they are 'gay children'
only after childhood, they never 'are' what they latently 'were.'"[35] In other
words, ownership of tomboy identity is claimed through shifting tenses.
"Tomboy" is used mainly as a retrospective term for late nineteenth-
century girls. Diarists of that period rarely call themselves tomboys, in
part because they engage in rowdy play alongside other girls and therefore
do not feel the misfit qualities conveyed by the term. Diarists also see the
term as a judgment used by adults to shame them. Adult women who were
those girls, however, often look back and claim the title in their autobiographies, memoirs, and autobiographical fiction. As adults, they are proud
to call themselves former tomboys, demonstrating that the evaluation of
the tomboy had shifted from negative to positive, but also suggesting that
the feeling of being out of sync with society felt a lot more positive from
within the safe space of adulthood looking backward, than experiencing it
in the present. Finally, biographers invoke the term to describe the origins
of great women such as reformers, rights activists, artists, and entertainers,
insisting that such iconoclasts came into the world with atypical ambitions
and views.

The tomboy emerged from northeastern print culture in the 1850s as
an ambiguous figure with which to work out society's ideas about female
youth and gender. She is classically depicted as a misfit because of her
enjoyment of sports and her disregard for self-care and fashion, but she
became more useful as modern girlhood and New Womanhood began to
take shape in the late nineteenth century. Now the tomboy became the
means for girls to express their discomfort with the requirements of femininity. Ironically, as tomboys became more ubiquitous in the culture, they
also became mainstreamed as ideal American girls.

The tomboy was a central transitional figure in the adoption of a more
modern girlhood in the United States. Understanding the emergence,
evolution, and popularity of the tomboy concept explains how modern
archetypal girlhood came into being both for girls themselves and for those
trying to define girls and girlhood. It gives us a way to consider girls' interior constructions of self in a world of competing depictions, but also how
those interior constructions had to be articulated through already existing
language. The tomboy remains an enacted identity and a cultural symbol because girls continue to struggle in that contentious space between

private ambition and public self-effacement. The tomboy character, real and imagined, was an attempt to come to terms with life "behind the veil," to use W. E. B. Dubois's famous metaphor for black identity in a white world. In the case of girls, they had to come to accept the bewildering sense of having a genderless self-identity that is denied at every turn by external perspectives and expectations. As tomboys, young women can, for a time, challenge the restrictions of femininity and maturity without denying their own female bodies. Tomboys serve as a playful assertion that, like boys, girls have a right to "be" irrespective of what they will "become."

1

Tomboys and the New Girlhood

On May 25, 1858, readers of the *Nashville Patriot* came upon an article titled "Our Daughters—Tom-boys":

> The "Tom-Boy" is an eager, earnest, impulsive, bright-eyed, glad-hearted, kind-souled specimen of the genus *feminae*. If her laugh is a little too frequent and her tone a trifle too emphatic, we are willing to overlook these for the sake of the true life and exulting vitality to which they are the "escape valves;" and, indeed, we rather like the high pressure nature which must close off its superfluous "steam" in such ebullitions.[1]

This snippet of prose appeared in papers nationwide for months, and frequently resurfaced in later decades. It was not an important piece even in 1858, but rather filler for newspapers far more focused on civil wars raging in Venezuela, Spain, and Mexico. Yet its popular reprinting across the country spoke to the American zeitgeist. Building on widely reinforced fears of enfeebled American youth, the writer scolds: "When our young men want so sadly what is tersely termed 'backbone,' when our young women want stamina . . . , there is a 'reform' upon this subject very much needed. . . . I would have [mothers] encourage their little girls to exercise effort, industry and energy, so as to give the them the health, vigor, activity, and power to expand into glorious womanhood." If we do not want our girls to be weak, they must be "encouraged to become real, *bona fide,* flesh-and-blood 'tomboys.'"[2] Acknowledging that "tom-boy" is usually used to rein in exuberant girls, the author suggests that for the sake of nation and (white) race, it is time for parents and girls to aspire to the term.

Positive portrayals of tomboys emerged with the notion that girlhood itself was a separate stage of existence with its own values, interests, and symbols.[3] This was not accidental, but rather reflected two contradictory forces at work in the creation of girlhood: in the popular culture, girls were defined to be the opposite of boys, and yet girls were now living more like boys than ever, in large part because of expanding primary and secondary education. As Americans began to define their national character as intrinsically independent, candid, and self-reliant, they searched for a girl type who could embody such traits. The rough and simple tomboy now became a viable approach to raising healthy girls.

By the second half of the century, didactic as well as prescriptive literature articulated fears that the Victorian emphasis on gentility and fashion was turning American girls into something that went against treasured values of American culture.[4] American as well as British audiences responded heartily to the widely disseminated 1868 essay "The Girl of the Period," by British gadfly Eliza Linton. Although she deplored the brazen forays of British girls into the public world—a theme Linton would expound on for the next thirty years with antifeminist zealotry—she directed the bulk of her criticism in the first essay at young women's participation in consumer culture. "The Girl of the Period," she charges, "is a creature who dyes her hair and paints her face, as the first articles of her personal religion—a creature whose sole idea of life is fun; whose sole aim is unbounded luxury; and whose dress is the chief object of such thought and intellect as she possesses."[5] Thus, by Linton's summary, the most visible new girls of the Anglo-speaking world embodied fashion and commerce. For Americans, such a girl clearly personified urban or European values; she was a corrupt extension of an overly cultivated girl. All the promise of American's economic development and social growth had led to this, writers suggested: a girl who expresses no moral value and is of no value to society. Tomboys—unaware of their attractions, beyond uninterested in fashion, and still so rooted into the earth as to appear unselfconsciously smudged and tangled—were a clear repudiation of the fashionable girls who began to populate imaginative culture.

This chapter examines how a growing belief in (white) childhood innocence, the expansion of female and coeducation, and popular narratives came together to forge a new girl archetype using an already familiar name. Allowed to be funny and engage in innocent but careless behavior, the figure of the tomboy helped girls and their parents navigate the gender tensions of a society in the midst of economic transformation from an agricultural to urban industrial economy. It was also no accident that the embracing of boy-girls gained new popularity in the wake of the Civil

War. The upheaval of war contributed to the viability of a tomboy ideal by throwing categories of race and gender into disarray, making it possible for an innocent white girl to "act like a boy" without imperiling her adult respectability.[6] And yet that same disarray also sparked a counter-need to reinforce white, female bodies as innately feminine. The tomboy ideal signaled changes in growing up female in America. But by licensing her free spirit only up until marriage, the tomboy also underlined the deep conflict between self and society faced by girls.

New Childhood and Gender

A growing need among the middle class to reinforce gender difference between children as well as adults led to an increasing preoccupation with how girls and boys should behave as opposites. Writings to entertain children were rare before the nineteenth century, and they did not focus on the gendering of boys and girls.[7] Boy-girls and girl-boys occasionally showed up in antebellum didactic fiction as the gendering of children increased, stressing the need for children to adopt the prevailing gender norms. The children in these stories are not presented negatively per se so much as needing to be redirected.

Eliza Leslie, a popular author whose work appeared in Boston's *Juvenile Miscellany,* wrote two such tales illustrating the problems of girls and boys crossing the gender line: "Lucy Nelson, or The Boy-Girl" (1831) quickly followed by "Billy Bedlow, or The Girl-Boy" (1832). Leslie participated in the new emphasis on the gendering of children at roughly the beginning of the rise of the middle class in urban industrial America. Although by the turn of the century scientists would argue that binary gender was a sign of higher civilization, in this earlier period writers like Leslie posited that gender was divinely or naturally binary and that respectable families kept that divide firm.[8]

Yet even if fictional depictions of rowdy girls were not celebratory in this period, heroine Lucy Nelson's lack of calculation is innocently appealing. Leslie begins the tale by implying that most girls naturally gravitate to more feminine company: "It was very strange that Lucy Nelson always preferred playing with boys, and seemed to take no pleasure in any girlish amusements." Lucy wants to play with her brothers. Like the tomboys who follow in her stead a few decades later, she discovers her talents among the boys: "She could fly a kite, spin a top, toss a ball, drive a hoop, and walk on stilts; and was delighted to race about the fields, and wade through the creek with boys." She most enjoys getting in snow fights, skating, and sledding. Too full of energy to move demurely, she jumps stairs "three steps at a time, and she did not hesitate to be on a horse without saddle or bridle, and gallop all over the fields." Moreover, Lucy foments mischief—leading her brothers into rambunctious and even dangerous play, essentially teaching *them* how to be boys.[9]

In the process of illustrating how girls should *not* behave, the story also emphasizes that girls should by nature be silent, tidy, graceful, and still. Real girls, such as Lucy's sisters, like to "dress dolls, and make feasts, and read story-books." Lucy's careless appearance is an important marker of her internal disorder: "Her clothes were torn to pieces in climbing fences and trees, her shoes were always covered with dirt." Cleanliness of the girl is important beyond hygiene, signifying the spiritual purity of the girl herself.[10] Perhaps most damning of all, "her skin was so sunburnt, that she might almost have been mistaken for an Indian child." Leslie concludes: "Every one called her a boy-girl."[11]

As punishment, Lucy's parents decide that she must spend a month dressed as a boy. Lucy is elated; she had, of course, been begging to wear trousers. But alas, this tale is designed to scare little girls away from gender-transgressive behavior, so her hard-won trousers lead to humiliation. When a family friend mistakes her for a boy, Lucy reaches the end of her tolerance: "I am not a boy!" She bursts into tears and flees. Her declaration dispels anxieties over ambiguities, and signifies that she will accept her female identity if it means she will not be shamed. But the transition pains her. At first Lucy's efforts to rein in her spirits give her headaches, but "at length she became a modest well-behaved little girl, and took pleasure in all the occupations and amusements that are suited to her sex."[12]

"Billy Bedlow," Leslie's bookend story about a sissy boy, highlights different attitudes toward boys crossing the increasingly polarized gender line. Gender scholar Ken Corbett stresses that "'sissy' carries the implication of weakness, unbecoming delicacy, and enervation, devoid of the possibilities born of resistance, agency, and action."[13] While Lucy is publically shamed for something she otherwise claims happily, Billy Bedlow is forced to recognize that feminine dress is irrational and unseemly for a boy. Billy's vanity marks him. Enthralled with his own reflection in the mirror, he sleeps with curling papers around his long golden locks, and with his hands in gloves to keep them soft. According to Leslie, he is happy "to sit with his sister and make pin-cushions, reticules, and purses, and to play and dress their dolls." A born ninny, he "screamed if a spider or a wasp came near him." In fact, Leslie states candidly, "he often wished in his heart to be a girl." He wishes this not because of an internal sense of gender identity, but out of shallow transvestite desires: he wants to "wear a large bonnet and carry a parasol." Billy's preoccupations impede his ability to take initiative and engage in the homosocial rituals so critical to boyhood. Naturally, Billy's mother's catering to his desires has only made the problem more acute.[14]

Things come to a head when Billy accompanies a group of children on a field trip, wearing a corset under his fussy frockcoat to look as "thin, small and feminine as possible." The corset hampers his movement, and when the laces slip into view, an older boy teases Billy in front of the others. Billy is so "vexed and ashamed" that he cries and hides. Luckily for him, the teasing boy is not a bully but the best example of budding manhood, who kindly convinces Billy to discard the fussy clothing, cut off his curls, and lay off the cologne.[15]

In the language of later tomboy fiction, Billy is a "sissy boy," a character who often served as the tomboy's sidekick. In contemporary parlance, he is made to suffer for being queer. Yet Leslie does not require Billy to change his desires, only his self-performance. Billy does not now bravely squash spiders or leave his sisters to their sewing patterns. For all we know, Billy still longs to wear a bonnet. Leslie's concern is that he now appears appropriate, unlike Lucy, who must feel as well as look conventional.

Another somewhat chilling story about punishing gender-bending children in this period can be found in a lighthearted children's picture book, *Little Miss Consequence*. "The Tom-Boy Who Was Changed into a Real Boy" appears as one in a compilation of playful, cautionary verses. The tomboy of in this story was "so rude and fond of noise" that

> She would mount a tree or wall
> To seek bird's nests, and would jump over ditches,
>   ditches, ditches;
> But at works of skill and grace
> She held the lowest place,
> And was very far from clever at her stitches, stitches,
>   stitches

At last she grew so coarse,
E'en her voice was rough and hoarse,
And her attitudes became so like a boy's, boy's boy's,
    That they thought it only right,
    On a certain Summer's night,
To change her sex completely, without noise, noise, noise.
    So a sailor she was made,
    And a ship's captain was paid
Quite quietly to take her off to sea, sea, sea;
    Where for anything I know
    This said Tomboy may be now;
And a caution may it prove to you and me, me, me.[16]

The tomboy cannot remain in the middle, so the mysterious and ominous "they" proceed "to change her sex without noise, noise, noise." And while there's something undeniably horrific about the idea of "them" doing this in the night, and sending the tomboy off to adventures far from everyone she knows, there is also something vaguely ambiguous about her punishment. Here the tomboy is rewarded with freedom, rather than shamed into headache-inducing conformity like Lucy. It is impossible to imagine this particular girl preferring "stiches, stiches, stiches" to embarking on worldly adventures.

But these were didactic tales, written to shape the behavior of girls and boys, not reflect it. Leslie's need to condemn boys and girls crossing the gender line implies that such desire was not uncommon. And even if the naughty tomboy was happy in the end to set sail as a boy, her fate nonetheless tells child readers that crossing convention too far may result in one never coming back. The need to clarify what it meant to be a good boy or girl suggests alarm over gender shifting in society as a whole.

For the most part, until the 1870s images of girls were used to define boyhood rather than girlhood, principally because new concepts of boyhood emerged slightly earlier than those of girls, a result of boys' earlier participation in wage labor. Free nations of boys, as E. Anthony Rotundo puts it, arose in the streets, alleyways, and fields of towns and cities when boys lost the adult supervision they had experienced through apprenticeships in earlier times. Now boys fraternized exclusively with each other in the time and spaces between home and work, bonded through the nexus of gender and age. "In this space of their own," Rotundo observes, "boys were able to play outside the rules of the home and the marketplace. It was a heady and even liberating experience." In their minds, the outdoors belonged to them. Indoors now became an alien space of femininity. Emphasizing the demure aspects of girlhood served to strengthen boyhood as girlhood's opposite. After outgrowing their home-bound early childhood, boys looked back and saw their sisters "still enveloped by the moral and physical confinements of domesticity and by the gowns and petticoats that were its visible emblems. With great clarity a boy saw that female meant fettered and male meant free."[17]

And yet girls' diaries, letters, and memoirs suggest that girls did not subscribe to such docile descriptions of their lives. Although girls might disparage rowdy behavior when critiquing themselves as individuals, they were prone to celebrate that same behavior when enacted by a group of girls. Ellen Emerson, for example, wrote with undiluted enthusiasm to her mother while at Miss Sedgwick's highly respectable private school in Lenox, Massachusetts: "Every night we do things which it seems to me I can never remember without laughing. . . . [T]he wildest frolics, the loudest shrieks, the most boisterous rolling and tumbling that eye ever saw, ear ever heard or heart ever imagined."[18] Emerson's letter suggests that such uncouth behavior was entirely normal and acceptable within the company of other girls. Leslie's depiction of Lucy suggests that behavior such as Emerson and her friends displayed should be curbed—certainly not *encouraged* as a natural expression of the "well-conditioned girl," as writers would assert only four decades later. The message in such didactic texts was that rowdy girls are by nature outliers—and unprincipled outliers are not celebrated in the social world.

Girl diarists themselves rarely express internal conflict over society's expectations until they reach an age for marriage—a view that aligns neatly with the observations of girls and wives made by Alexis de Tocqueville during his 1831 visit to the United States. In *Democracy in America*, Tocqueville's central concern is defining how democracy shapes society and culture. Thus his surprising decision to focus two chapters on American females suggests that he considered women's dilemma an important illustration of the virtues and drawbacks afforded by a democratic system. Speaking from the perspective of his own aristocratic French background, in which young women are entirely sheltered within the family, Tocqueville describes his amazement with the candor and self-reliance of American adolescent girls in the chapter "Education of Young Women in the United

States."[19] More telling still, he follows that opening with another chapter, "How the Girl Can Be Seen Beneath the Features of the Wife," famously opening, "In America the independence of woman is irretrievably lost in the ties of marriage."[20] Tocqueville's juxtaposition of the unprecedented freedom of girlhood and the unenviable subordination of married women makes it clear: young American girls were taught to enjoy a temporary level of independence unusual in European cultures, but were at the same time trained to relinquish autonomy upon marriage.

Respectable American girls were rarely chaperoned and shielded to the degree of their European counterparts. Tocqueville notes being "surprised" and "almost frightened" at the "happy boldness with which young women in America contrive to manage their thoughts and their language amid all the difficulties of free conversation. A philosopher would have stumbled at every step along the narrow path which they trod without accident and without effort." He muses that, rather than controlled by authority figures from without, these girls are taught self-control through their experience of a youthful freedom under the looming shadow of adult self-sacrifice: "She indulges in all permitted pleasures without losing her head to any of them, and her reason does not lose the reins though she often seems to hold them loosely." He saw this unusual way of training girls as a side effect of democracy, to make up for a lack of external social and familial control. Instead of inculcating mistrust in herself, adults "constantly seek to enhance her confidence in her own strength of character."[21]

The girl must willingly and lovingly choose her domestic cage, a requirement that would end the arc of the stereotypical "tomboy tale" later in the century. Tocqueville notes in the first paragraph of the next chapter, "If an unmarried woman is less constrained there than elsewhere, a wife is subjected to stricter obligations. The [young woman] makes her father's house an abode of freedom and of pleasure; the latter lives in the home of her husband as if it were a cloister." Tocqueville postulates the wife's relinquishing of independence as a direct result of Puritanical roots combined with a commercial ethos. A girl must be taught self-reliance in this new democracy, he summarizes, but when she becomes a wife "she must submit to narrower duties." Most of this is done not through law but rather "inflexible public opinion," which "prevails to contain women within the restricted sphere of domestic business and duties and to forbid them to step beyond it." Tocqueville thus describes American girlhood as a kind of bait-and-switch: raised to think independently, the girl "supports her new condition with courage because she chose it." Tocqueville suggests that the inner fortitude of American wives—their ability to sustain families in a nation of precarious fortunes and pioneering austerity—stems directly from their early education.[22]

Tocqueville's depiction of young American women foreshadows the heroine of tomboy tales who would become so popular within a generation: an independent-minded girl who willingly sacrifices agency for marriage. Between Tocqueville's writing and the end of the Civil War, that story of self-sacrifice began to change. At midcentury, popular fiction was serialized in magazines and papers, some of it written by girls themselves. Although stories continued to emphasize the personal fulfillment young women earn through domesticity, many stories about girls also glamorize youthful rebellion.

Elements of what would become the classic tomboy tale can be found in the early stories about girls published in *Godey's Lady's Book,* the most widely read women's magazine of the antebellum period. *Godey's,* though transgressive in the sense that it broke new ground by employing a female editor, Sarah Josepha Hale, and established female readers as a major market, nonetheless adhered to conventional domestic ideals. A good woman, the magazine posited over and over, was passive, maternal, Christian, and feminine. But *Godey's* was less rigid in its depiction of girls, opening the door to more assertive heroines. Stories of romps proved popular from its inception, and *Godey's* published a number of tales with jolly, mischievous girls squaring off against shallow, fashionable misses. The tomboy character, with a set of coherent signifiers, was a short leap away.

The narrative arc of romp stories soon crystalized into the American tomboy tale. One such example is "Old Truth and the Trout-Fisher," by Mrs. A. M. F. Annan, published in *Godey's* in 1845. A young beauty with a "nateral [*sic*] turn for running and climbing, and fishing and wading, and huckleberrying and blackberrying," in what appears to be generic rural America, enters the scene by captivating the attention of a vacationing male urbanite. As became typical in such tales, when the girl appears at dinner in appropriate dress, the man discovers that the saucy tomboy is the daughter of his hostess. Although he is fascinated by her free behavior, her demure dress assures him that she is also eligible. He can now admire that "the spirit of mirth did occasionally betray itself, but, in her low though ringing laugh, and the joyous twinkle of the dimples about her mouth, it never transgressed the restrictions of lady-like decorum."[23] The story ends with marriage, and the author claiming that the trout fisher is now a model wife because of her girlhood freedom.

Fondness for tomboys as fun and good-hearted underlines most of their depictions. For example, in the 1853 story "An Old Man's Yarn," the narrator remembers his sister Kate: "a romping, rackety, Tomboy of a thing, that used to get into more mischief, receive more scoldings and pettings, and make more noise in the old house than all the rest of the folks in it put together." Kate's story is the classic tomboy tale: men and boys love her, the older women despair over her, and in the end love tames the tomboy into a devoted housewife.[24] Then there are girls like Anna, heroine of a tale published in 1865, who whistles and has "an intellect almost masculine in its scope and force." Eventually, pain over the departure of her longtime love subdues her and she embraces womanly decorum just in time for his return.[25] Tomboys in these stories were not bad girls but rather heroines to be admired. Their central qualities—innocence and independence—were portrayed as positive traits for girls to emulate. Such a shift reflects the changing cultural and social conditions faced by white American girls.

Setting the Stage for the New Tomboy

Tomboys evolved as symbols of singularly American character, the equal of boys with the task of promoting American individualism and candor, because of slightly earlier shifts in cultural understandings of middle-class children as a whole. With the rise of the middle class and attendant elevation of women's moral role within the family and community alike, the cultural framing of childhood changed dramatically from one of innate sinfulness to equally innate innocence. Well-to-do urban industrial families increasingly regarded their children not as producers for the family, but as the product of the family itself.[26] Tomboys could serve as symbols because white middle-class children themselves had become symbolic of America's future.

In the United States, philosophies on childhood innocence took on nationalistic tones from the late eighteenth century. Ideas of rational and affectionate child-rearing put forth by John Locke and Jean-Jacques Rousseau, respectively, became critical in debates about the sovereignty of citizens and the importance of civic virtue.[27] Ministers delivered messages on Republican child-rearing. In preindustrial culture, fathers had been charged with nurturing their children (particularly boys) morally and intellectually, but as more fathers left the home in pursuit of wages, mothers increasing took over that role.[28] The historian Mary Ryan notes that as early as the 1820s, in the "burned-over district" of upstate New York where the fires of the Second Great Awakening revivals gave language to changing roles within the family, ministers began advocating cultivating affection to court children's souls.[29] In the 1840s a Congregationalist minister, Horace Bushnell, postulated that children are born innocent of sin and called the affectionate home "the church of childhood." Most importantly when considering the roles of youth (adolescents), he stated that children gradually achieve their own moral agency as they age. They must be protected and guided by God-fearing parents, even to the edge of adulthood, with mothers cultivating development beyond young childhood.[30]

By midcentury, literate Americans embraced an ideology that childhood (and increasingly, adolescence) should be a time of protected dependence, and that to press children into adulthood prematurely was bad for the nation as well as the child. Within two decades they would argue that prematurely pushing children into adult roles contributed to white racial decline.[31] Children, therefore, must be treated differently from adults and allowed to live as children for as long as possible. This was clearly a child-rearing philosophy for middle-class families, living primarily in northeastern urban centers, with the financial ability to shelter and cultivate children into adulthood. As middle-class youth gained a childhood and extended adolescence, the expanding market economy increased the labor potential of rural and working-class children and a majority began sharing responsibility for their family's economic survival as soon as they could be trusted with simple tasks, such as watching over pastured stock or foraging through city refuse. But because the middle class wrote the books that they read, their ideology reigned; normative childhood became a time set apart for play, self-cultivation, and gaining self-control.[32]

Belief in childhood innocence combined with an attenuating youth led to an ideal adolescent white girl as sexually obtuse. If there is one trait that holds true for tomboys of domestic fiction and prescriptive literature alike, it is that they are utterly unaware of their own sexual power even as onlookers (typically the narrator) stress their allure. The child-identity is what allowed for the term "tomboy" to be used positively—that is, to become descriptive of girls and not promiscuous older women, as the word had been used since the sixteenth century.[33] By the mid-nineteenth century, thanks largely to sentimental culture, children embodied the concept of innocence. Central to their cultural appeal, adolescent tomboys gamboled and cavorted with the obtuseness of younger girls, with bodies that suggest impending adulthood. And this child-embodied innocence, the performance scholar Robin Bernstein emphasizes, was "not merely an absence of knowledge, but an active state of repelling knowledge": it was "the performance of not-noticing."[34] Tomboys excelled at not-noticing.

Yet innocence and the need for protection did not preclude middle-class awareness that children must develop a sense of self-reliance in such an insecure economy. Adolescent girls were the first older children released from producing goods or wages for the family unit, largely because their compensation remained low and because earlier skills of weaving and food production were no longer useful for their middle-class families. Their loss of importance as producers made them critical as markers of family prosperity; a daughter at school served as a sign that her family did not need her labor.[35] And yet in such a volatile economic climate, middle-class girls must have the ability to move adroitly into the upper classes or survive among the working poor, as fate demanded. Even as middle-class girls were being educated and polished to a high shine more akin to socialites than shopkeepers, they were reminded of the fragility of their positions. Do not allow yourself to be rendered "helpless and dependent on men for support and protection," Catharine Sedgwick warns girls in *Means and Ends, or Self-Training* (1839). Accomplished girls might "secure an independent existence" through bookkeeping, copying, or writing, rather than going into the female work of the lower classes, such as domestic servitude.[36] Sedgwick's was a fundamentally pragmatic view of a girl's prospects. A girl might be the plum of the marriage market one day—in which case she needed know how to play the piano and converse in French—but if her father lost his job, she must be equally prepared to respectably earn wages.[37]

But again, if popular culture hammered home the message that girls were content to remain indoors and sew fine seams, girls' diaries demonstrate that in fact they enjoyed the same sports and games as their brothers. Male or female, life out of doors was the norm for most Americans. And, as much as prescriptive literature nagged girls to behave like domestic angels, most girls wanted to have fun and many played rough. Until a girl reached menarche, she often lived as active and unfettered a life outdoors as her brothers, after chores were done.[38]

Virtually every female memoirist, from Frances Willard of the temperance movement to the anti-suffragist Caroline Stickney Creevey, recalled a daring and energetic girlhood.[39] In an essay interrogating the disconnect between fictional depictions of children and historical evidence, Anne Scott McLeod writes that nineteenth-century girls recorded "freedom with a joy that rings down through the years and out of the pages of their autobiographies. Instead of being confined to house and hearth, many girls . . . 'lived as much as possible in the open' and thrived on it."[40] Rural and urban girls alike enjoyed sledding and skating in the winter. Girls with access to rural areas did their share of fishing, target-shooting, hunting, and daring stunts of all kinds. Girls who were enslaved or earning wages to support the family had less time for play, but as adults they, too, remembered the joys to be had in the natural world.[41]

Unlike their brothers, however, girls did straddle the outdoor world and the domestic sphere, which would become their domain in adulthood. In comparison with male diarists, girls write more consistently about visits with adult neighbors, family, and friends, and counted up their knitting and sewing projects. To extend Rotundo's metaphor of boyhood sovereignty, theirs was not "the free nation" but rather a "domestic dependent" nation, residing half within the world of domestic expectation and half in a world of youthful possibility. Rather than say that girls lived entirely indoors, it is more accurate to say that they enjoyed both a vigorous outdoor life and interior domestic arts.[42]

As they moved into adolescence, white middle-class male and female children shared not only playtime but also education. This was a huge shift in how females experienced gender as it related to age; young and female had been synonymous with private, but now girls were required to maintain a respectable public presence. And battles over how best to educate boys and girls were decided less by the culture of the country than by the curriculum, which is a fundamentally equalizing force.

It took nearly seventy years, from 1852 (Massachusetts) to 1918 (Mississippi), for public education to become nationwide.[43] And even though public schools became common, the school system itself never became monolithic in the United States. Besides preexisting private schools for elites, Catholic schools arose as a competing alternative for the common folk and proved particularly popular among immigrants.[44] But the philosophy behind the creation of public schools—called "the common school movement"—was egalitarian, and insisted that *all* children, regardless of class, race, gender, or religion, should be able to write, read, and do basic math, and know both history and geography. Common school advocates also applied a middle-class perspective to childhood, positing that a "real childhood" meant one focused on education and play. The segregation of children in age-determined classes also had formative impact in that Americans began to think about children in terms of chronology rather than function.[45] Strapping boys and girls who developed early were now seen as no more suitable for adulthood than their less visibly mature peers of the same age.

Definitions of white middle-class girls were largely determined by region, as was the education allowed them. This is one reason that tomboys as characters do not turn up in southern stories until much later (and quickly become ubiquitous in the early twentieth century). Although descriptive and prescriptive literature rendered northeastern ideals dominant, southern culture was too obviously different in terms of class and race to quickly adopt the same innovations in education or nuances of childhood definition. For example, the South was the last region to adopt compulsory education. For that reason alone—not taking into account the other vast differences in racial politics, economic structures, and population density—the northeastern press depicted versions of childhood and youth unattainable by all but a few southerners until industrialism began shaping the urban middle class of the New South in 1877.

Well into the twentieth century, education in the South was determined by class.[46] Most southerners were abysmally poor and had little access to basic literacy or reading materials. In direct contrast, both daughters and sons of prosperous farmers, planters, and merchants, as well as lawyers, doctors, and other professionals, routinely received an education equal or even superior to children in the northeast. With an eye toward making an advantageous marriage, elite fathers encouraged their daughters to study the classical languages and their literatures, often forbidden to girls in the Northeast.[47] The fact that so many southern families of means made tremendous financial, practical, and emotional sacrifices to send their daughters to school says more about the importance of girls as markers of class status than belief in intellectual equality.[48] Even within the white middle class and its relatively hegemonic print culture, girlhood and childhood were constructed regionally.

Republican ideas and emerging middle-class culture came together in support of education for all children, no longer just boys, in the northeastern states. It started with Massachusetts, where both boys and girls had been taught to read since colonial times, despite the fact that only boys were allowed in common schools until 1789.[49] Girls and women had proven themselves to be voracious readers, and by the time girls were officially going to school with boys they were already purchasing more than half of all books sold in the new United States. Likewise, despite early social patterns dictating that girls needed to learn sewing but not writing, girls had also proven to be prolific writers. Female authors accounted for over a fourth of the books sold by the end of the eighteenth century.[50]

Regardless of differing opinions on the appropriate political, economic, and social rights of women, nineteenth-century proponents of education agreed that men and women had similar intellectual capacities and the right to cultivate them.[51] As industrial capitalism transformed even rural households in the northeastern states by the 1830s, more prosperous households began to send their children to school full time. In that decade, Horace Mann in Massachusetts, Henry Barnard in Connecticut, and Calvin Stowe in Ohio strove to standardize state-supported systems of elementary education, for which they advocated a ten-month term, a uniform curriculum, and professionally trained teachers. Massachusetts alone had a state-wide mandate to integrate public schools, which it did in 1855, although there were other instances of racially integrated schools in various cities with small black populations.[52] It became the norm for children to go to school, and character formation was increasingly the focus of schooling. Education was widely promoted as an assimilating force, to shape the heterogeneous population into a more homogenous citizenry.[53] But expanded education also effectively reduced the control parents had over their children by removing them from the home for teaching. Also, through the printing of school primers, northeastern, Protestant values dominated early education.[54]

As historians have noted, the introduction of graded classes had a profound effect on the shaping of childhood and spurred the culture to make greater legal, as well as cultural, distinctions in a person's first twenty-one years of life. Because graded schools introduced mandatory attendance, schooling went from being a minor part in many children's lives to its defining element. And it helped prompt the shift from what Nicholas Syrett calls "functional age," or age determined by capabilities, to "chronological age," or capabilities determined by years.[55] The effect was greatest for rural children, who were caught between a family life based on natural seasons and a school calendar that never changed, regardless of external forces, and stood outside of the networks of church, race, and kinship. The new organization of classrooms, with lines of students at individual desks facing a teacher who stood at the front of the room, along with standardized measures of performance, formalized the new distance between their home lives and their individual identities as participants in a system outside of their family's control.[56]

At midcentury, the most consuming educational debate centered on coeducation, with doctors, educators, and cultural critics giving opposing prophecies of how genders would influence each other. This went on for decades. But most towns simply could not afford to run two schools (although some miraculously found the means when African American children entered public school systems), and coeducation quickly became the norm.[57] Western states proved the most amenable; in 1872 the far West boasted sixty-seven of the ninety-seven coeducational public and private institutions in America.[58]

In coeducational schools, boys and girls found themselves judged by the same criteria, in a world where men and women were seen as opposites. It was a heady experience for many girls, and it presented a forceful counter to domestic training that still demanded female subordination.[59] Girls quickly outnumbered boys—and also outperformed them. And as boys and girls increasingly attended school into their late teens, they also remained in a state of protected dependency much longer than youth of earlier periods. With the exception of sewing skills (which were still perceived to be a woman's main occupation other than mothering, regardless of status), middle-class girls began focusing more on intellectual than domestic training.[60]

Educators refused to change standards to accommodate girls. Within educational settings girls were expected to be intellectually aggressive, despite concurrent arguments that women were intrinsically passive by nature. The pioneering women's educator Joseph Emerson impressed upon female students that education demands "something more than sitting still and passively receiving . . . that information which you can scarcely avoid."[61] And, although northeastern schools were hardly educating girls to become spinster radicals, educators were vocal in supporting intellectual equality between the sexes.[62] They were determined to expand, not dilute, expectations of education.

Expansion in education irrevocably changed the lives and expectations of nineteenth-century girls in the United States, just as it continues to do the world over. By the 1850s northeastern girls were actively transforming the public world, not because they controlled the world—or even their own destinies—but because they began to see the world and engage with it differently. The school experience did more than teach academic skills to these girls, who were maturing earlier and marrying later than earlier generations of women; it trained them to treat their own cultivation as an occupation and buttressed the concept of self-sufficiency even as they were prepared to marry into economic dependence.[63]

Analyzing diaries primarily of middle-class northeastern girls, the historian Jane Hunter contends that education was at the center of how young ladies (the earlier term used for adolescent girls) came to be called girls in the late nineteenth century. By immersing themselves in school and pursuing their own ambitions, these young women embodied a new kind of girlhood, with time for self-cultivation between the dependence of childhood and the selflessness of adulthood. This new girlhood, disseminated through print as a national ideal, was in truth a product of northeastern urban centers.

Girls' more unconventional personal desires may have failed to materialize much of the time, but each time a girl tested the boundaries, she pushed closer toward asserting that fulfillment as an individual was as much an imperative for girls as for their brothers. School days brought girls into extended contact with peers, where, in unprecedented numbers, they enjoyed intense female friendships that began to produce a "girl culture," replete with leisure activity and consumer goods. Girl culture, created by girls themselves (though certainly encouraged by the market), had a "greater sense of fun and play" than adults tended to encourage.[64] Emerging girl culture created the audience for new print culture that spoke directly to American girl identity.

The New Tomboy in Print

The real force behind the emergence of the tomboy character came from the publishing opportunities available in the northeastern publishing world.

By midcentury, women authors such as Susan Warner and Maria Cummings dominated fiction sales with their phenomenally popular domestic novels. Inspired by this blossoming of female authorship, girls in particular sought out opportunities presented by story papers, weekly periodicals that looked like newspapers but contained mostly popular fiction.[65] In the late 1840s, in order to fulfill the promise of original works by American authors, editors found themselves compelled to include a significant percentage of contributions by women and girls.[66] Front-page authors Fanny Fern (Sarah Payson) and E. D. E. N. Southworth were the most successful of the story-paper writers of the mid-nineteenth century. Every literate citizen knew their names and many, if not most, had read some of their work.

Story papers became a favorite medium for amateur writers because publishers aggressively sought out new authorship, and publishing in story papers became a route to female agency. Examining the writings of Winnie Woodfern (the pen name of Mary Gibson) and her peers, Daniel A. Cohen demonstrates that adolescent girls published regularly in story papers from Boston to New York in this period.[67] These girl authors predominately wrote fantasies of youthful female ambition. Their heroines aspired to fame as artists, entertainers, and soldiers as well as to more conventional careers in teaching and writing. Many of the central heroines also flirt with male behaviors and dress, allowing for girls to "experiment with new forms of female masculinity in attitude, bearing, dress, ambition, behavior, and sexuality." At times their work was popular enough to win the coveted spot on the front page.[68]

The heroines of Woodfern's stories are unapologetic about their hunger for fame. "I must be wealthy and famous—then famous and wealthy—and then both together" proclaims Hero Strong, the central character of an 1855 story, who is determined to make it as an author. Hero is masculine in dress, with "short curls of thick, rich auburn hair, parted on one side, like boy's," tanned skin, and a face conveying both "good nature" and "pride"—and, like a young man, she is smoking a cigarito.[69] She gives up the man she loves to pursue fame as a writer. Nor does she compromise her intentions and choose to write from within the privacy of domestic life; she seizes public fame as one of her goals. Only after meeting her ambitions does Woodfern reward her with romantic love.

Woodfern's other heroines take similar paths and struggle between their drive for creative expression and fame and their hunger for romance and family.[70] Such stories proclaim that girls can make their mark in the world beyond the domestic sphere. Indeed, most of Woodfern's heroines choose to do so. For example, in "The Good Angel of Georgian Eden's Life," nineteen-year-old Georgian jilts her invalid fiancé, explaining to a friend: "I cannot marry Philip now, and settle down quietly as his wife. The world must hear of me first—I must have fame and wealth to satisfy my wildest dreams, and then I will return to make his life happy."[71]

Most girls could not live like the heroines in Woodfern's stories, but they could fantasize through them. And the lack of literary realism in such stories should not erase, in Cohen's words, "the very real *social, cultural* and *psychological* transformations" suggested by their plots.[72] Woodfern emphasized that a woman cannot find happiness without fulfilling the promise of her own talents. It is a version of the intense self-cultivation being taught to middle-class girls, except that it does not end abruptly with marriage.[73] Indeed, Cohen argues that the later coherent tomboy figure served to domesticate the ambitions expressed by such heroines, who were far more unconventional than the typical tomboy of later fiction.[74]

The edge of the Civil War, in 1859—the year after the "Our Daughters— Tomboys" article I discussed at the beginning of this chapter first appeared in print—proved to be a crystalizing moment for the tomboy character. It is impossible to pinpoint how much this shift had to do with impending national catastrophe or the increasing agitation for women's rights and abolition. We know, thanks in no small part to the controversial Fugitive Slave Act of 1850 and the subsequent reactionary publication of Harriet Beecher Stowe's *Uncle Tom's Cabin* in 1851, that abolition (the call for immediate emancipation) went mainstream outside of the South. In other words, even before the disruption of war, Americans were questioning the inviolability of categories of race and gender. Fearless, bold, and innocent, girls of antebellum American periodical literature suggested a tough self-reliance alongside tender and innate chastity.[75]

In 1859 E. D. E. N. Southworth's serialized novel *The Hidden Hand* became a literary sensation, principally because of its heroine, Capitola Black. The instant and lasting popularity of the work suggests that Southworth's playful use of gender struck a chord in American popular thought. Although largely forgotten today, Southworth was perhaps the most widely read female author of her time, and possibly the most widely read author of either gender. Beginning in 1857, her stories usually appeared on the front page of the *New York Ledger,* the top nationally circulating story paper from 1855 to 1898. *The Hidden Hand* proved to be the most popular of all of her stories; it was serialized twice more, in 1868 and 1883, before being published in book form in 1888, and remained in print for another thirty years.[76]

Thirteen-year-old Capitola does the near-unthinkable when she enters the tale dressed as a boy. But when Capitola is hauled before a judge, she makes it clear that she only assumed male dress to escape prostitution in New York City's "Rag Alley." Anyone familiar with popular fiction of the period will not be surprised to hear, several chapters later, that Capitola is in fact a wealthy heiress who was kidnapped by a heroic maidservant in order to save her from a (now deceased) demented uncle. Adventurous, hard-headed, resourceful, and daring, Capitola undermines patriarchal authority with insouciance and demands better treatment. She is not infrequently carried off and threatened with either marriage or a fate "worse than death," but she just as often rescues others—male and female—and follows her own inclinations.

In Capitola, Southworth constructed a heroine of feminine charm and masculine arrogance. On the one hand, Capitola expresses embarrassment over passing as a boy, but on the other, she defends and takes pride in the ruse. Although she later blushes when remembering her male attire, when called before the magistrate to explain her actions, she quickly asserts, "The only thing that made me feel sorry was to see what a fool I had been not to turn into a boy before, when it was so easy!" As a girl she could not find employment, but as a boy she "carried carpet-bags, held horses, put in coal, cleaned sidewalks and blackened gentlemen's boots and did everything an honest lad could turn his hand to. And so for more'n a year I was as happy as a king."[77] As a girl she had sold off pieces of her clothes to avoid outright starvation, and was to the point of selling her body. Capitola makes it clear: boys have it far easier than girls.

Despite her tenure as the heroine of what the literary scholar Nina Baym describes as a "recklessly unrealistic" story, Capitola is a relatively modern character who adheres to her own sense of self in the face of social convention. She enjoys feminine clothes and the attentions of handsome young men, but she shrugs aside the other trappings of femininity. She is in charge of accoutrements; they are not in charge of her. Capitola disregards femininity when it endangers her self-reliance. Her success and attractiveness lie in her ability to lay bare the false performances of true womanhood.[78] But while Capitola rejects superficial conventions of gender, she also subscribes to a belief in gender essentialism: that there is something morally and spiritually unique in female identity that is untouched by surface performance. She is not about to be turned into a boy by some mysterious "they"; she is a self-reliant girl, much like the ones Tocqueville described a quarter-century before, walking a precariously narrow line without seeming to recognize the danger.

Though marked as a tomboy from the outset, Capitola is not androgynous. Beyond the first chapter, she exudes femininity through dress, beauty, and wiles, while still claiming male freedoms through physicality, irreverence, hunger for adventure, and stubborn assertion of agency. She is most like a boy in her love of pranks, which she merrily plays on every authoritative man in the book. After her brief debut in trousers, Capitola remains in skirts. Yet domestic life soon bores her. When her guardian, Old Hurricane, likens her to a Bowery boy itching for a fight, Capitola agrees: "Yes I am! just decomposing above ground for want of having my blood stirred, and I wish I was back at the Bowery!"[79] Capitola craves fun and Southworth celebrates her brass—standing up to Old Hurricane, capturing the villain (his heart and the rest of him), and rescuing the more demure maidens.

As with many tomboys to come, Capitola's beauty allows her to behave boyishly without appearing manly. Alfred Habegger states that the "basic appeal" of *The Hidden Hand* is "an intrepid girl's casually assuming and getting away with all the old male prerogatives."[80] But she "gets away" with them thickly dressed in saucy charm. The freedoms Capitola claims are not threatening in a figure who is funny and pretty. Yet for her time—when "the term 'boy' was often synonymous with prankster"—Capitola's self-assertions were decidedly unfeminine.[81]

Capitola does not simply play pranks and outwit the men around her, but uses humor to critique society itself. Indeed, Habegger finds that she is "nothing less than the female Huckleberry Finn," calling the two characters "our great nineteenth-century orphans, female and male, whose scantily socialized points of view expose the absurdities of civilization and its masquerades."[82] Pairing Capitola with arguably the most famous "bad boy" of American literature is useful because it highlights how humor is used with the tomboy, much like the bad boy, to reveal social truths.[83]

Despite the farcical nature of *The Hidden Hand,* Capitola's humor and antics serve to highlight the ways in which conventional femininity undermines the autonomy of girls and women. It is telling that, like the heroines in Woodfern's stories, Capitola is allowed to keep her assertive personality after marriage. At the end she continues to give her husband the sharp side of her tongue, as Southworth suggests he deserves.[84] Capitola sacrifices no part of her self in achieving her goals.

The Hidden Hand had a life beyond the printed page—and indeed, beyond the United States, as over forty versions found their way to the stage over the next several decades, well into the twentieth century.[85] By December 1859 a burlesque version of *The Hidden Hand* began appearing in cities around the nation.[86] In 1905 the play was revised into a musical, *My Tomboy Girl,* by Charles E. Blaney, with a hit title song.[87] The play also became the basis of a silent film of the same name in 1915. Thus *The Hidden Hand* was not only a best-selling novel but was deeply enmeshed in popular culture for over half a century.

At roughly the same time, female entertainers began to break into comic theatre, playfully challenging gender more overtly. One of the most famous was the teenage darling of mining California, Lotta Crabtree, who stormed East Coast culture as a funny western tomboy. Habegger notes, "She smoked cigars, showed her stockings, and specialized in hoyden (not siren) roles. She hit the big time at the moment that the funny tomboyish alter ego of Louisa May Alcott became famous."[88] Likewise, Lydia Thompson and the British Blondes also captivated American audiences by dressing as young men and poking fun at gender assumptions through humor and burlesque (which was not about nudity, at this point, but turning expectations upside down). These tomboy performers used humor as their medium, moving emphatically away from sexualized cross-dressing into something more playful but perhaps also more socially provocative.[89]

Starting in roughly the 1860s, the "tomboy tale" formula of feminine redemption through love also became popular in periodical literature. The authors of such tales employed different environments (mountains, forests, farms, villages, cities, ranches), and their tomboys entered the story at different ages, although the most common age was early pubescence (around age fourteen in this period). But all stories come to the same ending: the tomboy falls in love and tames herself.[90] In this sense, tomboy tales are conversion narratives, which were arguably the most common stories written for girls before the flowering of the juvenile fiction market in the 1870s.[91] The tomboy heroine, chafing at the domestic space closing in on her, cannot be coerced into accept her "natural" place in the social order. Her change in character must be internal. In tomboy tales, love of the right man makes her see that what she had considered the burdens of womanhood are truly a gift. And yet the story typically ends with the narrator happily proclaiming that a trace of the tomboy remains in the health of her carriage or the sparkle in her eye. In every story the tomboy must tame herself, but not lose herself entirely.

By the late 1860s, writers in *Godey's* were alternately using "tomboy" favorably—for example, when a fond mother declares, "There comes my young tomboy!"—and as shorthand for uncouth behavior, as in the case of an "intolerable tom-boy" who munches taffy and makes mean remarks to the well-behaved heroine.[92] The time was ripe for tomboys to enter the cultural discourse not simply as a warning or even as a charming novelty, but as a character through which girls could seek temporary freedoms. Despite a tendency for early nineteenth-century writers to depict girls as opposites of boys, most girls continued to play the same games as their brothers. And as education, and particularly coeducation, expanded, girls increasingly saw themselves as the equals of (or smarter than) their brothers. Girls began to dream of more exciting lives, fed both by a print culture that produced such heroines and by their own life experiences excelling in school beside boys raised with greater freedoms. Furthermore, girlhood (like childhood) was lengthening, to accommodate schooling and the cultivation of middle-class social mores, at the same time that children were increasingly seen as immune to sexual knowledge. All of this created an environment in which girls had a longer time to be free as girls—free to dream of ambitions without being labeled as promiscuous, to play without running the risk of growing into "mannish women."

And yet even as tomboy characters gained favor—as more attractive, spunkier, smarter, and kinder than other girls—every reader knew that tomboy freedoms were bound by time. American women, married or not, were expected to accept nurturing, selfless roles. Girls knew this, and despaired in their diaries that their tomboy freedoms would expire upon reaching adulthood.[93] Because of the tomboy's ability to straddle the fence—to indicate both rebellion and conformity—she was a useful symbol for a culture in the process of creating a new girlhood. The increasingly coherence and popularity of the tomboy character and her story signified both an acceptance of modern girlhood as time of liberal celebration and its unavoidable demise upon maturation. It suggested that the tomboy could live freely and joyfully as long as she never grew up. The tomboy was acceptable only if her wildness could be tamed or put into the service of some greater social good, as was soon made clear by the blossoming of tomboy characters in juvenile domestic and western pulp fiction.

2

Tomboy Heroines in the Home

"I like best to read about 'Tom-boys,'" ten-year-old Eleanor Browne declares in her prize-winning essay "What I Like to Read." She explains that she enjoys going with fictional tomboys "in their games of ball, climbing trees, and kite-flying with their brothers; rowing boats and building rafts; picnics, chestnutting parties and rambles through the woods." She participates in unsupervised play through these tomboy characters. But she is also careful to point out the difference between expectations of herself in "real life" and the unfettered tomboys of her imagined life in books, hastening to add: "I am called a 'nice, quiet, ladylike little girl.' I never tear my dresses and never get into 'scrapes.'" She knows that "thoughtful and considerate" is the way girls must behave "in real life, but when it comes to the books I prefer stories of girls like 'Gypsy Brenton' and 'Joe' [*sic*] in 'Little Women.'"[1] Eleanor clearly wanted to be seen as a good, obedient, "thoughtful and considerate" little girl, but internally, adventure thrilled her. Safe adventures. Indeed, sweet ones that sound very much like how many real nineteenth-century girls spent their free time.

Unbeknownst to Eleanor Browne, the commercial success of the two tomboy heroines she noted—Gypsy Breynton and Jo March—were the engines behind the new juvenile publishing market that produced the books she enjoyed. Although tomboys already served as central characters in adult periodical fiction, Elizabeth Stuart Phelps was the first to center a novel and, eventually, a series on a tomboy heroine: *Gypsy Breynton* (1866). Phelps wrote for Sunday-school use but kept her moralism to a minimum, and girls consumed her books like candy well into the twentieth century.[2]

Gypsy's appeal is palpable from her initial introduction, when she climbs out of her bedroom window "without the slightest hesitation" before walking "along the ridgepole with the ease and fearlessness of a boy."

Gypsy has fun. She is full of faults, but they are benign and often illustrate what girls themselves find frustrating: the imperative to be neat and quiet and to dress in clothes that restrict physical freedom, and her struggle to rein in "bad" behavior when it gives her such pleasure.[3]

Phelps compares Gypsy to a boy often, but does not use the term "tomboy" until she clarifies in the preface to the 1895 edition that Gypsy is indeed a tomboy. The date is telling, because by this point tomboys had become beloved fictional characters. Phelps explains that we know Gypsy is a tomboy because "she paddles a raft, she climbs a tree, she skates and tramps and coasts, she is usually very muddy, and a little torn." Yet for all her dishevelment, Gypsy is joyful: "There is apt to be a pin in her gathers; but there is sure to be a laugh in her eyes. Wherever there is mischief, there is Gypsy. Yet, wherever there is fun, and health, and hope, and happiness— and I think, wherever there is truthfulness and generosity—there is Gypsy, too."[4] Gypsy sees through the hypocrisies fomented by fashion, and makes healthy choices even if she crosses gender lines to do so. Indeed, Phelps goes so far as to suggest Gypsy is *better* for being a bit like a boy: "There was not a trout-brook for miles where she had not fished. There was hardly a tree she had not climbed or a fence or stone-wall . . . that she had not walked. Gypsy could row and skate and swim, and play ball and make kites, and coast and race, and drive, and chop wood."[5] And these were *virtues* in the hands of Phelps. Gypsy approaches every challenge with good humor, exhibiting none of the mental self-flagellation that wrecked the lives of heroines of Sunday-school fiction.[6] The demon that Gypsy must conquer is her own impulsive spirit.

Yet even if Gypsy is a positively portrayed character, her gender transgressions nonetheless provoke anxiety in others. The central conflict of each novel is the survival of her engaging personality in light of the looming expectation that she must learn to subdue herself or face social ostracism. Like a steady croon of backup singers, her brother, her parents, and her neighbors wonder aloud what will become of her. Gypsy, much to their dismay, is utterly unconcerned. She likes herself. And although the central conflict is about loss of freedom upon maturity, she does not actually age. Gypsy remains in the freedom of girlhood.

This chapter explores the early postbellum tomboy of domestic fiction, stories largely idealizing the middle-class homes in which they were set, which established the tomboy as a marketable central heroine. Beginning

with Gypsy in 1866, the tomboy provided a fun-loving and highly imperfect alternative to the fictional girls suffering through Christian piety, and
a temporary detour for heroines finding themselves through romance. She
was both a good girl (in her natural morals) and a wild girl (not yet civilized) in the stretch between girlhood and womanhood. Part of her charm,
but also her folly, was that she pitted her will against adulthood—a battle
she could not win. By the 1880s, the tomboy heroine was fully established
as a vehicle for investigating the internal and external struggles of girls
growing up in the white, middle-class world.

Jo March: Archetype

With the publication of *Little Women* in 1868, Louisa May Alcott elevated
the tomboy into an archetypal American heroine. The success of her book
also revealed the market viability of a youthful female readership. *Little
Women* would have a lasting impact on readers' understandings of what
it meant to be a girl in America, in part because of the merits of the book
itself but also because it launched the fictionalization of girlhood.[7] The
development and persistence of the tomboy of juvenile domestic fiction—
literature produced for adolescents coming of age in well-supervised,
white, middle-class homes—provide a window into adult expectations of
girls in this period, how those expectations were successfully sold to girls,
and how and why girls responded so passionately.

Allowing the innocent and good-natured tomboy to grow up and
become a woman (dependent, respectable) without losing her spirit (independent, fun-loving) became the challenge of *Little Women*. It could be
argued that Alcott gave the tomboy new depth simply by allowing Jo to
be plain and often cross but also loved and admired. Sometimes easygoing
and other times consumed by temper, Jo expresses conflicts inherent to
being human. She stresses discomfort with the very *idea* of acting feminine, and utter disinterest in trying to change her gender behavior (though
she is entirely obsessed with flaws in her moral character, a personality trait
perhaps less about gender than about sentimental literature). Alcott found
a way, in the words of the feminist scholar Carolyn Heilbrun, "to appropriate the male model without giving up the female person"—to celebrate
a female-centered world in which the tomboy can have the freedoms of
a boy.[8] It was a fantasy that struck a chord, to say the least, and turned

Louisa May Alcott, a struggling writer and middle-aged New England spinster, into a household name and a heroine in her own right.

The novel began as a bread-and-butter assignment for Alcott, who was more concerned with feeding her family than transforming the publishing industry. Giving in to a suggestion by Thomas Niles, an editor at the Roberts Brothers firm, to write a "girls book," Alcott took up the task with the enthusiasm of a ditch digger. With Oliver Optic's proven commercial success with adventure fiction for boys, Niles recognized it was time to address the remaining market. Alcott simply needed the money. In May 1868 she famously confided to her journal: "I plod away, though I don't enjoy this sort of thing. Never liked girls or knew many, except my sisters; but our queer plays and experiences may prove interesting, though I doubt it."[9]

The fact that Alcott, who grew up in an almost entirely female household, claimed that she "never liked or knew many" girls makes sense only if she was defining "girls" through the prism of cultural discourse. The children's book trade, a century in the making, still focused on producing works for younger children, principally in three forms: the colorful chapbooks of fairy tales and Mother Goose rhymes, abridged versions of classics such as *Robinson Crusoe,* and the didactic fiction produced to counter the evils of the chapbooks.[10] If Alcott was thinking of the girls already in print—dutiful, passive, serene girls, or naughty girls who meet terrible ends—the success of her book soon proved she was not alone in finding such girls alien. As the novelist and critic Elizabeth Janeway summarized in 1968, "Her girls were jealous, mean, silly and lazy; and for 100 years jealous, mean, silly and lazy girls have been ardently grateful for the chance to read about themselves" and to learn with relief "that one's faults were not unique."[11]

The idea of girls or women as innately passive and dependent did not square with Alcott's own girlhood experience. By 1868 she had been contributing to her family's support for years. Although her father, the educator and Transcendentalist Bronson Alcott, was indisputably the head of the family, he did not earn enough to feed and house it. He was friends with Ralph Waldo Emerson and other illustrious thinkers, and his large, airy office made up half of the first floor of Orchard House, their home in Concord, Massachusetts. But he was financially impractical and could not earn the kind of money needed to keep a family of six within the realm of intellectual gentility to which the Alcotts so tenaciously clung. Abba Alcott,

Marmee in both the book and life, had long been the breadwinner as well
as the stabilizing force of the family.[12] As soon as they were able, Louisa
and her sisters also earned income to contribute to the family's support.
Yet despite the working-class status suggested by their need to earn wages,
they followed intellectual and creative pursuits suggestive of the middle
class. Alcott's own home was a topsy-turvy version of gender dynamics
that belied popular imagery of American family life. On a cramped writing
desk positioned between two windows in her bedroom, Alcott spun the
narratives that eventually kept her family fed, warm, and hopeful for the
future. In this sense, Alcott was a quiet precursor to the New Woman.
Although largely shielded from direct public gaze, she nonetheless became
a known public voice advocating female self-actualization.

Alcott's seeming innocuous "girls book" proved to have enormous
staying power. Indeed, her reluctance to write the typical girls' story along
with the self-discipline to incorporate the required conventions may, in the
words of the historian Barbara Sicherman, "explain how she managed to
write one that transcended the genre even while defining it."[13] It may also
have helped that Alcott, like Winnie Woodfern and other teenage story-
paper authors, had cut her writing teeth on blood-and-thunder tales in
the style of E. D. E. N. Southworth.[14] In a sensational novel, such as *The
Hidden Hand,* the drama comes in the form of villains and calamity and
the heroine's struggles against them. Alcott had to make the interior struggles faced by girls intrinsically valuable, vibrant, and active. The novelist
and critic Brigid Brophy notes, "You can measure Alcott's technical skill by
asking any professional novelist how he would care to have to differentiate
the characters of four adolescent girls—particularly if he were confined to a
domestic setting, more-or-less naturalism and the things which were men-
tionable when Alcott wrote."[15] While it is arguable, given earlier writings
by Woodfern among others, that the four types used by Alcott were already
well established in female fiction, it is the naturalism of Alcott's versions
that make them stand apart. The tension in the story had to come from
within the domestic world without offending the larger public that sub-
scribed to domestic imagery. Who better than a tomboy to lead the way?

Alcott opens the book with the four March sisters arguing in ways
that illustrate their differences and internal struggles when, in Jo's words,
they truly just want "to have a little fun." Meg longs for pretty things;
Jo "examin[es] her shoes in a gentlemanly manner" and pines for books;

Beth mumbles a desire for sheet music; Amy states that art pencils are her greatest "need."[16] There they are, in birth order, the pretty one, the tomboy, the good girl, and the fashionable girl, provoking as much as talking before a low fire on Christmas Eve. Jo and Amy posit themselves as opposites, mirroring a familiar pairing found in prescriptive literature and fiction: is it better for a girl to be authentic yet uncouth, or false yet appropriate?

> "Jo does use such slang words!" observed Amy, with a reproving look at the long figure stretched out on the rug. Jo immediately sat up, put her hands in her pockets, and began to whistle.
> "Don't, Jo, it's so boyish!"
> "That's why I do it."
> "I detest rude, unladylike girls."
> "I hate affected, niminy-piminy chits!"

By 1868 whistling was already a tomboy signifier on stage and in print, and readers would likely have understood that Jo was declaring herself a tomboy. Meg steps in as the public arbiter, giving Jo the first tongue-lashing: "You are old enough to leave off such boyish tricks, and behave better, Josephine. It didn't matter so much when you were a little girl; but now you are so tall, and turn up your hair, you should remember that you are a young lady."[17] To Meg, maturity should end Jo's boyhood.

But Jo's masculinity is innate, like Meg's femininity, so giving up such ways means hiding her core identity, not simply changing behavior. Thus she lashes out in frustrated fury: "I hate to think I've got to grow up and be Miss March, and wear long gowns, and look as prim as a China aster! It's bad enough to be a girl anyway, when I like boys' games and work and manners! I can't get over my disappointment in not being a boy; and it's worse than ever now, for I'm dying to go and fight with Papa, and I can only stay at home and knit, like a poky old woman."[18] To become forever bound to domestic life is not simply intolerable to her; it threatens to erase her sense of self. Jo echoes the experiences of many smart, spirited girls who find adult femininity a soul-numbing performance. Women such as the temperance leader Frances Willard, who, decades later, used much the same language to voice dismay at the restrictions that came with age: "I 'ran wild' until my sixteenth birthday, when the hampering long skirts were brought, with their accompanying corset and high heels; my hair was clubbed up with pins." As a girl she wrote in her journal, "Altogether, I recognize that my occupation is gone."[19]

Beth, who most closely resembles the classic good girl populating decades of books put out by Christian presses, sympathizes even as she stresses the inevitability of their female fate: "Poor Jo! It's too bad, but can't be helped. So you must try to be contented with making your name boyish, and playing brother to us girls."[20] Jo must be content to occupy the masculine end of the spectrum in an all-female household. Meg has declared that Jo's desires are childish and Beth that they are futile in the larger world, but they don't challenge her sentiment that feminine performance can be imprisoning as well as ridiculous. Because she is a girl, she must do something she does poorly (knitting), as opposed to something useful she believes she could do quite well (fighting).

Meg embodies middle-class social mores, and thus takes both Amy and Jo to task for their excesses. She scolds Amy: "You are altogether too particular and prim. Your airs are funny now, but you'll grow up an affected little goose." Meg herself is bland; indeed, she is designed, as one author points out, to be the "sort of girl whose character consists of having no character. Girls of this sort are the commonest to meet in life and the rarest in literature."[21] But that lack of definition conveys her central purpose: she is the voice of the mainstream social ego. Meg is stating a truism found throughout literature prior to *Little Women:* both tomboys and fashionable girls must grow out of their behaviors. Of course, unbeknownst to Meg, Alcott's Jo is about to adjust that perception.

Beth, a shadow of the now iconic tragic heroine of didactic fiction, demands to know her place in the narrative: "If Jo is a tomboy and Amy a goose, what am I, please?" And Meg answers the devastating truth: "You're a dear, and nothing else."[22] Her answer is prescient, as Beth never evolves or grows up in the novel. For thirty years, didactic fiction had cast the selfless Christian girl as powerful through her influence on others (usually by dying tragically young). Beth represents that girl: too shy to speak to strangers, almost too timid to leave the house, Beth serves as a source of obedient, selfless goodness—and she dies much as she lived. In some ways, Alcott reinforces that earlier didactic narrative by positing Beth's demise as fundamental in convincing Jo to accept the need to impose the kind of feminine self-control she has hitherto resented and avoided. But at the same time, Alcott allows Beth's death to remove her from the story, while Jo thrives and charts her own destiny. Jo's exterior aligns with the ways of womanhood, but she remains masculine in her drive to act rather than to influence.

There is no doubting Jo's tomboy status or her disdain for convention. She whistles, ruins her feminine clothing, longs to fight in the war, and claims to be the "man of the family" in her father's absence. She is also the source of humor in the story, a role that tomboys had been playing in periodical fiction for two decades.[23] But Alcott did something more with Jo: this tomboy was not simply funny and winsome, but smart, ambitious, and more comfortable defying feminine convention than trying to live up to its demands. At one point she declares, sounding like a heroine from a story by Winnie Woodfern, that she means to do something "heroic and wonderful that won't be forgotten after I'm dead," adding, "[I] mean to astonish you all, some day. I think I shall write books, and get rich and famous." Her dreams are not like those of her sisters, who long for domestic comfort, kindness, or beauty, but rather to earn her own fame and wealth.[24]

Within the book Jo struggles less against the constrictions of larger society than with quelling her own passionate and impatient nature. Indeed, as Judith Fetterley points out, "The imaginative experience of *Little Women* is built on a paradox: the figure who most resists the pressure to become a little woman is the most attractive. . . . Jo is the vital center of Alcott's book and she is so because she is least a little woman."[25] Jo must learn self-control, but Alcott supports gender differences among girls. Jo's disdain for femininity rewrites the typical tomboy story from one in which the tomboy must be made to conform into one in which the tomboy must conform only to the point of maintaining respectability.

Much like the "bad boys" who would take over fiction a decade later, Jo constantly fails to behave and in so doing reveals the hypocrisy of gendered social customs. Jo struggles to master her emotions throughout the book; her autonomy is hard won, and she approaches her dreams not as the daring heroines of story papers but more as a dutiful daughter who realizes she is transgressive, yet is convinced that convention is the problem, not her ambition.

With the success of *Little Women*, Jo overrode most of the depictions that came before her—she became *the* tomboy, and tomboys became much more than girls who needed to grow up and be tamed inside and out. Jo craves adventure and fun. She is disagreeable only slightly less often than she is "jolly." She unconditionally loves her sisters and shares their values, but cares nothing for beauty, fashion, or status like Meg, and is too active and internally disobedient to be accepting like Beth, and too straightforward and self-aware to resemble self-centered, affected Amy. Jo resides where most readers do as well: torn between the desire to please others and to get her way, her love of fun and her sense of responsibility, her female identity and her (so-called) masculine drive. Neither the author nor the readers truly wanted to see Jo "tamed" to the point of losing her internal convictions.

The ongoing relationship between Jo and Laurie Lawrence, her next door neighbor and best friend, is one of the aspects of the book that most sets it apart from both other tomboy tales and girls' fiction of this period, and also what makes this a story about a new kind of girlhood. Twentieth-century tomboy tales often include boy pals with whom the tomboy cavorts, but nineteenth-century versions were more likely to contain a male friend marked from the outset by his wealth or character as the tomboy's romantic future when she finally awakens to her feminine desires.[26] Jo and Laurie are simpatico spirits who immediately fall into a devoted friendship, but very early it becomes clear that their devotion differs in erotic potential. Laurie, handsome and heir to a sizeable family fortune, adores Jo from their first encounter, when he meets her standing against the wall at a party, trying to hide her burnt skirts. His ardor for Jo grows, regardless of her lack of fashion, unwitting destruction of property, and oft-expressed desire to be a boy. They trade inside jokes and innuendos. They have fun. Laurie's ardor is understandable: most readers of *Little Women* probably would have been aghast if he did not adore Jo along with them. But however much Laurie conforms to the designated marriage material presented in most tomboy tales, Jo roundly rejects a romantic relationship with him. What makes Jo's story different from the others—and turns Jo into a new tomboy archetype—is that not only does Laurie does not win Jo, but she does not change to please him or the reader.

After the publication of the first half of the story, in which Alcott primarily fictionalized the actual experiences of her family, fans demanded that she marry Jo off to Laurie. At this point, however, Alcott was not writing about what *had* happened, but imagining what *could* happen to herself and her family members. Alcott herself disavowed marriage, so she rebelled against marrying off her heroine-self. "Jo should have remained a literary spinster," she later confessed to a friend, "but so many enthusiastic young ladies wrote to me clamorously demanding that she should marry

JO IN A VORTEX.

Every few weeks she would shut herself up in her room, put on her scribbling suit, and

FIGURE 2: "Jo in a Vortex," from the original 1868 edition of *Little Women,* shows Jo March taken over by writing, existing only in the creative vortex of her own mind. Although she is respectably corseted and skirted, befitting a sedate middle-class woman, the electricity of her brain bursts her hair from its pins. AL 731.74. Houghton Library, Harvard University.

Laurie, or somebody, that I didn't dare refuse and out of perversity went and made a funny match for her."[27] She also prefaced Jo's fall into conventional marriage with several pages on why younger people should value spinsters and see them as full human beings. In her "perversity," Alcott allows her tomboy to choose a significantly different ending to the already classic "tomboy tale," in which the handsome, rich young man who has watched the tomboy grow up proposes and leads her to femininity. Not Jo. She turns down the plum pick of husband material. And although she appears tortured by hurting him, she remains secure in her reasons for refusing. Indeed, lest Laurie (and the reader) remain unconvinced, she repeats her refusal several times. He continues to pine for her—while she pines for worldly success through her writing.

More surprisingly still, the intimate friendship between Jo and Laurie ultimately survives the thwarted courtship intact. Thus Alcott depicts women and men as able to sustain loving, platonic friendships separately from romantic ones. Men and women could be equals within friendship; they did not have to occupy opposite ends of a social binary. Such a friendship must have been comforting to girl readers who, more than ever, were going to school and competing academically with boys, and befriending them.

The success of *Little Women* is fundamentally responsible for the tomboy character shifting from pulp fiction to American icon. And the fact that Alcott herself was that tomboy, and went on to have the kind of independent success pursued by her novel-version self, only made the tale more compelling. Alcott became a success alongside her heroine, Jo, because in many ways they became a two-sided coin of the same character. Girls and adults alike commented on the "authenticity" of the March sisters, and Jo in particular, and the thin membrane between fiction (March) and reality (Alcott) added immeasurably to that sentiment.[28]

The perceptions of Jo and "Miss Alcott" became entangled in part through a deliberate pairing by both the publisher and Alcott.[29] It was true that Alcott modeled the Marches on her own family and Jo on herself, but it was publishing sleight of hand to have pieces by Alcott, identified as "From Aunt Jo's Scrap Bag" (1872–1880), published as if Jo March were running about Europe, writing up observations. These stories were entirely unrelated to the March family, other than the series title. But the tangling of the two selves—Jo and Alcott—played a central role in making this tomboy heroine so powerful. It was also what gave the ending of the novel a wonderful openness, with Jo March marrying Professor Bhaer but Louisa May Alcott earning financial security and fame as a writer. Jo March went on to act as the matriarch of a family school that produced several New Women, most notably the tomboy Nan, who grows from a troublemaker in *Little Men* (1871) to an unmarried doctor in *Jo's Boys* (1886). Alcott, meanwhile, became the provider for her own family, finally digging them out of poverty and providing funds for European travels and education. Both Louisa and Jo succeeded by measures put forth in the book and the society embracing it. In 1982 the writer Cynthia Ozick spoke of reading *Little Women* "a thousand, ten thousand times" because "we identify in the end not so much with the Jo of the book as with 'some Jo of the future,' the independent woman she failed to become."[30] Jo may have failed, but Alcott did not, and that made for a wonderfully complex and satisfying close to the story.

Alcott's feelings about her own gender and sexuality may have contributed to her rendering of the complexity of Jo's female masculinity. According to Alcott herself, she not only felt she was truly a boy at heart, but that she was a boy who loved girls. In an interview by a fellow author, Louise Chandler Moulton, not long before her death, Alcott confessed:

> "I have often thought," she said, "that I may have been a horse before I was Louisa Alcott. As a long-limbed child I had all a horse's delight in racing through the fields, and tossing my head to sniff the morning air. Now, I am more than half-persuaded that I am a man's soul, put by some freak of nature into a woman's body."
>
> "Why do you think that?" I asked, in the spirit of Boswell addressing Dr. Johnson.
>
> "Well, for one thing," and the blue-gray eyes sparkled with laughter, "because I have fallen in love in my life with so many pretty girls, and never once the least little bit with any man."[31]

Alcott has Jo struggle mightily with the concept of marriage. Jo is disconsolate when she discovers that Meg harbors feelings for John Brooke, Laurie's tutor. She sees the marriage of her sister as a kind of death of their family, and Alcott allows her to mourn freely and without judgment. Likewise, Jo is dismayed by Laurie's proposal, and indeed it is only after her family circle is broken by the death of Beth and the marriages of Meg and Amy that Jo finds herself attracted to a man. And even then Alcott's language exploring Jo's feelings for Professor Bhaer are uncharacteristically vague, as if strong-willed, hard-headed Jo has suddenly caught a flu that makes her muzzy and out of sorts. She had to be loosened from her foundations to experience the desire to have a male partner. On the surface, Alcott's ending of *Little Women* is quite typical for the tomboy tale: when the tomboy falls in love, she ceases to resist maturity. But her rendering of that ending is far more ambivalent, with Jo choosing to marry someone who treats her as a fellow intellectual. And this tomboy does not go on to simply become a wife and mother but to become a matriarch who raises New Women as well as little men.

One of Alcott's puzzling choices in *Little Women* is how she handles the unnamed war that serves as the backdrop of the book. Writing only three years after the official end of the Civil War, perhaps Alcott felt no need to clarify which war removed the male head of household to create an all-female world. She had written extensively about the Civil War in *Hospital Sketches* (1863), recounting her experiences as a nurse, which first brought her to the attention of Niles. She may have already said all she had to say about the war. But it is also possible that depicting a generic war was a commercial choice, to sidestep the cultural chasm that divided the nation's girls by regional allegiance. The tomboy scholar Kristen Proehl notes that *Little Women* received enormous praise in southern papers, despite Alcott's widely known affiliation with "northern based reform movements"—namely, abolition.[32] Or perhaps it reflected a current belief that girls had no interest in politics or current events.

But it was still an odd choice for this semi-autobiographical novel, because by not naming the Civil War Alcott also ignores the racial injustices addressed by the war, which had profoundly shaped her own identity. Growing up in an actively abolitionist household, as a girl she taught black children to read. For a time, John Brown's daughters boarded in her home. Bronson Alcott famously jeopardized his school by accepting a biracial student.[33] By avoiding specifics about the war, Alcott and her publisher contributed to middle-class notions of appropriate material for youth, but in the process also participated in constructing a girlhood absent of color and the differences that color brings. Alcott chose instead to focus attention on gender and class alone, as if race was not part of such constructions.

It is possible that Alcott recognized that class resonated more than race with her audience. Personal records suggest that middle-class African American girls read and identified with the same materials as their white counterparts. Despite the whiteness built into the narrative, key African American cultural leaders, such as Mary Church Terrell and Ida B. Wells, claimed Alcott's work as integrally important to shaping their own ideas of girlhood and youth.[34]

The first half of the novel, titled *Little Women,* with a print run of 2,000, sold out immediately in 1868. As one newspaper noted, "The curiosity to learn the denouement of *Little Women* amounts to an epidemic." So when the second (and final) volume of the story, *Good Wives,* followed six months later, it sold faster than the first.[35] Newspapers noted the numbers sold: now 12,000, now 42,000, and so on. Although written for girls, it was—as one paper remarked—"read with avidity and zest by many 'children of larger growth.'"[36] Adults enjoyed the book for its storytelling but also approved of it as a "wholesome" family story. Girls loved it because the March sisters were shockingly realistic and useful for interpreting their own experiences. As one woman later recalled, the March family was "very real to us girls at home, and we were as familiar with the separate characters as if they were dear and intimate friends of ours. We not only discussed their doings, as portrayed in the book, but were constantly supposing them to be in our positions and conjecturing what they would say and do in like circumstances." Over a year after its initial publication, a Boston correspondent told the western Massachusetts *Springfield Republican* that *Little Women* was still "selling as if business was not dull, and books a drug."[37] By the time Alcott died in 1888, over 200,000 copies of the novel had been printed in the United States alone.[38]

Little Women remains a beloved book. In 1922 delegates from both the American Library Convention and the National Education Association voted it the most necessary children's book for one-room schools. In 1927 the *New York Times* printed an article headlined "*Little Women* Leads Pool: Novel Rated Ahead of Bible for Influence on High School Pupils." In 1968, a century after publication, it was the most commonly circulating book in the New York Public Library system, along with *The Diary of Anne Frank.*[39] One writer ardently confessed a not uncommon sentiment about *Little Women* and its lead character: "I loved it too much when I was young to evaluate it dispassionately, loved it so much when I was a girl that Jo was the second most important person in my life."[40]

Indeed, Jo's tomboy sense of independence and self-conviction in the face of society's insistence on passivity and dependence is what has consistently marked *Little Women* as an influential book for girls ever since its publication. As Elizabeth Janeway pointed out a century after the initial publication, "This Victorian tract, sentimental and preachy, was written by a secret rebel against the order of the world and woman's place in it, and all the girls who ever read it know it."[41] Girls' relief in finding a highly imperfect yet admirable heroine explains the lasting appeal of the tomboy as reconfigured through Jo March. Now the tomboy was not simply a girl who cared little for feminine pursuits, but a girl who actively pursued an independent life of the mind. The twentieth-century French feminist Simone de Beauvoir reflects this when she writes that, as a young girl, "I identified myself passionately with Jo, the intellectual. . . . Jo was superior to her sisters, who were either more virtuous or more beautiful than she, because of her passion for knowledge and the vigor of her thinking; her superiority was as outstanding as that of certain adults, and guaranteed that she would have an unusual life: she was marked by fate."[42] The rebellion of Jo's tomboy identity is not simply against social expectations for girls in terms of dress and decorum, but also against the idea that girls should care more about pleasing others than following their own moral compass and pursuing their intellectual ambitions.

In the Wake of Jo

The commercial success of *Little Women* spurred an outpouring of tomboy-themed works, including poetry, short stories, plays, and novels, as well as fueling the juvenile fiction market for girls. But not all of these heroines shared Jo's sense of tomboy identity as foundational. Teenage Jo's transgressions against social gender norms serve to highlight her strong character, but that was not true of all the tomboys who followed in her wake. Between 1871 and 1875, four relatively successful novels catered to the new hunger for tomboy heroines. Two of them—*Tattered Tom* (1871) by Horatio Alger and *Running to Waste: The Story of a Tomboy* (1875) by George Baker—present tomboys as inappropriate and uncouth, without celebrating their candor or self-conviction until they are officially tamed into femininity. Then both authors, like so many others of tomboy tales, suggest that a lasting glimmer of boyishness is what makes this feminine woman better than other women. The other two, *Hila Dart: Story of a Born Romp* (1871) by Mary E. Mumford and *What Katy Did* (1872) by

Susan Coolidge (Susan Chauncey Woolsey), are far more sympathetic to the integrity of the tomboy's internal spirit, but they fail, too, in allowing their heroines to remain independently driven into maturity.

With *Tattered Tom; or, The Adventures of a Street Arab,* Horatio Alger, the stupendously successful author of pro-capitalist boys' stories, attempted to expand his readership through a boyish heroine. Alger saw the tomboy as a means of writing about a girl without turning away his fans, for, as he states in the preface, "conventional girls" make for boring characters.[43] Indeed, his initial depiction of Tom the tomboy is shockingly rough. In a clear allusion to *The Hidden Hand,* Tom enters as a humorless version of Capitola, forced to dress like a boy to survive in a rough urban world. Yet she is essentially a street thug, violent and utterly lacking charm. When a kindly gentleman asks: "Which are you—a boy or a girl?" Tom answers, "I'm a girl, but I wish I was a boy"—and when asked why, replies, "'Cause boys are stronger than girls, and can fight better."[44] She enjoys fighting—which is unheard of for tomboy heroines of girls' fiction. Yet the rapid conversion of Tom into Jenny (because of poor editing, the name sometimes appears as Jane) suggests that internally she is a highly conventional girl. Alger did not seem to have a credible solution for a female central character who, unlike Ragged Dick and his other impoverished boys, could not independently climb the ladder of capitalism to respectability. Tom is by far the most aggressively masculine tomboy in nineteenth-century literature.

Tom's path to ultimate success in the world runs in the opposite direction from boys like Ragged Dick, who brought Alger lasting fame as the author of rags-to-riches, can-do fiction. His boys triumph through self-discipline and self-reliance—and naturally come to adopt the traits valued by the middle class. Tattered Tom tries that route, but other "street Arabs" steal the newspapers she plans to sell. When she tries to carry bags at the train station, "like others of her sex," she "found herself shut out from an employment for which she considered herself fitted."[45] She cannot live like a boy in a boy's world, no matter how she dresses.

In the end, Tom must be saved by someone other than herself. She captures the imagination of a ship captain, who declares, "I don't want a tame child. She wouldn't interest me. This girl has spirit." He places her in a boardinghouse run by his sister.[46] The captain actually does have fatherly intentions, despite how it reads from a contemporary standpoint, and Tom goes along with it because she has no other option.

Unlike other tomboys of fiction, Tom does not embrace femininity after falling in love; she simply falls into a bath. After a good wash and a corset, Tattered Tom goes from expressing herself as a rude and physically aggressive street tough to eliciting universal admiration for her beauty. Later Jenny is tossed back on the streets when a vain, fashionable girl falsely accuses her of theft. Yet she does not return to her rough ways: "The time had been . . . when she would have preferred to be a boy. But her tastes had changed considerably since then. Something of the instinct of her sex had sprung up in her, as she was brought to a closer knowledge of more refined ways of life. She was no longer a young Arab in her feelings, as before."[47] Tom's change in identity has nothing to do with her core personality, and everything to do with material comfort.

Luckily for Jenny, she turns out to be a long-lost heiress, and in the end returns to mansion life. Alger notes that she sometimes looks back with nostalgia, because she "missed the free life of the streets, which, in spite of all its privations and discomforts, is not without a charm to the homeless young Arabs that swarm about the streets." But her "new tastes" keep her feminine, though she never loses "that fresh and buoyant spirit, and sturdy independence, which had enabled her to fight her way when she was compelled to do so." And thank goodness, for those early fighting years are what Alger suggests make her an exceptional young woman: "It was evident that Jane, whether from her natural tendencies or her past experiences, was not likely to settle down into one of those average, stereotyped, uninteresting young ladies that abound in our modern society." Despite her change in manners, "nature was sure to assert itself in a certain piquancy and freshness of manner, which, added to her personal attraction, will, I think, eventually make Tom—the name slipped from my pen unintentionally—a great favorite in society."[48] Not only is Jenny now rich and well behaved, she has managed to escape the deficits of other wealthy, well-behaved girls because of her origins in boyhood.

If Horatio Alger wrote with an eye toward selling books, Mary E. Mumford wrote *Hila Dart: A Born Romp* (1871) out of particular passion for Alcott's Jo March. Unfortunately, it quickly evolves from its initial bold overtones into a tiresome version of the classic tomboy tale, which the publisher could rightly advertise with the heading "See how a Tomboy became a True and Good Woman."[49] But if the ending is banal, the opening is worth analyzing, because it presents one of the first pairings of a masculine tomboy and a sissy boy in American literature. Here Mumford raises the stakes for the tomboy tale by suggesting that her opposite is a boy who is overtly feminine.

Mumford introduces their gender positioning within the first few sentences of the book, when Sammy, "undersized for his age," cheers his sister in a sledding race: "Hurrah for our Hi! There she goes. She's the pluckiest girl in this whole town." When another boy scoffs at the claim, Sammy boasts:

> "What can she do? . . . Why, she can do everything a boy can. . . . You ought to see her at home. She beats us boys at everything. She finds out all the hens' nests first. She gets all the tally at barnball, she can climb every tree in the orchard, and she wont [*sic*] be dared to anything. Why, the other day, Fred and I dared her to jump from the big beam in the barn, down into the hay, and she did it."[50]

Actually, Hila can do more far more than her younger brother. And they comfortably take opposing gender positions when at play. Sammy is in his element when they play house: "He was more handy at dressing the dolls, and enjoyed them a great deal more than she. So while he put the babies in their morning and afternoon dresses, made the tea, set the table for meals, and washed the dishes, . . . she was the gentleman who came a visiting the ladies." Lest the reader think that the Dart children are not aware of their gender-bending ways, Hila later confesses to a neighbor: "I ought to have been a boy, and Sammy ought to have been the girl. We've got awfully mixed up in our family somehow. Other people's boys are boys, and other people's girls are girls, but ours ain't. Now, if I was a boy like Fred," she says, referring to her older, gender-typical brother, "I could get away from it, but, as I am a girl, I've got to stay at home and bear it."[51]

Hila annoys Fred by playing boys' games, but he does not mention his brother's effeminacy, which is probably more a reflection of Mumford's lack of understanding about boy culture than a commentary on boyhood masculinities. Indeed, once Sammy has served his purpose as a feminine foil to Hila, Mumford does not seem to know what do with him. He is a problem with no solution, unlike Hila, who has the classic tomboy reformation to save her from a life as a social outcast. Midway through the novel, Sammy disappears and Mumford drops her exploration of gender dissonance and embraces the story line that Hila's boyish girlhood makes her a better woman. It is by literary necessity a painful journey. Hila struggles with elders who disapprove of her boyishness, and she suffers when, with her habitual recklessness, she catches fire while shooting a gun. But her trials lead to her embracing feminine self-control and suffering, and she earns the heart and hand of a young minister.

Many other authors would try to answer the conundrum of the sissy boy over the next few decades, especially beginning in the 1890s, when concerns about an increase in "sissy boys" became amplified in the popular press. And the sissy boy became an increasingly popular sidekick for the tomboy, as if to balance out her gender transgressions and suggest that only a girly-boy would want to be with a boyish girl. For the most part, sissy boys remained subjects of derision and symbols of cultural illness. As the tomboy grows up and embraces femininity, the sissy sidekicks leave center stage by death, marriage, or simply disappearing.

In *What Katy Did* (1872), Susan Coolidge presented a significantly different trajectory for a whole range of genders. According to feminist and literary scholars, the central heroine, Katy Carr, is tomboy because she resists feminine restrictions.[52] She is exuberant, ambitious, daring, and fun, though not particularly aggressive or dismissive of femininity. Her little sister, referred to as Johnnie or John, is far more masculine, but she is not the central heroine. And, like many tomboys, she is paired with the sissy boy—in this case Dorry, "a pale, pudgy boy" who chiefly fantasizes about food. Coolidge addresses their gender variance up front and without judgment, noting that "Dorry seemed like a girl who had got into boy's clothes by mistake, and Johnnie like a boy who, in a fit of fun, had borrowed his sister's frock."[53] Yet Coolidge allows both Dorry and John to grow up across the span of four books as beloved members of the family who find their own place in society without much struggle. At no point do other characters bemoan their unconventional gender norms; John and Dorry are respected and accepted as simply individuals, with their own ways.

Alongside this pair, Katy's tomboyism appears more a source of delight than concern, but she is the one whom Coolidge posits as needing to learn self-control. As if to set off her masculinity, Katy is paired with a feminine best friend, Cecy, "a neat, dapper, pink-and-white girl, modest and prim in manner, with light shiny hair, which always kept smooth, and slim hands, which never looked dirty." Katy, therefore, is a mess by comparison, with her hair "forever in a snarl" and her clothes "always catching on nails and 'tearing themselves.'" But most importantly, despite being twelve and nearly as tall as her father, Katy "was as heedless and innocent as a child of six." She spends her free time "dreaming of the time when something she had done would make her famous," and reading anything available.[54] Katy, like Jo March and unlike Tom or Hila, is accepted and adored by her family and friends exactly as she is, even if elders foresee trouble ahead. As with Jo, Katy's problem is not her gender transgression but her desire to cling to childish fun past the time it is allowed for girls.

In tune with a refrain that was running through newspapers in the 1870s, their physician father encourages Katy and all five of her younger brothers and sisters to run freely outdoors. He wants them to be "hardy and bold" and encourages climbing and "rough play, in spite of the bumps and ragged clothes which resulted." Their far more conventional aunt who cares for the motherless brood, however, finds it "hard to quite forgive the children for being . . . so little like the good boys and girls in Sunday-school memoirs."[55] Aunt Izzie is only satisfied with the children when they are neatly dressed in the morning, saying their prayers. Through her, Coolidge makes it clear that such behavior would be inauthentic; real children are messy, loud, and prone to pranks.

And girls can be savages in groups, too, as becomes clear when the wind takes Katy's bonnet and sends it into the backyard of the rival school next door, Miss Miller's, just before the girls are about to flood out for recess. Katy eyes the situation: "Already she seemed to see them dancing war-dances round the unfortunate bonnet, pinning it on a pole, using it as a foot-ball, waving it over the fence, and otherwise treating it as Indians treat a captive taken in war. Was it to be endured? Never!" And "with very much the feeling of a person who faces destruction rather than forfeit honor," Katy slides down a roof and leaps into the yard. The rival girls are at the ready: "Out poured the Millerites, big and little. Their wrath and indigna-tion at this daring invasion cannot be described. With a howl of fury they precipitated themselves upon Katy," who scrambles up the fence, kicks away an attacker, and returns "alive from the camp of the enemy." One of Katy's cohorts stands ready with a tack-hammer to smash the knuckles of Millerites trying to climb over the fence in vengeance.[56] Are these the sweet little girls destined for selfless womanhood? If so, they will need quite a bit more shaping.

Pain is what turns this tomboy into a woman. In a study of disability and death in girls' fiction, Lois Keith observes that there is hardly a girls' novel after the mid-nineteenth century that does not "have a character who at some crucial stage defied their guardian and fell off a swing or out of a sled, became paralyzed through tipping out of a carriage or was suffering from some nameless, crippling illness from which they could, indeed must, be cured." Curing girls of their boyish rebellion through dire and painful consequence became nearly as popular as curing them through marriage. Although boys' "books of war, derring do, adventure and brave encounter" certainly led to some painful experiences, the illness or injury is not presented by the authors as a lesson in why boys should stay home and be safe. But the girls' books that focus on "family life, self-denial, love (without sex, of course), and personal stories of triumph over tragedy" present such outcomes as solid reasoning for a change of personality.[57] And sometimes tomboys receive similar lessons through causing pain in others, such as when Jo repents her anger when her sister Amy nearly drowns. Or when George Baker's tomboy, Rebecca Sleeper, finally connects to her femininity through guilt over exacerbating her mother's illness with her misbehavior.

Baker's *Running to Waste: The Story of a Tomboy* (1875) harkens back to the older images of the tomboy, in that Rebecca Sleeper is a gorgeous girl who inspires desire in young male onlookers even as she enrages elders. Becky enters the novel stealing apples with her fat brother, Teddy, who is "ambitious to emulate all of her achievements." Despite muddy stockings and an apron stained with berry juice and grime, Becky is radiant, with her "plump, round, rosy face, with a color in the cheeks that rivaled in brightness the coveted fruit above her, blue eyes full of laughter, a pretty mouth, . . . teasing smiles," and "a profusion of light hair, tossed to and fro." She is clearly a diamond in the rough. Teddy, the archetypal sissy, is, by comparison, simply pathetic. He admires his sister for exhibiting the masculinity he covets, and so essentially cedes his own claim to manhood. Becky, meanwhile, excels at "*boyish* sports": she "could climb a tree with the activity of a squirrel, ride a horse without a saddle or a bridle, pull a boat against the swift current of the river, 'follow my leader' on the roughest trail, take a hand at base ball, play cricket, and was considered a valuable acquisition to either side in a game of football."[58] Indeed, Becky elicits the respect of peers if not adults, including Harry Thompson, the pride of the community, who will eventually become her tutor and suitor. Teddy, on the other hand, receives only disrespect and aversion.

But adults in the novel express far more anxiety over Becky than Teddy, as they see her behavior as selfish, yet fixable. When Becky's mother nearly dies of a stroke because of her daughter's reckless behavior, Becky dissolves into a puddle of remorse. At the height of her misery, her neighbor Mrs. Thompson kindly thrusts the knife in deeper: "Had you given the same attention to learning to keep house that you have to playing ball and tag, to robbing orchards and shooting the Basin, you would have been ready to take your place at your mother's bed-side, or to take charge of cooking. You would have gained the good opinion of everybody, instead of being shunned as a tomboy." Becky, of course, resolves to turn around her behavior, and the rest of the book details her struggles to tame herself and apologize for past deeds. "I came to beg your pardon for being so much trouble to you when I was a wild tomboy," she pleads with the owner of the orchard where she once stole apples; "I was young then; didn't know how wrong it was. I'm older now, and see my error." He responds with wonder that this "little woman, with her sweet voice and penitent air" could be that same terrible tomboy.[59]

Yet despite the fact that the story emphasizes the imperative of girls embracing the female role, in the end Becky reaches her more worldly goals because of her tomboy proclivities. Determined to support her family, she applies for a job at a Boston engraving office. The owner, Mr. Woodfern, scarcely gives her the time of day because she is a girl. So she wheedles him into allowing her to take a look at the cricket bat decorating his office wall. In the middle of the printing office, Woodfern gets so excited to see "a cricketer in position" that he bowls her a ball—which she hits true and smashes into a glass globe. Despite the property damage, Woodfern hires her on the spot. In no time at all Harry Thomas, who sees that Becky has "grown into a strong and beautiful woman," proposes, and "the 'Tomboy' became a lovely bride."[60] Becky wins it all—the respect of neighbors, love of the community's golden boy, and even a meaningful career—because she remains just boy enough to make her womanhood more admirable.[61]

Tomboys and Bad Boys

Although the tomboy is often paired with sissy boys and dainty girls as sidekicks, her cultural parallel is the "bad boy" who came to prominence in boys' fiction beginning in 1869, a year after the publication of *Little*

Women. This was not coincidental; just as the tomboy is connected to the emergence of women in public life, so, too, is the bad boy. The tomboy suggested a way to raise healthy, domestic girls in the midst of modern opportunity; the bad boy signaled a way for adult male readers to reclaim the masculinity that many felt was threatened by the feminization of modern American life. Both characters display the hearty American values that are culturally tied to white identity. And they are not permanently marked by their rebellion against civility, but instead reveal its hypocrisies on their unhindered way to adulthood. But popular culture sanctioned bad boys as symbolic American rebels in a way that no tomboy of the period could claim.[62] The bad boy is truly a "good bad boy," just as the tomboy has a good heart, but he is also, as Leslie Fiedler remarked, "American's vision of itself, crude and unruly in his beginnings, but endowed by his creator with an instinctive sense of what is right."[63]

Tomboys and bad boys are gendered versions of the same compulsion for realism that would reshape American literature at the end of the century, even if the female version remained tethered to the domestic space and framed in sentimental language. Earlier tomboys who populate short stories in newspapers and *Godey's Lady's Book* had laid some of the groundwork, simply by being allowed to ignore social cues and misbehave without meeting dire consequences. But the tomboys who appear in fiction for girls go further; Jo and her followers harbor ambitions that go beyond the domestic hearth. Although they never reach the full-throated declaration of ambition voiced in the story papers by adolescent-fiction authors like Winnie Woodfern, they are nevertheless adamant in their desire to earn income. They follow their aspirations even as they struggle to accept the languages of femininity and domesticity, and they give attention to the social cues that baffle and frustrate them. Tomboys agonize over the struggle to control unfeminine characteristics such as anger, envy, and self-centeredness, but they also revel in their unfeminine strengths. Most importantly, the reader is able to take part in their adventures, as girls like as Eleanor Browne could attest.

Much like the tomboys, bad boys appeared in earlier short stories and sketches, but they were effectively launched as an archetype by a lightly fictional autobiography, *The Story of a Bad Boy,* by Thomas Bailey Aldrich, serialized in 1869 and published as a book the following year.[64] "In short I was a real human boy such as you may meet anywhere in New England,"

Aldrich asserts, "and no more like the impossible boy in a story-book than a sound orange is like one that has been sucked dry."[65] Didactically entertaining children's stories by Oliver Optic, Sophie May, and others remained beloved, but the heavy moralizing in such works marked them as outdated and feminized in contrast to these robust and authentic depictions of youth. William Dean Howells suggested as much in his gleeful review of Aldrich's book in 1870: "No one else seems to have thought of telling the story of a boy's life, with so great desire to show what a boy's life is, and so little purpose of teaching what it should be."[66] Aldrich's celebration of "real" boyhood became a popular strain of juvenile fiction that persisted until 1914, with the publication of Booth Tarkington's *Penrod*, often seen as the last of the good bad boys.[67]

The bad boys populated what came to be called "boy books," which were not so much stories *for* boys as stories *about* boys and written to delight grown men as well as their younger counterparts.[68] The great purpose of these books was to reclaim a real boyhood in the midst of a late nineteenth-century masculinity crisis promoted by economic changes that also moved female workers into the male realm. The novelist Frank Norris looked back in the early twentieth century at the bad boy phenomenon and gloomy queried, "Do you know who he is? He is the average American business man before he grew up. . . . It is the study of an extinct species, a report upon the American boy of thirty years ago."[69] The good boys of middle-class domestic fiction were left behind as creations of sentimental Victorian culture, while male authors strove to recall (and thus reclaim) the rowdy and raw behavior of their boyhoods. As Sarah Wadsworth points out, Aldrich and later Mark Twain "trivialize human suffering and sorrow in order to celebrate the more capricious, mischievous side of human nature through the misdeeds of their bad-boy protagonists," who "engage in pranks, seek out daring adventures, and, on occasion, fight, thieve, and dissemble."[70]

Although many authors built the genre, Mark Twain elevated the bad boy in the public consciousness with *The Adventures of Tom Sawyer* (1876) and *The Adventures of Huckleberry Finn* (1884). Twain humorously records Tom's magical thinking, unkind pranks, and self-aggrandizement while habitually stepping in to share wisdom with the reader, much like Alcott's voice in *Little Women*.[71] Twain does not state that Sawyer is "bad" but introduces him engaged in a sly but affectionate war of words with his

Aunt Polly, who is trying to catch him in the lie she knows he is spinning. When she finally gets him cornered, he dashes out the door, leaving Aunt Polly to ruefully reflect that because breaking the rules is what he does, and catching him is what she does, they will remain in their volatile dynamic.

Twain notes drily of Tom, "He was not the model boy of the village. He knew the model boy very well though—and loathed him."[72] Here the bad boy enjoys a freedom unavailable to tomboys, who must reform to survive, and therefore must learn to *want* to be better. The freedom to loathe the better-behaving girl was not yet available to tomboys. Tomboys can be rough, careless, selfish, and prone to play pranks, but in the end they have to recognize self-control and appropriate behavior as an unmitigated good. Bad boys, on the other hand, must not struggle against the superego; indeed a truly good bad boy pays little mind to society's rules. The bad boy, written to soothe nostalgia and masculinity anxiety, is best as he is.

Thus Tom soon proves his loathing for model boys when he encounters a newcomer who immediately arouses his ire: "His cap was a dainty thing, his close-buttoned blue cloth roundabout was new and natty and so were his pantaloons. He had shoes on—and it was only Friday. He even wore a necktie, a bright bit of ribbon. He had a citified air about him that ate into Tom's vitals."[73] As Howells later explained in reference to his own childhood self, "A fellow who brushed his hair and put on shoes and came into the parlor when there was company was looked on as a girl-boy."[74] Civilized boys were feminized, and the central purpose of the bad boy literature was to reinforce that masculinity was rooted in feral boyhood. Therefore Tom and the boy immediately get into a fistfight.

When bad boys inhabit the domestic space, they do so as visitors. Although both tomboys and bad boys struggle with the assault of "civilization" on their personal freedoms, the tomboy must come to accept her confinement. She succeeds when, like Jo March as Mrs. Bhaer, she makes the most of the freedoms she finds within the cage. Bad boy tales celebrate the freedoms of feral boyhood, and in that sense mourn the onset of adulthood. But the adult men in these stories are, for the most part, active agents in the public world. Bad boy tales suggest that boys will eventually lose the freedom to run around in the woods, but they will channel those impulses into running the larger public world. Tomboys, by contrast, must learn to suppress their spirits. It is not a coincidence that many authors, diarists, and biographers compare tomboys to young horses before they are broken.[75]

And yet the bad boy and the tomboy alike critique social convention. Huck Finn, Twain's most celebrated bad boy, clearly exposes the absurdities of convention through his inability to conform—like Jo March before him.[76] Huck and Jo consistently believe they are at fault for their inappropriate behavior, while readers see them as obviously superior in their simplicity.[77] The books are entirely different in setting; the March girls grow up within Orchard House, while Huck Finn gains insight and maturity while traveling along the Mississippi River, in partnership with the slave Jim and, later, a pair of white con men. But the two characters align in spirit, with their instinctual questioning of convention when they find themselves unable to move with society's currents. Yet even while Alcott emphasizes the absurdity of social convention, she supports the community as largely moral. By contrast, Twain suggests that morality is often subjective, and social convention a symptom of class- and race-based myopia.

And for both the tomboy and the bad boy, in an age when darker skin color is linked with "savagery" it is their whiteness that allows their rebellious behaviors to be seen as a manifestation of age rather than an intrinsic lack of civility. Even Huck Finn, who enters Tom Sawyer's novel swinging a dead cat and described as being "cordially hated and dreaded by all the mothers of the town because he was idle, and lawless, and vulgar and bad," is believed fixable.[78] Out of Christian piety, he is taken in by the Widow Douglas to be civilized: cleaned, educated, and given a financial stake. Of course, her effort at civility does not take root, allowing Huck to launch into his own set of adventures.

The historian David I. Mcleod observes that in the 1890s "adults were complacently embracing an artificial cult of the 'bad boy'"—fed by the bad boy books but also the theories of "boy nature" promoted by psychologists, scientists, educators, and youth leaders who would come to be known as "boyologists."[79] But even as early as the first bad boys of the late 1860s and early 1870s, we can see the white boy's native savagery asserted as being temporary but necessary to his higher development, and the tomboy, likewise, evolving past her boyish girlhood to embrace the "best" elements of womanhood (namely maternity).

Tomboys, like bad boys, give social recognition to instinctive wants and impulses of youth that are not tolerated in adults, but they also suggest that the spirit of their youth lives on into adulthood. The tomboy and bad boy identities are both temporary; they are acceptable because authors like

Alcott and Twain, by all accounts successful and respected adults, are living testament that naturally incorrigible youth will mature into the ability to control impulse and act responsibly. At the same time, both authors suggest that, when finally reaching adulthood, their characters house a seed of that original tomboy or bad boy at their core. Looking back at his childhood friends, Aldrich comments, "Some of those dear fellows are rather elderly boys at this time—lawyers, merchants, sea-captains, soldiers, authors, what not?"[80] And Jo March can occasionally be found cavorting with her young charges in Alcott's subsequent novels *Little Men* and *Jo's Boys.* When she enters *Little Men,* now all grown up as Mrs. Bhaer, Alcott introduces her: "She had a merry sort of face, that never seemed to have forgotten childish ways and looks, any more than her voice and manner had," and these qualities make her "jolly" in the eyes of the boys in her care. Authors suggest that the youthful spirits of former tomboys and bad boys can be seen their sense of freedom and playfulness not dimmed by adult responsibilities. And "these things, hard to describe but very plain to see and feel," make grown-up Jo March, for example, "a genial, comfortable kind of person."[81] Both tomboys and bad boys are allowed to be funny and real, but their paths to maturity split at adolescence. Then the tomboy must struggle internally to prepare herself for adulthood, while the bad boy moves nearly seamlessly from boyhood savagery to the competition of the marketplace.

By the 1880s tomboy characters were symbolic figures in books and on stage, asserting an emerging idealized gender role that was "conspicuously unmannerly, outspoken, and challenging."[82] A version of the tomboy even gained popularity in western pulp fiction, targeted to male readers. These western tomboys would reflect more on national white solidarity and the importance of the frontier than on the tomboy's maturation into the New Woman of urban life. But across genres, by the 1880s tomboy imagery was so well established that such behavior in girls began to be viewed as natural—"a life stage" particularly suited to Americans. So girls adjusted. Now "American girls" blossomed from tomboy origins, expressed tomboy spirits, and served as a juvenile bridge to the "New Woman" of the late nineteenth century.

3

Tomboy Heroines on the Manly Frontier

Edward Wheeler's 1877 dime novel *Hurricane Nell, the Girl Dead-Shot; or, The Queen of the Saddle and Lasso* opens with a rowdy band of whites and Indians coming to remove a family from valuable ranchlands, advising a "pretty half grown girl" to drag from the cabin her parents dying of smallpox and warning that in ten hours they will set fire to the prairie. Too weak herself to save anything, Nell watches her house and parents reduced to ashes and finds her life's purpose: "As sure as there is a god and a ruling power on earth, I will have revenge! . . . Girl though I am, and young and feeble. . . ."[1] Revenge soon forges her into a woman of the frontier, thrust from the domestic sphere into the heart of savage wilderness. Hurricane Nell is a smart, disrespectable but admired heroine who takes charge of the narrative, and her story apparently proved popular enough to reprint under different titles up to the turn of the century, by various publishers inside and outside of the United States.

Just as the tomboy heroine increasingly took center stage in fiction for girls, another kind of tomboy rose to prominence in the western pulp fiction marketed to male youth. Writing at a time when "sport" meant a young man, the authors of these dime novels often refer to these genderbending young heroines as girl sports, which is the term I will use here to distinguish them from the tomboys of domestic fiction.[2] In these novels, the girl sport is allowed to transgress gender norms in service of white triumph. Only when in the presence of the hero does the girl sport move firmly into the feminine end of the gender spectrum, much like her domestic tomboy parallel. Otherwise, she rides, shoots, and cusses as much as the men around her. Formula westerns, capitalizing on questions raised by westward national expansion, contributed to solidifying frontier mythologies. Though designed as lowbrow entertainment, they nonetheless played

73

an important role in the evolving narrative of the Far West as a place of white male dominance, where civilization was depicted as both a desirable outcome and a tragic conclusion. The girl sport thrived as often as she failed on that thin frontier line.

Although clearly in violation of the middle-class norms of respectability that gave domestic tomboy characters cultural power, girl sports share significant similarities with them, such as courage, verbal candor, and a preference for outdoor life. Tomboys and girl sports alike revel in their physical agility; they ride horses, climb trees, make noise, and mark social conventions by defying them. And, although there are exceptions, tomboys and girls sports often have similar features, suggesting a blurring of racial signifiers—most often dark "unbound hair," "snapping" black eyes, and tanned skin. A streak of natural gentility runs through nearly all of these boy-girl heroines, no matter how rough their dress or speech, or—in the case of girl sports—how many people they kill. Narrators and other male characters constantly assert that the girl sport cannot afford feminine softness if she is to survive in this savage environment—not unlike the strategies employed by Capitola Black and Tattered Tom to survive their urban environments.

But girl sports differ critically from fictional tomboys in one distinct way: they exude sexuality. The adolescent boy-girl heroine takes on male freedoms in both domestic and western fiction, yet behaviors designed to reveal the tomboy's innocence suggest the opposite in the girl sport, laying bare her knowledge of sex and violence. While the girl sport's eroticism is clearly for the titillation of a male readership, it is also part of what allows her to thrive on the frontier. She cannot survive in the wild without being part of the wild. Yet her innate savagery also emphasizes that the girl sport is not a meddling civilizer bent on changing male ways, but rather changes to suit the masculine world in which she lives.

The sexually charged beauty of the girl sport may be her most salient trait, and she is typically already "ruined"—sexually defiled in her mysterious past—when the reader meets her. Defiantly, the girl sport emphasizes her independence rather than expressing shame for her lack of virtue. In *Hurricane Nell,* for example, when the "feeble" Nell returns as the jaded, shapely Hurricane Nell the narrator lingers over describing her, creating an oasis of luxurious language in the midst of a novel of scattershot phrasing. He savors the depiction of her "form of exquisite contour, that was attired in a close-fitting suit of buckskin, tastefully ringed and ornamented with Indian beads, which all the more enhanced the beauty of the supple body." She is strong and lithe, but not soft. Hurricane Nell also presents as a mysterious mix of racial signifiers. She has an "almost purely classic face," "browned to a nut hue by the wind of the prairies and sun of the plains, from years of constant exposure."[3] Her facial bones assert an Anglo-Saxon identity, but she is literally colored by her life in the savage Wild West.

The girl sport's spunk, courage, talent with a gun, and ability to ride a horse are lauded as virtues in these violent settings. Elders urge the tomboys of domestic fiction not to go too far in their quest for freedom, but girl sports have already passed that line. Weapons, culturally understood to be tools of manliness, are suggestively placed all over the girl sport. Enhancing the eroticism of her gender transgression, she inevitably has pistols or knives nestled in her cleavage, strapped to her tiny waist, or housed along a shapely thigh. Hurricane Nell sports a glamorous pair of silver revolvers and a lasso lashed to her belt. Clearly she is at the ready; she will fight rather than wait to be rescued. Yet despite the sexually charged placing of weapons, Wheeler also suggests that guns and rope are so encoded with masculinity that they confuse onlookers even when looking at this emphatically female body. Distracted by her guns, a side character preposterously exclaims: "That's Hurricane Nell? Impossible! . . . Why that is a man!" But the hero sees through the weaponry. "A girl in man's clothing," he laughs.[4] He is too masculine himself to be fooled by a fake.

And in fact, though Hurricane Nell is well armed and independent, she dresses like a girl. She wears skirts, like domestic tomboys of the nineteenth century, as do most other girl sports. Even when regularly fighting (and living) with outlaws, Indians, Mexicans, and wolves, most girl sports wear skirts—albeit dashing ones, with elaborate beading and buckskin fringe. Indeed, the distinction may be more important than in domestic novels, because westerns were written for a male audience. Trousers were a sacred marker of maleness—one that most male readers were not allowed to wear until young adulthood. But the skirt that reinforces the domestic tomboy's domestic future signals sexual availability in the girl sport because it marks her as female in a world made up mostly of men. The skirt emphasizes that she is female, regardless of her usurpation of masculinity. It is not a signifier of respectability, because she is already ruined.

In the 1880s girl sports became increasingly commonplace in the mythical West. In this age of the New Woman, eastern fantasies of western

FIGURE 3: Cover of the 1908 dime novel *The Woman Trapper,* from Beadle's Frontier Series. The skirted girl sport triumphantly holding up a fresh scalp to show her male companion brazenly reveals the white imperial sovereignty at the heart of these gender-blurring works of entertainment. "The Woman Trapper (Beadle's Frontier Series no. 35)," *Dime Novels,* accessed January 23, 2018, https://ds-carbonite .harverford.edu/dimenovels /items/show/40.

adventure required not only the expected assortment of schoolmarms, good daughters, and Indian princesses, but also girls asserting masculinity. And the chief value of the girl sport was that she did not want to civilize or tame that male West; she was not set apart from the West, but a white woman made integral to the male setting. She was allowed to transgress the parlor-fiction norms for two reasons, neither of which involved actually empowering independent women in the West: she was white, and therefore her gender transgression was seen as temporary as long as she bonded with the white hero against the villains; and the girl sport brought sex to a violent adventure story.

The Mythical West: Emergence of the Girl Sport

Female heroines taking action spoke to tensions surrounding how westward expansion challenged gender and racial ideologies. Westward expansion of the nation accelerated after 1848, with the acquisition of Texas,

Oregon, and the lands of the Mexican Cession, transforming the United States into a transcontinental nation. Anglo-Americans saw the expansion into the West as the right and duty of white civilization, their "manifest destiny." History textbooks mark westward expansion as integral to the nation's descent into the Civil War, but it also triggered a wave of white nationalism expressed in numerous ways, from the removal and destruction of the nation's indigenous peoples to violence against Chinese miners. After the Civil War, violence and legal restrictions on nonwhites only accelerated, leading to Jim Crow laws, the Chinese Exclusion Act, and what many historians refer to as the genocide of Native Americans.

Western dime novels were so ubiquitous that they identified the entire dime novel market, and they functioned as symbols of the racial and cultural confrontation taking place outside of fiction. The western genre mythologized the Far West as a place for real (white) men. By far the most lasting and influential formula centered on the frontier, which by the late nineteenth century was understood to be in the Trans-Mississippi West, signified by wilderness, plains, and dramatic canyons, and populated by whites, Indians, and Mexicans.[5] The American frontier itself was less a geographic place than a process of cultures contesting for dominance; in formula westerns, it was understood to be the meeting place of "savagery" and "civility."[6] If the tomboy of middle-class fiction gave readers a figure for adjusting to changes in domestic urban life, the girl sport of dime novels functioned as a vehicle for sorting out white racial solidarity at a time when neither whiteness nor "other" was clearly defined but in a constant state of flux.

Tension lay in the fact that in order for the West to be made white it had to be civilized—which meant feminized in the eyes of many nineteenth-century Americans. Within larger western civilization, women had long been subordinate to men by religion, custom, and law. But over the course of the nineteenth century, women also became signifiers of civility—that condition that Anglo-Americans stressed separated white people from the savagery of nonwhites. Thus with the expansion into the lands west of the Mississippi, white women became important cultural signifiers of white dominance on the frontier as well. And indeed, Anglo expansion was also characterized in American ideology as domesticating the "wild" land, even as many Americans (especially those in the East, where they wrote and read about the wild lands but never saw them) considered that domestication emasculating.[7] The West made men manly, yet by settling the West those men also brought domestic life to the wilderness.[8] It was a losing game. This raised the inevitable question: Could masculinity survive in a civilized world? If the frontier remained undomesticated, what kind of white woman could survive there?

In came the girl sport: threatening to sully the parlor, but with honor to spare when it counted. Over and over, the girl sport, who has long since lost her feminine virtue, proves her manly honor. And like her domestic tomboy counterpart, she often outgrows her girlish adventures when she meets a man more masculine than herself. Girl sports evolved in western pulp fiction as a means of positing whiteness without compromising the centrality of masculinity in the mythical Far West.

The United States was racially diversifying more rapidly than Anglo-Americans could culturally process, between immigrants from southern and eastern Europe flooding the East Coast, Native Americans increasingly crowded together on the Great Plains, Chinese workers in the western mines and railroad construction, Mexicans in recently annexed portions of the Southwest and Texas, and, of course, recently freed African American citizens. The expansion of the United States into the West jeopardized Anglo-Saxon America's understanding of the relationship between race and national identity. White Americans theorized racial character, debating how they managed to reach the top of the evolutionary scale, against a backdrop of intense competition for land, culture, and legal and economic dominance. Labor leaders in the East expanded the white tent to cover those of northern European stock.[9] Romantic racism—a belief in separate tribes and races—provided the ideological basis of the western dime novels.[10] Jockeying not only for racial dominance but for the moral *right* to that dominance played out in western pulp fiction.

Such thinking was also undeniably problematic in an era obsessed with addressing the parameters of what made one "American." A century before, Hector St. John de Crèvecoeur answered his famous question "Who is this American, this new man?" by celebrating how the land itself reshaped Europeans of various extractions into true Americans. At the end of the nineteenth century, in 1893, Frederick Jackson Turner put Americans on notice by saying that recent census data demonstrated that the "frontier" was now closed (according to his definition, at least). In his now famous "frontier thesis," Turner reinforced his contention that the struggle from savagery to civility on the frontier was what made Americans intrinsically different from

Europeans, and opened the question of what would happen to American character now that the story was ending.[11] And yet this was also the age of great nations—indeed, of the rapid rise of American imperialism. How was American nationalism to flourish with so many diverse races in competition within its borders? And with the frontier essentially gone, and the western lands so crowded, what other forces might shape American identity? White Americans responded to all of these threats with a legal, economic, cultural, and social strengthening of the ideology of white supremacy. Western novels and their young readers were part of that effort.

Dime novels were essentially adventure fare tailored to youthful male readers. They enjoyed popularity in the last quarter of the nineteenth century, and died out in the early decades of the twentieth. There were literally hundreds of dime novels, some reprinted from story papers and others written as stand-alone publications. The term "dime novel" began as a brand name, Beadle's Dime Novels, first published 1860. Within three years, George Munro, a former employee of the Beadle firm, began another series, but by then "dime novel" had become accepted as the term for similar pulp fiction—including the "half-dime novel" series that took over the industry in the 1870s, marketed specifically to the more limited budgets of boys between eight and sixteen.[12]

Buffalo Bill's Wild West show heightened the potency of western formula fiction when it began traveling internationally in 1887. Joy Kasson suggests how very real the Far West seemed in the minds of ticket-buyers: "At the turn of the twentieth century, millions of people around the world thought they remembered the American Wild West because they had seen it, full of life and color, smoking guns and galloping horses." Buffalo Bill's Wild West and western dime novels played off of each other, and strengthened the mythology. And the Wild West show had up to thirteen celebrated female performers.[13]

Although many authors included girl sports in their novels, the most prolific and successful was Edward Wheeler. Thousands of writers made money in the dime novel industry from 1860 to 1915, writing as hacks for nominal fees, but only a few authors gained a public following.[14] For eight years, from 1877 until his death in 1885, Wheeler churned out scores of stories featuring strong female characters that principally catered to a white audience of tradesmen, clerks, and dreaming boys who would probably never leave the industrial centers. And that was fine, since Wheeler, who himself hailed from upstate New York, wrote from an office in Philadelphia.

His American West was wholly imaginary. And yet he shaped how the world would come to imagine the America frontier: its people, towns, struggles, and importance. Indeed, Wheeler became so beloved that his name lived on long after he passed away—a common publishing practice when a writer became too profitable to give up to mortality.[15]

Wheeler gained fame through two particular characters: Deadwood Dick and Calamity Jane, whose lives were entangled, without much rhyme or reason, in thirty-three books. Sometimes they married, sometimes they were already married, other times they refused to marry each other—Wheeler (and his successors) clearly saw no intrinsic need to maintain continuity on that front. Wheeler went on to introduce many other beloved girl sports, including Baltimore Bess and Rowdy Kate, but Calamity Jane became the reigning girl sport of half-dime novel fiction and had fans around the globe.[16] For many young English-speakers growing up in the late nineteenth century, Deadwood Dick and Calamity Jane defined the American West.[17]

Dime novels were widely considered forbidden fiction, rendering them both extremely desirable and unlikely to be claimed by readers. Newspapers regularly contained stories of young male and female criminals led astray by the graphic depiction of violence and crime in dime novels. Typical was the attitude expressed in the *New York Times* in 1882: "In the departments of theft, highway robbery, forgery and counterfeiting, together with those fascinating branches, train-wrecking and gambling, dime novel textbooks are beyond praise."[18] Samuel Hopkins Adams, a popular author, noted that in his youth dime novels were "taboo, strictly so. To be devotee of this kind of reading was as bad as smoking the surreptitious cigarette or going to a 'leg show.'" Yet despite all of the warnings issued by ministers, educators, and other adults, "reading circles gathered in the barn on rainy days when some adventurous spirit" would produce a dime novel for sharing. Half the fun was hiding it from the adults. Indeed, according to another reminiscence, the nickel papers were popular because they "could be spread open inside a school geography and entirely concealed from any teacher." Although few young diarists mention dime novels, as adults many of them waxed nostalgic about their love of cheap adventure fiction. When Edmund Pearson informally polled men and women in 1929, he found that four in five had read at least one dime novel when younger.[19] A hunger for entertainment undermined the effects of parental aversion; dime novels brought adventure to an otherwise quiet life. It was also a relatively safe and easy form of rebellion.

Perhaps the most amusing example of the worries over the effects of dime novels can be seen in an 1888 *New York Times* article about sixteen-year-old Mary Abbott of Stockton, California, who became so enamored with westerns that she attempted to run away and join the cowboys. The journalist declared that Abbott "is the victim of dime novels, and says she wants to be a cowboy," before recounting the tale according to her father, who claimed that Abbot had tried running away "two or three" times before this final dramatic stand-off. Each time, she had "arisen at night, saddled a pony, and with a lot of provisions, a camping outfit and pistol, started for the mountains." In the past, she had been rounded up by neighbors. This time she holed up in a barn, fired a shot to scatter the pursuing crowd, and thrust her pistol into the face of a parson who tried to approach her. Finally she "ran out of the barn and made for the river." The "crowd started after her," the constable fired a couple of warning shots, and she was finally captured.[20] One has to wonder if she was a girl inspired by dime novels or simply desperate to escape her father's home—or if the story was true at all.

Girls undoubtedly read the books, but it is impossible to know if they identified any more with the girl sport than other central characters. Wheeler and other authors who favored girl sports, such as Prentiss Ingraham and Joseph E. Badger, clearly catered to male fantasies with shapely girl sports, but they also allowed them to direct the action, not merely as damsels in distress but as aggressors and rescuers. Female readers were accustomed to identifying with male heroes, of course, since stories about white males functioned as universal stories about human beings. Many girls, such as thirteen-year-old Mary Sheldon Barnes of Oswego, New York, enjoyed adventure stories as much as boys. In her diary, Barnes recorded reading "a book of thrilling adventures by my favorite Captain Mayne Reid." Theodore Roosevelt would later hold up Reid as critical reading for raising manly boys.[21] Early in the game, publishers tried to target adventure tales to female audiences, but nearly all of those ventures quickly folded.[22] Apparently adventure stories featuring a girl sport but written for male audience proved far more marketable.

Girls may not have recorded their dime novel reading because, as Caroline Stickney Creevey, an unabashed tomboy and supporter of women's higher education, later commented, "They represented to me, not only trash, but positive evil." The one time she even saw one as a girl, her father picked it up with tongs to put it in the fire: "He said he would not defile his fingers by touching it." Yet when teaching school as a young woman a decade later, Creevey discovered that many girls "and nearly all of the boys" belonged to a secret dime novel "club" of three years' standing.[23]

The blurred cultural and social boundaries of the western frontier setting rendered the girl sport an unusually exciting heroine. And, at least within the dubious morality of the novels, girl sports remain remarkably sympathetic characters despite shocking, unsexing behavior. Readers (and characters) understood that rules might be bent for a young woman to survive on the frontier. If the tomboy of domestic fiction is about taming the interior self and learning to accept limitations and self-restraint, the girl sport by comparison is about adjusting to the exterior—the hostile world of the frontier, which is beyond her control and clearly "outmans" her.

While girl sports were hardly role models for readers, they spoke to the fusing of white masculine aggression and national identity as authentically American and as an imperative bulwark against the feminizing effects of urban modernity. Even more than tomboys, girl sports suggest that defying gender convention was not only admirable within particular settings, but necessary to protect the expansionist aims of righteous America. Girl sports serve to influence how readers understood the roles of white men and women in a nation increasingly depicted as a white civilizing influence in a world of savage darkness—a darkness represented in these novels by Chinese, Mexicans, Native Americans, outlaws, and the wilderness itself. The actions of girl sports, who are almost always paired with white male heroes, illustrate a coalition of whiteness against others. Girl sports enact gender transgression in the service of racial solidarity and, in fact, become conventional in those moments when they are aligned with the hero. If tomboys spoke to how real girls might behave within the confines of respectable middle-class change, girls sports spoke to the need for white heroes and heroines to align against a darker world.

The Girl Sport in Action

Calamity Jane, the breakthrough girl sport, became a major character in *Deadwood Dick on Deck; or, Calamity Jane, the Heroine of Whoop-Up,* published in 1878. She enters the novel as a sweet voice wafting across the night sky over strangers sitting around a campfire. A miner describes Calamity Jane to the visiting tenderfoot as morally degenerate, the "most reckless buchario [buckaroo] in ther Hills," who "kin drink whisky, shute, play keerds." Then the miner murmurs an aside: "Twixt you an' me, I reckon the gal's got honor left wi' her grit, out o' ther wreck o' a young life." The West has made Jane, just as the West would shape the character of all its inhabitants. Yet the hearsay is slander, the old miner insists: "Because she's got grit and ain't afeard to shute ther galoot as crosses her, people condemn her. I reckon you know how it is out hyar in the Hills, Sandy—ef a female ken't stand up an fight for her rights, ets durned little aid she'll git."[24] In Wheeler's novels, Calamity Jane and other girl sports represent an idealized female independence—painfully won, isolating, and dangerous, but honorable, and respected if not respectable. In these half-dime novels that were by all accounts marketed to male youth, the West was the domain of men, but girls and women were not always forced to the sidelines as agents of civilization or vulnerable damsels in need of rescuing. A few girls stood up for themselves and thus earned the respect of local men, and often the heart of the hero.

The physical description of Calamity Jane echoes Wheeler's earlier vision of Hurricane Nell, and it is replicated in form again and again in subsequent novels by various authors. She enters a "female of no given age, although she might have ranged safely anywhere between seventeen and twenty-three." Her figure is "graceful and womanly" and her face is memorable, with beautiful lips of "full, rosy plumpness" and eyes of "dark, magnetic sparkle." Like most girl sports, she has "long, raven hair that reached below a faultless waist."[25] Everything about her physical self emphasizes female identity.

But then there are her clothes: Jane wears pants! This is significant: the skirt of the girl sport is often the most tangible item that sets her apart from the men and boys around her; it is what suggests an opposite pairing with a man, which reinforces the heterosexual structure.[26] Calamity Jane, by contrast, is ambiguously gendered yet fully sexualized. Her "buck-skin trowsers [were] met at the knee by fancifully-beaded leggings, with slippers of dainty pattern upon the feet; . . . a boiled shirt, open at the throat, partially revealing a breast of alabaster purity; a short, velvet jacket, and Spanish broad-brimmed hat, slouched upon one side of a regal head."

Despite their male design, her clothes are splashed with femininity in the form of "dainty" patterns and sparkly beading. And, as with her dime novel male counterparts, her flashy dress suggests ill-gotten wealth: "diamond rings upon her hands, a diamond pin in her shirt bosom, a massive gold chain across her vest front." And finally, this curvaceous body in its male clothes, with outrageous jewelry in the midst of dark wilderness, is elaborately armed: "a belt around her waist contained a solitary revolver of large caliber, . . . along with a rifle strapped to her back." She rides a black horse "richly decorated and bespangled after lavish Mexican taste."[27] Calamity Jane is a delicious tangle of contradictions—womanly, available, exotic, angry, dangerous, immoral, honorable, and even nurturing when compelled by innate female compassion. And she influenced the depictions of most girl sports that would populate the nickel-paper western world well into the twentieth century.

Thus Wheeler establishes the cultural relativism that made his westerns so captivating. Calamity Jane and her ilk are sexually aware; they were brought to their present circumstances by ruination, and they sometimes assert their sexuality to male characters. By their very presence in the fictive West, girl sports are hybrids of masculinity and femininity—embracing adventure over respectability because their surroundings leave them little choice. Female elders in these novels are invariably rough and somewhat masculine as well, as if to say that this is simply the way it has to be out west; women must be tough to survive in these parts. But the heart of the girl sport—her emotional will and tenderness, hidden beneath a carapace of hard living—is largely chaste and responds instinctively to the hero, as if she had been waiting for his presence to set her true self free.

Part of the allure of Calamity Jane, as is true of other dime novel heroes such as Billy the Kid, is that her character was based on a living person. And just as with most of those dime novel heroes, the author had never met Martha Jane Canary, the living version of his character; Wheeler simply embroidered on rumor. From a historian's perspective, Calamity Jane in the flesh was far more interesting than the character created by Wheeler. Colorful and opportunistic, she made the most of the celebrity conferred on her by Wheeler and eventually peddled hyperbolic tales of her adventures in the Buffalo Bill show of the 1890s.[28] Wheeler's Calamity Jane inspired plays, musicals, and films in her name, and other dime novelists to feature nearly identical characters in their novels.[29] There is little correlation between the woman and the character, but for readers to know she actually existed out in the Far West gave the books an added thrill of authenticity.[30]

Annie Oakley (born Phoebe Ann Mosey or Moses) was far more famous than Calamity Jane, but she did not figure much in dime novels, perhaps because she emphasized herself as a lady as well as a sure shot, and was famously happily married.[31] Oakley had genuine talent with a gun, and playing up her femininity increased the spectacle of her sharpshooting.[32] After she joined Buffalo Bill's Wild West show in 1885, she became an international celebrity. But if Oakley in many ways defied the imagery of the tragic but triumphant girl sport, such imagery still served as her context. She was the opposite of the girl sport in her gender performance, and yet she was also living proof of the girl sport simply because of her comfort with a gun and association with the Far West.[33]

By the late 1880s, after Wheeler had died and other dime novel authors were writing under his name, girl sports in Wheeler novels, as well as those inspired by Wheeler, took on an almost mystical allure. For example, in *Girl Rider,* by Joseph E. Badger, a hunter describes having once seen a mysterious girl: "Now I could see that she was white—though her complexion was that of a rich brunette. A more beautiful face I never saw. I can't describe it—only that her great big eyes were black and shining as those of a deer." She is a white girl and yet part of the wild. And she is ravishing, with an hourglass figure no male attire can hide, moving the hunter to confess, "Boys, that face and figure have haunted me ever since. If that woman is as good and pure as she is beautiful, she would be well worth dying for!"[34] The girl's masculine dress not only highlights her female form but makes earthly a woman who otherwise appears too extraordinary for mere mortals.

In the same period, some girl sports also became figures of dread desire, when their thirst for revenge eclipses their femininity. For example, in Badger's *The Girl Cowboy Captain* (1889), vibrant Maria enters the story with "black eyes flashing" as she views the charred remains of her family and home. Two months later, a "stranger would have shuddered at her ghastly pallor. Only for the eyes, she looked like a corpse. . . . [But] nearly two score brave men owed allegiance to the Girl Cowboy Captain." Her female tenderness lost in bloodlust, she dies at the end of the novel, while another female character assumes the romantic role.[35]

Dime novels make full use of simplistic stereotypes, but they are surprisingly complex in how various characters relate despite racial difference. The Mexican and Chinese characters fare by far the worst; they are consistently depicted as of low, and even bestial, character. For example, in Wheeler's *Apollo Bill, the Trail Tornado; or, Rowdy Kate from Right Bower* (1882), Chin-Chin, a Chinese passenger in a stagecoach with white travelers, is called "pig-tailed son of a washee-washee . . . almond-eyed, flat-mugged nigger! . . . chop-stick rat eater."[36] Yet even though racial stereotypes rule these books, race alone does not predict who will turn out to be bad, victorious, or loyal. Given who wrote and who read them, the books are unsurprisingly and unabashedly white supremacist and male-centered, but that does not mean that all morally superior characters are white. Both Native American and African American characters are allowed innate nobility, particularly when juxtaposed with a white villain. Of course, there are lots of nasty male Comanches, Arapahos, and Sioux, but the books just as often depict individual Indians who are loyal to the good whites, despite the atrocities taking place in the real world outside of the novels. Rife with stereotypes, the dime novels imbue whiteness with connotations of valor and honor, and yet also reflect the confusion many Americans felt about race.

Although African Americans could be found throughout the West in this period, as missionaries, farmers, cowboys, prostitutes, and homesteaders, they are usually lone figures in dime novels, and black women rarely appear.[37] Indeed the term "black" in these novels can mean African or Native American; it defines characters who are "not white," and white is itself defined against that blackness. For example, Mabel Calmet, the title character of Badger's 1871 Beadle dime novel *The Black Princess,* is an "Indian maiden" of eighteen rescued from a Native American whom the white hero refers to as a "Nigger." Her "skin, clear and soft, glowed with a tint that betrayed the presence, in some faint degree, of aboriginal blood. Her hair, black as night, silken and glossy, hung far down her back, secured only by a scarlet ribbon that crossed above her forehead. Her eyes [were] large and lustrous as those of yearling doe's." She is a male fantasy, of course: "the graceful neck, the heaving bosom; all in all, the picture of a wildwood beauty, such as seldom is ever beheld, save in a poet's dream." Yet the author dresses her in a short, beaded red dress and gives her the dialect of a debutante, and the white hero sounds like a southern hick. As if to emphasize their shared whiteness—and to clarify the meaning of "white" in these novels—at one of many points of danger the hero refuses to leave her side, saying "I ain't no nigger! We'll live or die together."[38] And indeed he does marry her by the end of the novel, by which point her description has evolved into true ladyhood, and she is tired, pale, and worried most of the time. Yet on the whole the novels appear to tacitly accept miscegenation as part of frontier life. Indian girls in these stories fall in love with white men, of course, but even Native men are allowed to marry mature (not virginal) white women with impunity.[39]

Many girl sports are themselves racially ambiguous, such as the title heroine of *Wistah, the Child Spy*, by George Gleason (1892). Fourteen-year-old Wistah rescues two white men at the outset of the story, marking her as on the side of good. Yet she is "semi-savage," as is expressed by her dress: "a neat-fitting tunic, embroidered with parti-colored needlework, with a skirt fancifully fringed and reaching just to her knees—leggings of dressed dear-skin, little moccasins of the same material, and a scarlet mantle drooping from her shoulders behind." She is beautiful, with hair as black "as an Indian's" (emphasizing that she is not an Indian) "but soft as silk," which "fell about her shoulders in a shower of ringlets, and was adorned by one or two eagle-feathers." Her appearance is racially mingled: "Her features were of the European cast, but there was a tinge in her complexion that might have been imparted by a mixture of blood. She was decidedly pretty, with a voice as musical as silvery chimes, and teeth that glistened like genuine pearls." From the outset she is a blurring of opposites, as is demonstrated by her eyes, which "were large, lustrous, and burning in their gaze. Sometimes they were meek and gentle in their expression; again they flashed and blazed as if governed by some wild passion; at other times, they glowed with a strange, uncertain light, suggestive of a weakened mind."[40] By this point, an experienced reader of dime novels would quickly read the doom written into the description of those eyes.

Biracial heroines are often good, but they rarely survive, and they are usually of Native American and Anglo or, more rarely, Mexican-Anglo descent. Their heritage may allude to mythologies of noble Indian princesses, but also, in the discourse of the period, they represent the untenable union of civilization and savagery. Despite her Anglified beauty, Wistah is dangerous, armed to the teeth and sporting a large rattlesnake about her shoulders.[41] A heroine so racialized cannot survive as a central heroine, but must remain an exotic fetish at best.

Sexuality

Sexual awareness is what most clearly sets the girl sport apart from tom-boys, and what makes her, despite her masculine dress and freedoms, wholly female. In marked contrast to the norm in American popular culture as a whole, the sexual purity of white women is not positioned against a supposedly natural promiscuity on the part of dark women. Her sexuality is no doubt attributable to the male target audience, for whom the distant girl sport provides only fantasy.

The novels' covers advertise the girl sport's sexual allure even before one reaches the story. Although several of the more celebrated dime novelists were female, the illustrators—the ones responsible for grabbing the atten-tion of purchasers with covers that struck a balance between enticing and inoffensive—were uniformly male.[42] Dime novels were simply made, with an illustration on the cover that often did not connect to the story. The girl sport almost always wears a dress on the cover, even if in the story she wears trousers. In those few instances when the heroine is depicted wearing male clothing, she is also feminized, with a tiny waist and long hair. Yet it would be misleading to say that she is depicted more femininely than the heroes on the cover, as they are also illustrated with the same large eyes, long hair, and small mouths associated with sentimental fiction. The distinguishing difference between males and females on the covers tends to be facial hair and waist circumference, and the behavior they assume when juxtaposed. The heroine often plays an active role in scenes against male bad guys, but the hero takes the lead if he is alongside her.

Although some girl sports, such as Calamity Jane, manage to develop into full-blown central characters, all of them function as erotic elements in the story. The narrators worshipfully describe their bodies for the benefit of the male audience. Leadville Lil is typical; she has "magnificent black eyes, a mouth of tempting ripeness," and "a figure perfect in every proportion."[43] Hurricane Nell, as we've seen, has "a form of exquisite contour."[44] Kit Keene is shocked when the hero sees through her male "disguise," despite the fact that she has "mild girlish blue eyes, and long auburn hair, soft and silken like a maiden's."[45] Although secondary characters consistently voice confusion over the sex of the girl sport because of cross-dressing, the descriptions of her are sexually charged and emphatically female.

In the later decades of popularity, some girl sports move beyond mere objects and made their own sexually aggressive moves. One example is

Leadville Lil, who is known as the "girl who took her whiskey straight." She dares a man to try to kiss her in exchange for a hundred dollars. It turns out he can't take the bet because he's been robbed. "Well, I'm sorry you're broke," Leadville Lil says as she leans up against the bar and puffs away at a cigarette. "Was in hopes I could make a raise out of you, or have a smack at your luscious lips—one or the other. Any other gent fond enough of kissing to risk a hundred?" Yet despite her provocative ways, Lil marries the hero and converts to feminine invisibility at the end of the novel.[46]

Heterosexual Coupling

Heterosexual love transforms tomboys and girl sports alike, though to different ends. If love for a man saves the domestic tomboy from a life of thwarted and immature masculinity, the possibilities for the girl sport are more extreme, going so far as to erase her past ruination and life as an outlaw. Heterosexual coupling tends to save the hero as well; through it the hero and girl sport redeem themselves as a united front of white solidarity in a savage environment.

Even the most disreputable of the girl sports is redeemed by her devotion to a man, particularly if it ends in marriage. For example, Hurricane Nell steps outside of all bounds of propriety in far more ways than cross-dressing. She ropes mustangs. She kills Indians and brands them on the forehead with a half-moon stamp dipped in their own blood. At one point she explains, "My life is one of constant peril, and strange as it may seem sir, the greater the danger, and the more exciting the adventure, I glory the more in it. You will doubtless think me a wild and strange creature, without a heart or a woman's instinct, but I cannot help it."[47] Yet she falls in love at first sight with a white city lawyer, whom she saves and marries. They appear in their elder years at the end of the book, and Nell has become feminized and husband has gained masculinity.

The taming of the girl sport, however, was not necessarily a welcome solution. After Calamity Jane finally marries Deadwood Dick in *Deadwood Dick's Doom* (1881), she becomes a secondary character. Deadwood Dick immodestly proposes: "Come to me, at Death Notch, Calamity, and the hand you have so long sought shall be yours." And as he assumes, Calamity indeed looks forward "to claim[ing] the love and protection of the only man she had ever worshipped."[48] Independent, give-no-quarter Calamity Jane embraces dependency on Dick, which is illustrated in the next installment of their adventures, *Captain Crack-Shot, the Girl Brigand; or, Gipsy Jack from Jimtown.* Calamity, who has rescued Dick countless times in previous novels, now requires rescuing. A lawless young woman named Captain Crack-Shot captures Calamity to use as bait to lure Dick into her clutches. With silver revolvers at her waist, a knife at her hip, and a "face fresh and fair," Captain Crack-Shot replaces Calamity Jane as the brash girl sport of the novel. When Deadwood Dick finally reaches the camp, Calamity cries in relief, "Oh! Dick! Dick! . . . Have you come to rescue me?"[49] In earlier novels, canny Jane had taken the measure of those who tried to trick her and staged her own escapes. But marriage has erased what had made her remarkable. She becomes so passive that even the dog, Skipper, ends up being more resourceful at thwarting Captain Crack-Shot.

True to the tomboy/ girl sport story, marriage *did* redeem Calamity Jane, but the transformation proved unworkable. While that redemption may have been acceptable for less beloved characters like Hurricane Nell (who disappears from print after her marriage), it was not a characterization that Wheeler (and subsequent ghostwriters) chose to sustain. To permanently feminize Calamity Jane was tantamount to killing her off, and yet fulfilling the expectation of marriage to Dick could not be entirely avoided. So the writers did both. In later books Calamity Jane goes back and forth between being Dick's equal partner in adventure and, more rarely, his passive wife—at one point giving birth to their son, Deadwood Dick Jr., who goes on to have his own series.

But Wheeler may also have stepped away from a marriage of his two most famous characters because a domesticated Deadwood Dick was equally problematic. The heroes of dime novels are entirely unlike the young men of superior character who save the tomboy through marriage. Indeed, part of their charm is their blemished character; they are not designed to be husbands. They are flawed, like the girl sports, because the frontier requires them to accept the violation of certain codes of respectability. When Calamity Jane and Deadwood Dick finally marry, Wheeler describes them as equally besmirched: "two wild spirits who had learned each other's faults and each other's worth in lives branded with commingled shame and honor."[50] The girl sports and tomboys alike marry the hero, but dime-novel husband material is no more conventional or respectable than the female characters. Moreover, Deadwood Dick and Calamity Jane were internationally beloved characters; they could not simply disappear into domestic life, however much that would conform to the typical narrative arc.

The kind of men who save the tomboy and the girl sport reflect the concerns of their market audience. The tomboy becomes "normalized" through marriage, while the girl sport's marriage confirms that the masculinity of a real man will eclipse her own. Tomboys consistently marry kind, smart, upstanding young men able to provide a middle-class life. Girl sports, for the most part, disdain such men. When a girl sport falls in love, it signifies that she recognizes a man with masculinity superior to her own; she allows herself weakness in response to his overt masculinity. For example, the girl sport Zoe in Wheeler's *Bonanza Bill* (1879) turns down a suitor, declaring: "He is soft, shallow and effeminate, and, I suspect, has a disposition to be treacherous. When I marry, I want a *man* whom I can respect and look up to, as brave and fearless."[51] Characters like Zoe emphasize to their male readers the importance of masculinity in allowing women to play a subordinate role. Even disreputable girl sports acknowledge their males as superiors: a real woman knows a real man.

But changes in gender expectations of the larger social world are also reflected in the western novels, as the New Woman of the late nineteenth century was increasingly challenging the notion that women would have to sacrifice womanhood to participate in public life and pursue nondomestic ambitions. Within western novels, the girl sport is allowed to transgress these gender norms in large part because she does so as a white woman alongside a white hero in a savage land. The explicit whiteness of the western heroes and heroines became more pronounced by the turn of the century.

One of the western pulp series most obvious in connecting whiteness and gender norms is *Young Wild West,* which first appeared in 1902. Throughout the stories, various characters reassert that the hero is the "whitest boy in the whole West" because he has principles.[52] "White" in these stories is shorthand for the many virtues supposedly inherent to the white race: courage, rationality, self-control, compassion, and independent action. And Young Wild West (yes, that is his name) is matched by an equally white soulmate: sixteen-year-old blonde-haired, blue-eyed Arietta, who, though "light hearted and as graceful as a fairy," can "handle a gun or pistol as well as the average man in the West" and spends every issue expressing zestful violence until literally brought into swoons by the greater masculine presence of Young Wild West.[53] The caricatured charm of Young Wild West and Arietta, along with their need to voice racial philosophies, suggests how ideas voiced by adults filtered into fiction geared toward children.

When Young Wild West first comes upon sixteen-year-old Arietta, both are held captive by a band of "red devils," and she is "pale from fear and her eyes were red from weeping." Making his escape the next day, he pulls her across his saddle horn and, not missing a beat, she soon grabs one of his revolvers and shoots a pursuing Indian. Then she faints when they jump across a deadly-looking abyss.[54] Throughout the series, Arietta kills easily and often, but the presence of Young Wild West makes her fragile. He exhibits a similar shyness in her presence, overtaken by blushes whenever they converse. Indeed, one reader, the playwright and noted wit Marc Connelly, later remembered, "I don't believe Young Wild West ever even kissed her. He just spent his life rescuing her." In fact Arietta spends a fair amount of time rescuing herself, but only if her lover is not available. Connelly, who as a boy read the *Young Wild West* series hidden inside more acceptable books, recalled Arietta as "the most guileless girl that ever got into a villain's clutches."[55] And yet she shot to kill regularly and often faced death without a murmur.

True to the girl sports before her, she coolly kills with a revolver hidden in the "bosom of her dress," and stands up for her man, but she connects his virtue to white identity: "The idea of his insulting you—Young Wild West, the Prince of the saddle, and the whitest young man in the whole Wild West!"[56] In every issue both Arietta and Young Wild West explicitly prove their whiteness. Yet even as racist language and supposition fuel these stories, progressive Arietta and Young Wild West spout paternalistic compassion and constantly extemporize on the need to see nonwhite people as capable of good.

Arietta's greatest and most consistent danger is marriage; in story after story, evil men—from lawyers to millionaires to Mormons—try to marry her against her will. She is routinely sexually assaulted—kidnapped, tied up, tricked, and attacked—but she fights back hard: "If the scoundrel wants a kiss," she tells a kidnapper, "I am ready to give it to him, but it will be a hot lead kiss."[57] Because she consistently swears loyalty to Young Wild West, one would presume that marriage also has the greatest potential to save her, yet both she and he refuse to admit to being engaged, let alone marry.[58] Clearly, what makes Arietta most vulnerable is also what makes her free. Her heroism is made possible by her identity as a "guileless" young woman.

Although a two-dimensional character at best, Arietta is important here for what she represents in the evolving genre. Her transgressive behaviors—hard riding, easy killing, provocative weaponry—are the stuff of postbellum pulp western heroines like Calamity Jane and Leadville Lil. But she significantly departs from that company by being younger (sixteen) and unambiguously white, and by being seen as entirely respectable, even dainty, within her environment. Her face and body do not show hard usage and toil; she does not, like Calamity Jane, light up cigars and whoop "like a full-blown Comanche warrior."[59] Arietta reacts to danger; she is otherwise as wholesome and sweet as the girl next door. In many ways, she is the tomboy evolved into the American girl: the qualities of the girl sport have become tamed and softened, and normalized, in a figure like Arietta.

If Arietta complicates gender norms by being feminine in every way but her comfort with violence, Young Wild West complicates them through his appearance. He is a strikingly feminine "bright, handsome boy of eighteen, with a wealth of waving chestnut hair hanging down his back," big eyes, and "lush" lips.[60] Yet despite his beauty, no character questions the masculinity of Young Wild West; no one teases him about his curls or pretty features because time and again he proves himself to be bloodthirsty, courageous, and honorable. In the first installment he confides to onlookers, "I could have dropped the other fellow [a Sioux warrior] with no trouble whatever, but he did not show fight, and I would not be guilty of shooting any man, white, black or red, unless I was compelled to." One soldier interrupts: "'That's a grand principle, ain't it? . . . I haven't know Wild very long, lieutenant, but I'll stake my life that he is the whitest boy in the whole West.' 'There is not a shadow of a doubt but that you are right,' was the reply."[61]

Young Wild West was one of the more successful formula westerns vying for children's nickels. By the turn of the twentieth century, dime novels had transformed into juvenile stories increasingly marketed to adolescent male readers, and Arietta was one of the most successful of the girl sports of this changing genre. She quickly emerged as a central character second only to the hero, with every third or fourth issue focusing on her adventures. If race relations and gender norms in the earlier novels were complex, the ones in these later versions defy all rationality, conveying to young white readers that while gender and race were shifting and flowing, white men were still on top and youthful whites were particularly graced.

Through heterosexual coupling, the gender transgressions of the hero and heroine are muted in service to their white solidarity. The hero and heroine alike can be beautiful and principled, as long as they embrace violence when they need to assert their dominance. The *Young Wild West* series presents a hero and girl sport who are remarkably alike, and echo the national context of white supremacy and tension over women's greater participation in public life, education, and wage labor.

The girl sport and the tomboy appear alike in multiple ways, but the target audiences of their different genres require them to function significantly differently. Writers of domestic fiction present tomboys to girl readers as models for negotiating the unbearable tension between a free girlhood and fettered womanhood. The girl sport, by contrast, assures male readers that masculinity can continue to reign in frontier environments without giving up heterosexual satisfactions. Both tomboys and girl sports function to solidify whiteness—the former as the unspoken normative girl, and the latter as explicitly asserting white superiority in a savage world.

The Far West created by eastern authors provided a masculine alternative to "feminized" middle-class culture dominating so much of American life, and also soothed male fears over the concurrent rise of the New Woman. Tomboys and girl sports alike suggested that modern women would play an increasingly public role, but also that, with maturity, heterosexual coupling would continue to trump female masculinity.

4

The Tomboy and the New Woman

In June 1900, the *Boston Herald* observed: "A tomboy used to be described as a girl with the tendencies of a boy, but how are we to differentiate this from an accurate definition of the New Woman? Perhaps only the greater maturity of the latter. This would make a New Woman a tomboy grown up."[1] The arc of the classic tomboy tale was of an adolescent boyish girl coming to embrace the destiny of marriage and maternity built into her female body. The New Woman was that tomboy demanding to choose her own destiny.

Embedded in the newspaper's observation was dismissal: New Women are just girls wanting to be boys, unwilling to grow up. But there was also fear: What if young women refuse to take the female role? Are women becoming men? Yet because tomboys were now widely depicted as healthy and strong, there was also hope: the New Woman heralds a healthier young woman, able to rise to the challenges and embrace the opportunities of modern life. Or, as the historian Martha Patterson succinctly summarizes, "Was she to be celebrated as the agent and sign of progress or reviled as a traitor to the traditional family and by extension her race?"[2]

In the last two decades of the nineteenth century, prescriptive literature almost universally praised tomboys at roughly the same time that America became enthralled with, and horrified by, the image and concept of the New Woman—that is to say, the notion that there *was* a New Woman born of modernity and asserting her right to a public presence. Her actual definition remained ambiguous, which made the concept extremely useful. In real life as well as in images, she spanned class, race, and ethnicity in urban areas. She also appeared in many different guises in popular culture, although by the turn of the century her caricature took on reliable dimensions that typically placed her as white, young, and conventionally pretty.

In print culture the New Woman was often a college girl who asserted rights to her own sexuality and the freedom to choose between marriage or a profession. In more critical illustrations she typically wore pants below her nipped-in waist as she smoked a cigarette, bellied up to the bar, or loomed over a cowering man.

Because the New Woman was a public figure who took many forms, women and girls across social classes claimed the image, even if the press largely ignored them. Immigrant daughters adopted New Woman styles, often to the distress of their parents. African American women welcomed a respectable womanhood that did not require being cloistered in the home, since that was a life few of them could afford. In all of her many guises, as athlete or office girl, suffragette or socialite, union leader or clubwoman, the New Woman of print culture enjoyed freedom as a consumer, autonomy outside of the home, and homosocial as well as heterosexual leisure time in public spaces that had hitherto belonged to men.

But the observation made by the *Boston Herald* did hold true, because the New Woman also amplified an aspect of identity that had long been the subtext of tomboy fiction: the desire to express her internal sense of self beyond her external female identity. The article states that tomboys earn their title for having the "tendencies" of boys, but the American tomboy that developed in postbellum print culture had struggled far more with a sense of failing feminine norms. Both the tomboy and New Woman spoke to the conflict between what the feminist Charlotte Perkins Gilman called "myself as a self" and the self bound by a female body.[3]

By the 1870s and '80s, concerns over female health led to tomboys becoming common figures in newspapers, plays, books, and magazine stories; by the 1880s, with the spread of women's higher education and athletics, the New Woman played a similar role. Tomboy promoters laid the groundwork for the idea that girls embracing boyish play made for healthier future mothers. Often explicitly, they posited tomboys as ideal in a modern world, where the greatest concern about girls was how to preserve their reproductive health in the face of new opportunities.

With the blossoming of magazines and consumer culture, images of the New Woman appeared everywhere. In the 1890s, ten-cent magazines changed the culture of the periodical press, with a new reliance on advertising and a need to attract readers through entertainment and sensation. Oppositional images of the New Woman sold magazines, and illustrations of attractive women sold even more.[4] The New Woman, glamorously and dangerously modern, was easily signaled through dress and activities that became stereotyped by the turn of the century. As a type, the New Woman was educated, independent, frank, fearless, and physically strong.[5] Negative portrayals cast her in men's clothing, dominating her emasculated husband. She became the most potent symbol of the Progressive Era (1880–1920), and yet, despite her ubiquity, voices in popular culture suggest that she remained hard to pin down. She seemed to belong as much to advertising as to politics, to social reform as to entertainment. As with the tomboy, the ambiguity of the New Woman was part of what made her such an effective symbol. And like the tomboy, her transgressions against gender conventions were linked, positively and negatively, with white evolution.

The New Woman was the tomboy who pursued her own inclinations well into adulthood. She claimed a right to personal freedoms and a public presence long understood as the province of males. Linking the demands and opportunities of modernity to tomboyism in earlier decades had tied such gender transgressions to immaturity. Yet by the 1890s, as more and more girls and young women adopted behavior formerly labeled as "tomboy," the term lost not only its sting but also its purpose. In earlier decades, real girls such as Louisa May Alcott, growing up in Massachusetts, or Kathie Gray in Ohio (see chapter 7), embraced tomboy identity as a means of asserting physicality, candor, and ambition. But they knew it ended at the door of womanhood; indeed, this was their struggle. Now the New Woman suggested that such rights were not tied to age. In regard to tomboys, the New Woman confirmed, as Jack Halberstam puts it in another context, "the dread possibility . . . that the tomboy will not grow out of her butch stage and will never become" joined with others in conventional life.[6] Worse still, she might do this by choice, for the New Woman asserted the right to choose something other than marriage and also asserted that a professional life might provide meaning equal to motherhood. Thus the New Woman threatened not only male dominance, in the eyes of many, but the evolution of the white race itself.

The term "New Woman" entered popular discourse in the 1890s, but articulations of young middle- and upper-middle-class women demanding a right to personal liberty appeared in the early postbellum years. Historians credit Henrik Ibsen's 1879 play *A Doll's House,* a scathing indictment of Victorian gender roles within conventional marriage, with inspiring

New Woman advocates in western culture.[7] By the mid-1880s, discussion of this new kind of womanhood peppered the papers.[8] In 1885 the *New Haven Register,* for example, sought to remind voters that modernity was changing female instincts as well as male: "Instinctively she sees old forms crumble away and upon the ruins she sees the new structure of life." Meanwhile, Edward Bok, editor of the *Ladies' Home Journal,* the most widely read American women's magazine, scathingly wrote, "I have not been able to find out exactly in what respect this woman is 'new,' unless it be that her newness lies in her being unwomanly, or different from what God intended a woman should be."[9] Most commentators agreed that regardless of how she was depicted, the New Woman symbolized a reconceiving of woman's roles and place in the society. Through education, work, and politics, young American women increasingly asserted their right to a public voice without losing respectability.

Tomboys were a safe way of advocating physical activity for girls, since most prescriptive literature concluded with assurances that tomboys grow out of their boyishness. But many who championed the advancement of women now posited the tomboy as the seed not only of ideal womanhood, but of the New Woman specifically. By 1873, when Mrs. E. B. Duffey expressed her opinion on the topic, in *What Women Should Know,* she was largely repeating what was already accepted among the "experts" of prescriptive literature: "I would, at this period [as a girl approaches puberty], allow a girl to be as 'tomboyish' as her inclinations lead her to be. . . . Let her ride, drive, row, swim, run, climb fences, and even trees, if she has a mind to. She is only laying the foundation for future good health."[10]

Indeed, by the 1880s there seemed to be a national call to encourage tomboyism. In 1888, when Elizabeth Cady Stanton queried "What does this country need most?" a reporter for the *Omaha World Herald* volunteered: "A change in the system of bringing up girls. The country needs less art and artificiality and more health, strength and muscle. It needs old-fashioned tomboy girls who will develop into robust women with vitality enough to do their own housework and have plenty of time for social duties besides."[11] It was as if the culture had decided collectively that only tomboy girlhoods could account for the New Woman becoming successful in a man's world.

Girls got the message. In 1880 young Emma B. Sonedecker wrote to the *Ohio Farmer:* "I live on a farm. . . . I got my hair shingled this summer and pa calls me his little 'tom boy,' but I am quite proud of that name. I will be 14 the ninth of September."[12] Indeed, by the 1880s print culture in the United States became fairly overrun with self-proclaimed tomboys, and they often mentioned being steered that way by their own parents, particularly fathers. For example, in 1887 a Georgia girl told an area paper that her parents call her a tomboy, "and father says he is glad of it."[13]

Girls themselves were aware that adults expected tomboy days to end in her mid-teens. In 1887 one fourteen-year-old wrote in the Louisville, Kentucky *Courier-Journal:* "I'm very healthy, like fun and boys (in fact I like boys better than girls). I am called 'Tom Boy' at home, and think the name suits me." The problem was the adults around her, who constantly suggest she is either too old or too young: "One of my great trials is this: If I go climbing out on the chicken coop mamma says, 'You ought to be ashamed; a great big 15-year-old girl, thinking about beaux, to be climbing about like a boy.' Then again, if I walk home from town with a boy, mamma says 'You little 13-year-old-child, not quit playing with dolls, to go flying around with a boy.'" Clothes, once again, became the symbol of her imprisonment: "It is about this age a girl begins to squeeze her feet into shoes two sizes too small and wear her gloves and bonnet in doors and out."[14]

Alongside the championing of raising tomboy girls, stories of successful women as former tomboys appeared regularly. In an 1872 newspaper article titled "A Tom-boy Grows Up," for example, a girl who "made sleds and wagons and kites" for her brothers, and preferred "saws and hatchets" to dolls and tea, found that she simply could not "drone away her life at the family fireside" but instead went "to work like a man" in a paper-bag plant. Eventually, Martha Knight earned the first patent awarded a woman by inventing a paper-bag machine, and supposedly amassed a respectable fortune. "This tom-boy has done it!" the reporter crows.[15]

Tomboys also became popular stock characters in entertainment and consumer culture. *Cad, the Tomboy,* first produced in 1882, became a sensation and rocketed the lead actress, Carrie Swain, into international celebrity.[16] The success of *Cad* prompted copies, and the classic tomboy tale (rowdy girl grows up and tames down just enough to nab a husband) became such a cliché that by the century's end it proved ideal for early nickelodeon and silent films, which tended to rely on familiar storylines. Indeed, by that point, canned goods, fashion styles, fabrics, shoes, horses, and yachts were using the tomboy label. It had a lingering and endearing feistiness associated with girls mimicking boys. Although still not entirely positive as a term applied to actual girls, within popular culture "tomboy" suggested something playful and wholesomely American. And yet prescriptive literature tying healthy tomboys to the future of white motherhood was all about white fear, even as the term was used commercially to indicate a joyful acceptance of new gender codes.

The extension of tomboy freedoms into young adult life reflected shifting conceptions of life stages among the middle class. After all, the entire point of the tomboy tale was to emphasize that all girls grow into femininity. But the New Woman suggested that such freedoms should not pass with maturity, since they were needed to make the most of changes in the larger culture. In this industrialized and corporatized America, with widening urban spaces and a new national movement advocating women's legal and political equality, middle-class Americans were having a hard time tracing out an appropriate yet advantageous path to womanhood. In the Progressive Era, the regulation of rights according to age, such as the right to vote, marry, consent to sex, or go to work, suggested a growing sense that chronological age should determine appropriate behavior.[17]

Much of the emphasis on new freedoms sprang from a shift in the training of white middle-class girls and women from the private to the public sphere. It began with adolescent girls entering the public world through expanses in education and print culture, and extended to slightly older girls through the growth of higher education for women and attendant fears about how education would impact female health. The line between high school girls and college women was indeed very fine. Athletics for young women became a proposed solution to the poor health brought on by too much education, further extending the pastimes of tomboys into young womanhood. The tomboy had already broken trail for white middle-class girls by claiming freedoms in the name of health and nationalism, and the New Woman extended that mentality.

The New Woman's presence confirmed that while tomboys might make healthier women, there was no guarantee that they would come to embrace the selflessness expected of their mothers. For some Americans this was a sign of progress, but for others it foreshadowed white race suicide—the increasingly widespread conviction that modern choices were leading to poor health among future mothers and a dangerous drop in white birthrates, combined with a new sense of the importance of genetics.[18] America was in the initial stage of what the historian Wendy Kline calls a "'country-wide crusade' to strengthen family and civilization by regulating fertility—more commonly known as eugenics."[19] Tomboys gained a positive gloss in print culture because they worked in favor of eugenics by focusing on the health of white girls as future mothers and reinforcing masculine aspirations as a sign of immaturity. Raising girls as tomboys became positive in response to the New Woman, who was equally seen as a threat to manhood and a sign of progress.

Reform and Regulation

The Progressive Era, the forty-year spread at the turn of the twentieth century (1880–1920), was marked by accelerated change, and bewildered and alarmed Anglo-Americans reacted by embracing greater organization of the public world and using science to reinvigorate conventions of race and gender. Looking back, we can see the contours of heightened industrialization and the attendant pattern changes of intensified urbanization, immigration, and technological advances that must have baffled native-born Americans at the time. A national population of 57 million in 1885 grew to 76 million by 1900, of whom 67 million were legally defined as white.[20]

Urban and government-minded Americans responded in various ways, but they can largely be summarized by the words "reform" and "regulation." Reformers tended to be activists who focused on humane (but typically ethnocentric) ways to reassert "civility," which they considered threatened largely by the influx of immigration from southern and eastern Europe.

Regulation became the tool of reform, as progressives strove to create order. But in the hands of a white middle class expressing deep fears about the shape of the future nation, regulation and reform also translated into the oppression and dehumanizing of nonwhite, foreign born, and/or impoverished peoples. Proclamations of white racial superiority saturated the culture and found expression not only in more dramatic forms such as lynching and minstrel shows, but also in the conscious portrayal of only white men as fully human in dominant mainstream depictions.[21] Similarly, Anglo-American women expressed a heightened racial consciousness about themselves as civilized women and fundamentally different—physically, morally, and culturally—from women of other races and ethnicities.

The flood of immigrant low-wage workers from southern and eastern Europe to American cities may have felt threatening to older populations of whites, but they also made it possible for many more native-born whites to climb the social ladder. The managing middle class expanded. The late nineteenth-century middle class hewed to the same markers as the earlier (smaller) middle class—fashion, respectability, and cultural knowledge—but within a vastly different context.[22]

Print culture often linked the New Woman with the suffrage movement, though the two were not intrinsically related. The New Woman moved into public spaces, forecasting a breakdown of the "separate spheres" that had governed gender roles since early in the century, but New Women were not necessarily interested in enfranchisement. In the public mind, however, the two separate developments of suffrage and the New Woman became "one grand movement of women toward equality with men."[23]

The strategies taken by the woman suffrage movement of this period also differed significantly from earlier efforts to obtain women's rights. Racism now became a tool used to unify white, native-born women, while women's rights had earlier been advocated by abolitionists. Adopted in 1868 and 1870, respectively, the Fourteenth and Fifteenth Amendments, which recognized black male citizenship, sundered the shared political status of women and black men. The relationship between "woman" and "the Negro" had to shift to a new context, with black women in the untenable space between them. Previously activists for rights had emphasized their common victimization, but now the woman suffrage movement stressed white women's racial and cultural superiority to both African American and immigrant men, and no longer addressed the added oppression faced by black women.[24] Although many white middle-class men saw woman suffrage as a threat to their own freedoms, white suffragists proved just as threatening to the freedom of people of color in their efforts to pass pro-female legislation. They sought out white racial solidarity in their attempts to change gender norms in their favor, and woman suffrage became in many ways not only a racially segregated movement but also an explicitly racist one that strengthened the zeitgeist of white, nativist oppression and encouraged American imperialism.[25]

Now girls were being cultivated within the public, not the domestic, space, and thus were becoming creatures of that space, regardless of their expected futures as home-centered mothers and wives. The True Woman of the earlier era, originally a source of empowerment for women in the hands of people like Catharine Beecher, was now a liability—at least for young women wishing to avail themselves of modern opportunities. Most girls growing up in this period, regardless of class or race, probably experienced a family life not so very different from that of their mothers. But now white girls who did not have to work for wages went to school and read magazines reflecting and shaping the contours of their gender, class, and age.

Higher Education for Women

The opening of liberal arts colleges for women and coeducational land-grant universities expanded the self-cultivation period promoted for middle-class adolescent girls into young womanhood. The tomboy who emerged in a girl culture created by expanded secondary education transformed into the New Woman born of the move toward female higher education, and particularly coeducation. From the 1830s through the 1980s, coeducation steadily became the norm.[26]

In the 1830s, most higher education open to women was through seminaries or normal schools; both trained teachers, and the seminaries also trained women to work in the missionary field. Young women of color and immigrant as well as native-born white daughters pursued higher education whenever available, recognizing its potential personal and communal ramifications.[27] By 1855, with the University of Iowa leading the way, state universities started admitting female students.[28] In 1862 the Morrill Act structured funding for land-grant colleges in every state, and many of those west of the Mississippi were founded as coeducational institutions, though those in the South were closed to African Americans. In 1867 African American women also gained access to higher education with the opening of Howard University in Washington, DC, which had no requirements for race or sex, as well as normal schools such as Bennett College in Greensboro, North Carolina, in 1873. In 1870 both Cornell and the University of Michigan began admitting female students. By 1897, 60 percent of undergraduate women were enrolled in a coeducational institution.[29]

For the most part, the coeducational experience was not one of equality. In most coed institutions female students were second-class citizens, held to a high standard of morality in an environment that also supported male rowdiness.[30] The *image* of women at coed institutions was, however, path-breaking. The concept of women competing with men in higher education essentially extended the experience of girlhood in secondary schools to young women of marital age.

But the Seven Sisters liberal arts colleges shaped the public's image of college girls far more than the coeducational schools at this point.[31] While women in coed schools were constrained by rules and custom as second-class students, women at the Seven Sisters held the primary social position in their schools. Beginning in 1865 with Vassar, women could attend a college designed to have the same rigor as all-male liberal arts colleges, but still protective of women as creatures of the private world. Vassar was a closed community, patterned after Mount Holyoke Seminary (founded in 1837). Faculty and students conducted all parts of their lives within a single building. Protecting the virtue of young women motivated the system, but it also had the unintended consequence of creating insular communities that outsiders viewed with suspicion.

Tellingly, rather than cut back on the college girl's new freedoms, educators went in the opposite direction: creating college living situations for women that more closely resembled those of men. When planning began for Smith College (which opened in 1875), a group of alumni and current and former faculty of nearby Amherst College was charged with designing the campus. Wanting to nullify what they saw as the negative effects of a cloistered female community, they planned separate buildings and cottages for students. Regulation and oversight also loosened, allowing Smith women a closer approximation to male college life. Wellesley soon followed Smith's lead. Under the leadership of M. Carey Thomas, Bryn Mawr became the first women's college to follow a male liberal arts curriculum.[32] All of these changes contributed to the image of the college girl as living much like young college men; they were New Women in training.

Magazines and newspapers participated in creating the college girl/New Woman connection with an almost voyeuristic obsession with Vassar and Wellesley girls. Such images were indeed revolutionary: young women of the same age, with little supervision (none of it familial), and engaged in activities hitherto allowed only to young men.[33] They also suggested an elite existence now in the grasp of young middle-class women. An informal reading of popular fiction suggests that college girls also disproportionately populated domestic schoolgirl fiction, encouraging girls to imagine college as part of their future. By 1890, as historian Jean Matthews notes, "even the conservative *Ladies' Home Journal* offered a four-year scholarship to Vassar, Wellesley, or Smith to the girl who could sell the most subscriptions to the magazine."[34]

Thus, theoretically at least, by the 1880s ambitious girls could pursue higher education just like their male peers. In practice, of course, few women attended college, but the ones who did had a tremendous impact on changing gender norms. In 1870, when less than 1 percent of Americans attended college, 21 percent of the college population was female, a figure that jumped to 36 percent in 1890. By 1900 America boasted nearly 85,000 females currently enrolled as undergraduates.[35]

Fears about female college graduates eschewing marriage and motherhood, and thus white citizens losing their majority status, were borne out by statistics. Only 40–60 percent of female college graduates remained single, at a time when 90 percent of all women married—both by custom and because, with high-earning jobs available only for men, most unmarried women suffered lives of abject poverty.[36] On top of that trend, physicians still firmly believed that the blood used in the brain for study took energy from the reproductive organs. So even if college-educated women did marry, fears abounded that they would not be able to reproduce.[37]

The normalizing of secondary and higher education for young women, combined with fears about white racial deterioration, sparked a debate among scientists and educators about how best to educate girls while preserving their health. Since the late eighteenth century, advocates had argued that educated women raised better citizens. But would college-educated women be able to bear those citizens? Educators took the question seriously and strove to regulate the lives of their female students, encouraging exercise and limiting study hours. Consequently, by the 1890s girls were playing a host of sports beyond the pale of earlier depictions of tomboy antics. They were not merely climbing trees and walking along fences, they were sweating and running and vigorously competing in games like basketball, tennis, and baseball. When the bicycle entered the scene, young women took off; they were now independently mobile, and able to explore the public world without chaperones. As sports like basketball and bicycling became "crazes," clothes for young women also changed to accommodate their new physical freedoms. It all seemed to unfurl swiftly, a brilliant ribbon of opportunity for girls with the means to grab hold.

Female Maturity and Evolution

Age may have been the most obvious difference between the tomboy and the New Woman, and that age difference was critical because it signified the end of innocence and the onset of sexuality. Both tomboys and New Women were unmarried, self-focused, idealistic, ambitious, and fun. But the budding sexuality of the New Woman was palpable in popular images. Indeed, claiming sexuality was central to both popular images of the New Woman and ideologies fostered by particular female public figures, such as Gilman, and also in new literary fiction, such as *The Awakening* (1899) by Kate Chopin, *The House of Mirth* (1905) by Edith Wharton, and *Sister Carrie* (1900) by Theodore Dreiser. By contrast, the adolescent tomboy was sexually inert because of youthful innocence, but the fact that she was straddling puberty made her a ticking bomb.

At the turn of the century, psychologists, educators, and physicians would focus on adolescence because of concerns over young white manhood, but in the 1880s the focus was on girls, and the issue was not adolescence but puberty. These men of science asserted that puberty was the most crucial event in a woman's physiological life—which meant it happened in girlhood when she was (thankfully!) still under the control of parents. A few vocal physicians depicted puberty not as a natural transition from childhood to full reproductive capacity, but as a time of heightened fragility. They contended that a girl's behavior during puberty, and particularly during her monthly menses, would have lasting repercussions on her future physical and psychological health. And, extrapolating from the girl's primary identity as a mother-in-the-making, they tied her healthy experience of puberty to the future of civilization and continued white evolution.[38]

Concerns about female puberty contributed to the need to find a way to educate daughters of the middle and upper-middle classes without weakening the race. Physicians and evolutionary scientists posited that treating girls like boys during such a volatile, transitional stage of life not only threatened fecundity and mental health but could also lead to the passing on of mental and physical problems to subsequent generations. Their theories responded to popular anecdotes about the increasing sickliness of American girls—ignoring the fact that a wan appearance and delicate health had recently been fashionable, and that Europeans expressed similar concerns over the health of their own girls.[39] Instead, they harnessed such fears to recent expansions in higher education and concerns that extensive study impeded a girl's reproductive development. Educators posited exercise as the solution, and college girls responded with unbridled enthusiasm. In the process they subverted the social understanding of education and athletics as fundamentally masculine.[40]

In 1873 Edward Clarke, a professor of medicine at Harvard University, published *Sex in Education,* the most influential text positing the dangers of educating girls in the same manner as boys. The book went through seventeen printings over the next thirteen years and sparked a national debate over coeducation and the best way to structure higher education for women.[41] M. Carey Thomas later recalled of her time as dean of Bryn Mawr College, "We were haunted in those days by the clanging chains of that gloomy specter, Dr. Edward Clarke's *Sex in Education.*" At the University of Michigan, where women had been attending for three years, two hundred copies sold in a single day.[42]

Using anecdotes to make his point, Clarke recounts stories of accomplished young female graduates with "undeveloped ovaries" and current students plagued with "dysmenorrhea, chronic and acute ovaritis, prolapses uteri, hysteria, neuralgia, and the like."[43] As the historian Crista DeLuzio notes, Clarke was in agreement with evolutionary theorists in believing that boys experience puberty as "steady, protracted, harmonious growth," but that girls' bodies grow too fast, too soon, and are weakened by excessive demands.[44] Although Clarke gives a nod to the potential harm of effeminacy for boys, he depicts the fate of studious girls as catastrophic, running the gamut from infertility to insanity. "In the education of our girls," he states, "the attempt to hide or overcome nature by training them as boys has almost extinguished them as girls." Revealing his ignorance of the strenuous work and drudgery of preindustrial housekeeping, he harkens back to a past when girls worked peacefully alongside their mothers until marriage. Stating that boys can handle six hours of study a day while the average girl cannot tolerate more than four, he argues that girls must be allowed fewer hours of study and monthly breaks to accommodate menses.[45] His book promotes the belief that how girls experience puberty shapes their future mental and physical health and that of their offspring.

Clarke's text was fundamentally a story of white middle-class female development. As DeLuzio points out, it was only the "western, white middle-class girl who warranted such assiduous protection." Many of those focusing on puberty as critical for white girls were quick to state that because of both "inferior heredity and less complex social environment, . . . girls of the 'Orient,' of the European peasantry, and of the American working class possessed desirable physical strength but not the refined physical, mental, and emotional natures that portended both great risk and significant possibility for their civilized counterparts."[46] Middle-class white girls were at risk from puberty because they were so highly evolved.

Clarke built his work onto the theories of Herbert Spencer, a leader in the concept of Social Darwinism who vigorously and prolifically insisted that puberty arrested the evolutionary development of girls.[47] Drawing heavily on Darwin's 1871 *Descent of Man,* Spencer argued that higher civilization produces distinctly different sexes of oppositional characteristics: a fragile female sex and a robust male sex. According to Spencer, problems arose for women only when social ambitions overtaxed their inherently weak bodies.[48]

Of course, not everyone read girls' earlier physical development as a sign of weakness. The Congregationalist minister Antoinette Brown Blackwell, for example, countered concerns over girls' rapid growth by suggesting that since girls were more advanced than boys in mental processes as well as physical maturity, they were up to the task of deciding what they could safely handle. She also pointed out the blatant class prejudice embedded in such theories by noting that that many girls worked very hard in fields and factories, without raising public concern: "Why single out the poor little school-girl-class, between thirteen and twenty, as the one group above all others from which to draw the most impressive moral? There are tens of thousands, both of American and foreign-born maidens, also in their teens, who have left school, who are toiling in country homes and in city work-shops, having no day of rest except Sunday, and not always that. Are they stronger in physique than the others—the more favored class?"[49] But voices of reason did not captivate the larger public as much as the prophecies of doom.

Menstruation itself came to attention for several reasons, some of them the result of dramatic changes in physiological realities. Better nutrition and lower rates of infectious disease led to an earlier onset of menses in late nineteenth-century middle-class girls. Girls reached menarche at an average of age seventeen in 1780, but by age fourteen in 1900.[50] White women went from having an average of seven live births (in an era with a high incidence of miscarriage and stillbirth) to just over three.[51] On top of these biological shifts, education and economic changes also began extending the period when girls were postpubescent but not yet ready for motherhood. The combination of these factors meant that monthly periods became a more common life experience just as the physical body itself was coming under increased scientific scrutiny.

Medical theorists at the time considered menstrual irregularity a sure sign of future peril.[52] In 1875 one physician, A. F. A King, went so far as to suggest that menstrual periods were themselves new. He argued that a "women's natural state was pregnancy" and that what he called "cultural interference," such as higher education, later marriage, and family planning, were contributing to irregular menses.[53] His assertion that menstruation was both new and pathological set off a debate on whether periods were a sign of disease or natural. Medical advocates strenuously argued that if a girl did not begin her reproductive life correctly—with regularly spaced periods and a consistent flow of menstrual fluid—she was doomed to a life of disability and infertility. White girls' bodies and even the quality, quantity, and regularity of their menses became attached to the health of white civilization.[54]

The racial underpinnings of the debate became more blatant as experts began to cite anthropological studies on menarche in girls of "other" regions and climates, ignoring the fact that many "American girls" were not of western European ancestry. Race, climate, latitude, social conditions, and even hair color were brought to bear on the timing and characteristics (heavy, light, painful, etc.) of menarche. Different theories arose about which girls matured earlier and why, but the white medical world largely settled on the notion that white girls reach menarche later because of their higher place on the evolutionary ladder. Thus the later onset of menstruation also came to be viewed as a sign of greater civilization, and experts fretted quite a bit about girls leaving the protected innocence of childhood too soon.[55] Indeed, as the historian Joan Jacobs Brumberg writes, "most Americans came to believe that a hallmark of Christian civilization was its ability to nurture and protect girlhood innocence: in effect, to guarantee a safe time between menarche and marriage, when girls would be sexually inactive."[56]

In their effort to express concern about these future mothers, scientists implicitly supported the notion that white middle- and upper-class females are by nature fragile. Again, Antoinette Brown Blackwell pushed against that narrative by asserting that physical vigor must be demanded of girls if they are to strengthen: "She is not porcelain to be easily broken, nor are the adjustments of her nature so weakly put together that they can be readily disturbed, or so fearfully balanced that the slightest overwork in one direction must mean weakness or disease in some other as penalty."[57] But the princess-and-the-pea delicacy attributed to the gently bred girl was equally how white women could justify the chivalry demanded by Victorian etiquette. And many women did not fight back against such theories, because asking for freedoms in one area meant risking privileges in others, and not all women favored the exchange.

Contributing to the push for tomboy girlhoods, in the late nineteenth century many cultural commentators accepted as fact that American girls were the weakest in the civilized world. In *Sex in Education,* Clarke compared the "sturdy German Fraulein" and "robust English damsel" with the "fragile American miss" and declared that if the situation was not soon reversed, American men would have to cross the Atlantic to find healthy wives.[58] An 1888 *Harper's Bazaar* article, for example, compares the health of women of different nations hiking the Alps and argues that the weakness of American girls illustrates the danger they posed to their country. And the writer took a more controversial turn, declaring that sports were the solution and that it is necessary "for parents to defy public opinion in the boyish freedom of exercise they demand for their growing daughters."[59] S. Weir Mitchell, the physician later famously vilified by Gilman in *The Yellow Wallpaper* (1892), declared that the only solution was to raise girls more like boys up to puberty: "Train your girls physically, and, up to the age of adolescence, as you train your boys. . . . To run, to climb, to swim, to ride, to play violent games, ought to be as natural to the girl as to the boy."[60] Paradoxically, despite all of this talk of female ill health and education, images of college girls in the bloom of health became commonplace across print culture.[61]

Again, notable women pushed back against the narrative of female fragility. Mary Putnam Jacobi, physician and ardent suffragist, used scientific data to demonstrate that the poor health of American women was overstated.[62] In 1874 she contributed to a compendium of medical studies, *The Education of American Girls,* edited by Dr. Anna C. Brackett, challenging Clarke's anecdotal theories. Brackett mocks Clarke's suggestion that girls be sent home to grow up at their mothers' sides, engrossed in domestic tasks, to "spend their hours and try their eyes over back-stitching" when "a hundred cheap machines can do it not only in less time but far better."[63] In her essay in the volume, Jacobi, tongue in cheek, notes: "A remarkable change has taken place in the tone of habitual remark on the capacities and incapacities of women. Formerly, they were denied the privileges of an intellectual education, on the ground that their natures were too exclusively animal to require it. To-day, the same education is still withheld, but on the new plea that their animal nature is too imperfectly developed to enable them to avail themselves of it." After summarizing Clarke's argument in five sentences and then rebutting it point by point, Jacobi declares that American schoolgirls are weak because they "arrive at the period of adolescence already enervated by the senseless training of their childhood, on which distinctions of sex have been obtruded long before they are established by nature."[64]

But although Jacobi argued that boys and girls should be raised alike until puberty, she agreed with Clarke's call for gender-segregated education up to age eighteen—not because of an inherent weakness in girls but because she agreed with the need to prolong innocence in the service of white evolution. Her proposed solutions—more exercise, a longer adolescence, and an extended education for girls—are limned with the same celebration of white civilization found in arguments by Clarke and Spencer. She asserts, "Unless the education of girls be continued beyond the conventional retiring-point of eighteen, and unless they be permitted access to the State Universities, they cannot participate in the highest intellectual education of the race."[65]

Tomboys became a way to assure white Americans that independent-minded girls would make fine women. In 1886 a Kansas City newspaper retitled the 1858 article "Our Daughters—Tom-boys" (quoted at the beginning of chapter 1) as "The Grown-Up Tomboy," focusing on the reassurance that "the glancing eye, the glowing cheek, the fresh, balmy breath, the lithe graceful play of the limbs tell a tale of healthy and vigorous physical development which is nature's best beauty." The tomboy's uncouth behavior will smooth out with maturity, and both soul and mind "will be developed also in due time, and we shall have before us a woman in the highest sense of the term. When the tomboy has sprung up to a healthful and vigorous womanhood she will be ready to take hold of the duties of life to become a worker in the great system of humanity."[66] The repetition of the "Our Daughters—Tom-boys" piece, alongside a greater outpouring of conventional tomboy tales, nurtured the growing acceptance that female individualism and maternal devotion could be corroborative, rather than competing.

Athletics: Basketball

Both print and entertainment culture tended to focus on the boyish play of tomboys and not their misfit identity—in part because the culture was in the midst of celebrating tomboys as normal and healthy. By the 1880s, the clearest indication of a tomboy spirits was a girl's love of boys' pastimes, and participation in athletics became the hallmark of the young New Woman as well. Athletics were taking American society by storm, and all of the celebration of its health- and character-building qualities promised advantages to white girlhood as well as boyhood. But this promotion of the athletic girl came at the same time that athletics were becoming the principal means for boys and men to perform their masculinity. The question for athletic promoters was how to emphasize the positive benefits and minimize the negative in a situation in which there was such hypersensitivity to gender definition and performance. The tomboy held the place in line for her older counterpart, but she also tied a love of sports to immaturity—the free state of girlhood before the work of womanhood.

Educators in women's colleges and girls' schools became tireless diplomats in promoting athletics as an essential part of modern education in an effort to calm fears about the danger of education to female reproduction. The drawback to athletics, many feared, was that competition would turn girls into "mannish" women. In 1885 the Association for the Advancement of Physical Education was founded to further women's participation for health reasons. They particularly promoted nature-related sports, such as mountain climbing and hiking, alongside more established sports, such as croquet or archery. Not surprisingly, sports already enjoyed by elite women, such as horseback riding and golf, slipped into public culture with barely a ripple; no one was disputing the intrinsic femininity of elite girls and women. Individual recreation, such as bowling, hiking, archery, skating, and fencing, also received little question. Sports requiring "awkward positions, physical contact, or great vigor," however, were immediately deemed unfit for girls.[67] In other words, team sports.

The advent of new sports, as yet untainted by rigid gender connotation, made girls' participation in team sports possible.[68] For example, baseball, still a relatively new sport in the 1860s, was all the rage for both boys and girls, according to the journalist Jeannette Gilder, remembering her girlhood in Bridgeton, New Jersey, where two all-girls baseball clubs met regularly. Parents forced the girls to disband their clubs only after a reporter from a neighboring town—without having actually *witnessed* the games—used his imagination to depict girl players as rude and violent.[69] Yet despite such stories, girls continued to play baseball. In 1866 Vassar College already had two baseball clubs, and by 1877 had seven teams competing in intramurals.[70]

The need to shore up modesty in sports meant that women in the early years played in clothes designed for a more sedentary life—and thus they were soon mimicking the heedless tomboys of domestic fiction with their mussed and dirtied clothing. Within the privacy of gymnasiums girls wore bloomers, but they were deemed too immodest for outdoor sports, so girls played baseball wearing "train dresses" with long skirts and full corsets.[71] In 1896 the *Cleveland Plain Dealer* noted that when the women of Flora Stone Mather College played ball, "nearly all of the players went in bareheaded, heeding not freckles and sunburn. All lamented that they could not wear their 'gym suits' consisting of bloomers and blouses. In these they felt they could do much better playing. But the nearness to the public street and sidewalks made such attire well nigh impossible for modest girls."[72] But early baseball players made the most of it by using their skirts to catch an inside hit or protect their legs when sliding into bases.[73] Regardless of the handicap presented by corsets and cumbersome skirts, the women played hard.

The sport that became the first true athletic craze among female Americans, however, was not baseball but basketball. According to newspaper reports, in the last decade of the nineteenth century girls in high school, women in recreation leagues, and even high-society women took up the sport. But it was basketball games at Smith, Wellesley, and Vassar that initiated and dominated the image of female basketball players. Senda Berenson, the new director of physical culture at Smith College, read James Naismith's 1891 article introducing his new game of "Basket Ball" in the monthly YMCA newsletter.[74] Seeing that this was an inexpensive game that could be played indoors in a limited space, she immediately reconfigured

FIGURE 4: Vassar baseball team, 1876. Vassar College Archives & Special Collections Library.

the rules and court to make the game more appropriate (that is, less vigorous) for her students. By January 1892 Smith students were playing women's basketball. Within ten months, Berenson's version had become so popular that the University of California at Berkeley and Miss Head's School in nearby Oakland had the first inter-institutional game. And even though physical education was still a novelty in the South, by 1893 Sophie Newcomb College in New Orleans, under the leadership of Clara Baer, also had an active basketball league.[75] In 1896 Stanford University and the University of California at Berkeley staged the first intercollegiate women's game—a competition that lead one reporter to remark with admiration that basketball "wasn't invented for girls, and there isn't anything effeminate about it."[76]

Early articles were, for the most part, complimentary to girl athletes and promoted basketball as forward-looking and healthy. Reporters took pains to reinforce the decorum of female athletes: "In a Harvard–Yale football contest one does not hear opponents saying at an exciting crisis: 'Pardon me, but I think that's our ball,' or 'Excuse me, did I hurt you?'"[77] Indeed, Berenson and Baer alike made strenuous efforts to keep basketball within the bounds of propriety, creating new rules for the female version to reduce physical contact.[78] And yet the increasing popularity of basketball among women rendered the initially polite behavior unsustainable in such a vibrant sport, soon spurring one observer to point out that, in fact, "basketball is to the women's college what football is to the men's."[79] And it did not take long for women's basketball to lose its feminine reputation once it moved beyond the control of elite women's colleges.

Soon, according to one reporter, basketball spread "like an epidemic" to public schools. Within three years, the comments of a high-school athlete in Trenton, New Jersey, unwittingly refuted the earlier assertions of decorum: "We don't stop and say, 'excuse me, dear,' when we are after the ball. We just pile into the one that has it and grab it, and if she happens to fall down and get walked on we don't stop to say 'Darling, are you hurt?'" She claimed her fellow athletes rejected Berenson's rules against scrimmaging and full-court play because they made the game "too tame." In open rebellion against the efforts to feminize girls' sports, the athlete boasted, "I am the heaviest man on our team—you know we call ourselves men." Then to attract attention, of course, the reporter used that claim in a subhead in the article: "She Is the Heaviest Man."[80]

And that pattern fairly accurately summarizes the evolution of coverage of women's basketball in the national press. When elite college women began playing basketball as part of their curriculum, the sport was largely praised as healthy and appropriate for young women. When private girls' schools and society women took up the sport, the press continued to depict it as a suitably decorous sport. As one reporter remarked, basketball "gives all the exercise that football does but the very rough plays and dangers are eliminated. . . . The fact that a society girl can play the game in the afternoon and dance at a cotillion until well into the next morning without harm to her physical well-being is a goodly tribute to basketball."[81] But when recreation leagues and high school teams formed, reporting began to include hyperbolic depictions of female competition.

Comparisons to men's football were soon used to condemn women's basketball. In 1896, for example, a game pitting a New Haven club team (with a Yale coach) and a Cambridge club team (with a Harvard coach) resulted in disparaging comparisons to the famous college game: "The big company which had gathered to witness the sport was simply paralyzed to see the spirit which was suddenly developed by the gentle players. At the end of the first half of the game it began to dawn upon the young women that their conduct was better suited to a game of football."[82]

And although most articles of the period praise the beauty of the athletic girl, there were also "scare pieces," such as one suggesting that sports were deforming women's feet. The manager of a Chicago shoe store explained: "The college women, who jump hurdles, run races, do pole-vaulting, play basket-ball, and tennis, and exercise an hour or two a day on the field . . . , all wear shoes with no heels or very low ones. Their feet spread out and develop." He claimed to be able "to name a dozen women whose feet have become two inches broader and longer" because of sports—particularly golf and basketball.[83]

But Berenson had configured the rules of women's basketball specifically to counteract criticism and avoid rough play, as well as to emphasize team cooperation, and so basketball persisted.[84] As athletics became more popular for girls and women, it became normative for girls to play boys' games, but not play like boys. In public discourse, competition in sports belonged to boys, while girls played sports to strengthen cooperation.

The association of modern girlhood and sports became so commonplace that in her popular 1893 book *The American Girl at College*, Lida Rose McCabe defines the "modern girl" as one who dresses in "Turkish trousers, crosses swords with a fencing master, vaults bars, climbs ropes, plays ball, rows and swims."[85] Now the odd girl out was not the one playing the games, but the one sitting them out. A few years later the popular journalist Kate Masterson noted that a properly raised girl "can row, run, and jump and play basketball as well as quote Latin and Greek and is doubly armed for the fray. She is a splendid specimen of up-to-date-womanhood. If circumstances force her into public life, she is physically strong for the contest. If she enters domestic life she becomes the mother of children representing the highest type of civilization."[86] She gets a choice. In other words, she grows into the New Woman.

The Bumpy Road to Acceptance

Even as both tomboys and New Women were being celebrated within popular culture, they were equally a source of worry. One of the most cogent symbols of the long road to acceptance of the grown-up tomboy, the New Woman, can be found in depictions of the 1890s "bicycle craze" that overtook America, England, and Europe. The fad was enjoyed by men as well, but the freedom gained by women and girls was transformative. And the public was both enamored with the image of healthy young women peddling under their own power and fearful of how such independence would work across class lines.

Popular culture paired New Women and bicycles. The typical New Woman heroine of commercial representation was not only young, pretty, and single, but "almost invariably a keen bicyclist." Just as whistling and climbing signaled tomboy identity in popular fiction, bicycles marked new womanhood; as one literary historian notes, "If a character makes her first appearance on a bicycle, it is almost inevitable that she will turn out to be single and well-educated, with strong views on women's rights."[87] In conflating the two, the press also ostensibly transformed a recreational fad into a political statement.

In 1885 the "safety bicycle"—the modern bicycle with two identically sized wheels—replaced the older version, making it possible for women to cycle in skirts. It immediately proved so popular that within that year there was a women's six-day race, won by a woman named Frankie Nelson.[88] As one woman put it in 1896: "Nothing short of being in love can so utterly change and electrify a woman as the bicycle craze. In many cases it opens up a new existence and introduces a life of action and enjoyment which hitherto has not seemed possible."[89] An aging Susan B. Anthony declared that the bicycle did "more to emancipate women than anything else in the world" because bicycling gave women "a feeling of freedom and self-reliance." The bicycle was called the "freedom" machine.[90] Almost immediately, it became the symbol of modern young womanhood.

The bicycle craze particularly raged in towns and small cities, bringing modernity to places that usually looked to larger cities for change. One

FIGURE 5: "The 'New Woman' and Her Bicycle," by Frederick Opper (1895), aptly represents the variety of fears raised by the figure of a young woman moving independently, dressed in clothing meant to allow her to bike swiftly and safely, but also suggesting a new world of shocking new freedoms. Courtesy Library of Congress, Prints and Photographs Division.

paper claimed that in smaller cities such as New Haven and Hartford in Connecticut and Springfield in Massachusetts, "women ride about the streets almost as much as men." That is understandable, the reporter sniffs, since "these girls also skate, play base ball, tennis, and a dozen other manly games." Their love of bicycles, the writer suggests, goes along with the fact that they are "more careless of appearance than the city bred woman, who dreads ridicule as the burned child does the fire."[91] But soon Parisian and London fashion houses took up the cause of designing sportswear, and there was all the more reason for women to ride bicycles.[92]

The bicycle also finally wrought the change that health reformers (who also tended to be women's rights advocates) had been seeking for decades: less constrictive dress became fashionable. Bicycles finally made a contemporary version of bloomers fashionable in London and the United States (those daring Parisian girls, by contrast, wore "tight breeches, long stockings, and short jackets").[93] In the United States, a "compromise garment," with a series of drawstrings that could transform skirts into bloomers, became particularly popular.[94] The British novelist John Galsworthy remarked that the bicycle had created "more movement in manners and morals than anything since Charles the Second. Under its influence, wholly or in part, have wilted chaperons [*sic*], long and narrow skirts, tight corsets." Also "under its influence," he noted, "have bloomed weekends, strong nerves, strong legs, strong language, knickers, knowledge of make and shape, knowledge of woods and pastures, equality of sex, good digestion and professional occupation—in four words, the emancipation of women."[95] Carolyn Kitch notes that in 1897 every issue of *Ladies' Home Journal* "contained ads for bicycles and all sorts of related products, including corsets that produced a 'bicycle waist' as 'graceful as the New Woman.'"[96]

Soon working girls took to "the wheel" as often as the fashionable girls of the leisure class, and when the bicycle crossed class lines, depictions in print culture became less celebratory. In 1897 the *Cleveland Plain Dealer* quoted one man's exasperation with his domestic servant: "She was as good a girl as ever lived till the bicycle came into such general use, and then she seemed to lose her head. She couldn't become interested in anything but wheels and riding and things of that kind." The reporter noted that employers were willing to pay more for servants who did not "wheel": "The women who need servants don't want bicycle servants." Bicycling servants were far more interested in their own lives and pleasures than in their duties.[97]

Reporters did not label these adventurous girls "tomboys" per se, but they did criticize girl cyclists in terms that echoed descriptions of tomboys. For example, in an 1893 article reprinted extensively around the nation, the *Boston Herald,* under the headline "*Fin de Siecle* Young Lady and the Bicycle," quoted a stablemaster bemoaning the damage the craze had wrought on his business. He was particularly shocked by the gender transgressions of female cyclists: "These girls wear men's caps and shirts, and ride just as boldly as the men themselves. They laugh and chat as they roll along, and they look perfectly at home on the things." The reporter noted that "the young female sex are enjoying the hope of further freedom from the shackles of social traditions by the successful experiment of this young [fin-de-siècle] lady with the laws of gravitation."[98]

Indeed, bicycles were also routinely blamed for fulminating delusions of masculinity in girls. One sensational story, "Gay Girls in Bloomers," tells of two sisters who ran away from home to take jobs as male waiters in a resort town. When their father managed to find and expose them, he declared: "I lay this on the bicycle craze. . . . Both girls insisted on having bicycles, and then got to bloomers. Finally they have adopted male attire entirely. A month or six weeks ago they left home, intending to visit relatives. . . . Thank God they are good girls yet."[99]

One of the most vocal proponents of the bicycle was Frances Willard, longtime president of the Woman's Christian Temperance Union, one of the largest and most successful social reform organizations in the nation. Willard, who still went by the childhood name "Frank" among her family members, took up bicycling at fifty-three because it returned a sense of self she had lost with maturity. In the bicycle Willard saw the means to recapture unfettered tomboy days: "From the day when, at sixteen years of age, I was enwrapped in the long skirts that impeded every footstep, I have detested walking and felt with a noble disdain that the conventions of life had cut me off from what in the freedom of my prairie home had been one of life's sweetest joys." She declares that she took up cycling "from pure natural love of adventure—a love long hampered and impeded, like a brook that runs underground, but in this enterprise bubbling up again with somewhat of its pristine freshness and taking its merry course as of old."[100]

And then there were the more colorful women of competitive cycling, who suggested a swaggering heroism normally associated with men. Mrs. A. M. C. Allen set a national record for miles pedaled in one year. When attacked by a dog during one ride, she drew out her revolver and shot it, before pedaling another sixteen miles to seek medical treatment.[101] Allen advocated that "women who ride a wheel should go armed" and, in fact, carried her firearm in the "right hip pocket of her bloomers." She told reporters, "I consider that the day has gone by when women should turn to man as her natural protector and never venture abroad except under the sheltering care of his arm. The world is hers, and she is capable of defending herself." She went on to tell of a rough character who attempted to rob her: "As quick as flash my revolver was out, and its shining barrel pointed full at his astonished face."[102] Allen was not simply setting records on her bicycle, she was asserting the emancipation of women through the modern technologies of a wheel and revolver.

Although there was some grousing in the popular press about lack of decorum among female cyclists, arguments against bicycles for health or moral reasons went nowhere. The Women's Rescue League, an organization dedicated to protecting the moral and physical health of working girls, launched a crusade against bicycling in 1896, sparking national ridicule.[103] The group deplored the "evil associations and opportunities offered by cycling sports" and claimed that "seventy-five percent of the cyclists will be an army of invalids within the next ten years." One Michigan newspaper called them "rabid" and countered that both common sense and medicine affirmed the health benefits of cycling.[104]

Society's attitudes toward active girls had changed markedly. By the 1890s there were too many bicycle-riding, sports-playing girls for them to be classified as tomboys—a term that had consistently signified a girl whose boyish behaviors set her apart from other girls. But the normalizing of daring physical activities for girls and young women did not result in the term "tomboy" dropping from practice; its use simply changed. Although still sometimes used to scold girls or their parents, it was more often employed to suggest a significant break with the past. Writers began asserting that since progressive minds now embraced female health, autonomy, and confidence, "tomboy" was an outdated term. In fact, "tomboy" grew in popularity over the next century as women gained rights. The tomboy served as the origin of the New Woman and an increasingly common version of the modern girl.

But if the tomboy was the origin of the New Woman, it was because educators and writers were looking for an origin. In this way, the New Woman elevated the status of the tomboy by connecting her to progress. Tomboy tales appeared in newspapers more than ever, and those stories did not change; they remained the same story of self-taming to participate in heterosexual relationships. It was the reception of the tomboy that changed. With the coming of the New Woman, she gained a purpose beyond maintaining freedoms in a modern girlhood that was increasingly separated from boyhood; she became about a new path to a more progressive womanhood.

Positing the tomboy as the New Woman as girl soothed mainstream fears, for the cultural figure of the tomboy was a good, white, middle-class woman in the making. She looked like a rebel, but when push came to shove she shored up convention. Likewise, few advocates of the New Woman truly wished throw out domestic ideology altogether—they merely wanted to render it less confining. New Women asserted their rights to having a career, a public voice, and visible power—in other words, the rights of their male counterparts; they did so as "women," but in mainstream culture that meant white, native-born, and middle-class.[105]

And this New Woman—the tomboy who did not outgrow her love of sports—was far more desirable than her feminine cohorts. Tying nationalism and capitalism to young women's demeanor in 1888, a London article reprinted in the *Kansas City Times* suggested that American girls were "cutting" English girls out of the "matrimonial market" because the "American girl is not so 'missy' as her English sister" and "she is brought up to run down her own game."[106] Likewise, an 1891 article titled "The American Tomboy: She Often Becomes a Woman Men Admire and Worship" states, "When sensible men meet a grown-up tomboy and take involuntary note of her royal mien, her elastic tread, her lithe movements, her relish of the fresh air and of beefsteak, they hasten to lay at her feet their loyal admiration." The grown-up tomboy brings out the best in men, as her admirers "quickly understand that she is no moaning drone, whose happiness consists in misery, but one of themselves, so to say, ready to front the responsibilities of life, with joy that she has found the world a theater of action. Such a woman is a man's exemplar and prod."[107] According to such accounts, overt femininity weakens society as a whole. Girls and women with a trace of the boy in their makeup build a better foundation for the nation.

California went so far as to commission a white marble statue of a tomboy to represent its women at the upcoming 1893 World's Columbian Exposition in Chicago. Countering arguments that "the California girl is not pretty" because of her sun- and wind-ravaged complexion, California boosters retorted that she is better than pretty.[108] She is a tomboy, self-reliant and unpretentious—the ideal American in female form. The *San Francisco Chronicle* asserted that the tomboy was the ideal representative for their state's forward-thinking women, as she is "neither a drudge nor an aesthetic simpleton. She does not care to spend the whole of her time cleaning plates and dishes or darning stockings, but neither is she too proud to do these thing." Rather, she is "brave, honest, single-minded, and takes no stock in the saying that is a disgrace for a girl to work for a living."[109]

But these observations in the white press that New Women were tomboys grown up did not hold true for nonwhite or wage-earning women. The *Chicago Defender*, the most widely read national newspaper of the

African American middle and aspiring classes, immediately took up the term "New Women" without carrying a single reference to tomboys. Although the New Woman was a direct descendent of the True Woman for middle-class whites, in many ways she represented an opening of respectable womanhood for minority and working-class women. Respectability was of central concern to middle-class African American women, as was demonstrated by the ideologies and rhetoric employed within the black women's club movement at end of the century.[110] But white concerns about females crossing into privileged male worlds of mobility—for that is what education and athletics were all about, both materially and metaphorically—did not challenge respectability across lines of race and class, because so many of these women already lived public lives. The New Woman was a challenge to patriarchy for the white middle class; for most other women she presented a respectable way to claim what they were already doing out of necessity. Tomboys continued to belong to the white middle-class world alone, even as the New Woman came to belong to women across race and class lines in large and small cities.

As the Age of the New Woman became a celebrated fact, a new tomboy narrative emerged in the mainstream press: the tomboy was used to highlight the present as progressive. Tomboys used to be seen as ungovernable aberrations, but now modern-minded Americans recognize that rowdy girls are simply normal and healthy. Indeed, the comparison of how tomboys were seen in the past (negative) and how they are seen currently (normal) became a consistent depiction of the past and present. For example, a columnist in 1895 noted, "It was not so many years ago that a woman's sole ambition seemed to evince itself in a desire to be thought delicate," so she engaged in harmful practices to "reduce her symptoms of good health." "Tomboy," the reporter observes, was what a girl was called if she refused to follow such practices, noting that her grandmother "was so fond of boyish pursuits, hunting, fishing, riding to hounds and the like that she got the name of 'tomboy,'" and she sensibly took pride in the term, despite the "despair of her mother" and being called "masculine' and 'advanced.'"[111] In the past women blindly followed social mores, but now they have the intelligence to embrace health in themselves and their daughters. Girls called tomboys in the past were ahead of their times.

But although writers increasingly asserted that changes wrought by the New Woman and modern thinking made the tomboy outdated, they were overlooking a competing phenomenon exacerbated by the rise of the New Woman: the threat such changes appeared to pose to masculinity and men's social roles. Tomboys were not only young New Women, they were also the female version of boys, at a time when many physicians, youth organizers, and cultural critics were asserting the importance of distinctly male boyhood in growing good American men. If tomboy girls were increasingly embraced vis-à-vis adult women, they remained problematic in the raising of little men.

5

Boyhood for Girls

"There are a many varieties of boys," noted an 1874 article in New York's *Commercial Advertiser*, "among which are found the good boy, the bad boy, the big boy, the little boy, the wild boy, the fat boy, the tom boy, the fast boy and the Bowery boy." After waxing fondly on these various kinds of boys, the writer reaches the "tom boy" and states: "The Tom boy is a snare and a delusion. He is not a boy at all. He is a girl, and we are not discussing girls."[1] Boy identity was not open to girls—even the ones who behaved like boys. But within a couple of decades the message shifted a bit. No, girls could not claim to *be* boys, but they could claim many traits, interests, and behaviors that supposedly belonged to boys. They just had to call themselves something else: young and American.

This chapter is about how, as a solution to fears about modernity halting white evolution, boyhood became an exalted category that, paradoxically, allowed girls to emulate boys with impunity. Boyhood became a more powerful concept in this era. Boys did not simply grow; they evolved. Scientific promotion of the "recapitulation theory" placed a premium on raising boys correctly if the white race was to continue to evolve to the top of the ladder. As the historian Don Romesburg observes: "The construction of modern adolescence was part of this larger process that reworked binaries of racial difference (i.e., savagery vs. civilization) into developmental stages (from savagery to civilization). Through recapitulation, individuals supposedly carried with them the evolutionary traces of their forebears. This allowed all societies, 'races,' and youth to evolve as they matured, but limited the pace and heights to which many could progress."[2]

Tying the origins of idealized American citizens to the raising of boys explains how tomboy traits became adopted as those of the American girl by the early twentieth century. According to the rhetoric of Theodore

Roosevelt and others, the valorized American grew straight from a vigorous, playful boyhood. Boys and their boyhood became symbolic of America's freedoms and promise; indeed, as Leslie Fiedler wrote in 1948, "The
mythic America is boyhood."[3] And as certain characteristics—such as
candor or courage—became idealized as germane to white boys, girls as a
group strove to adopt or amplify them as well.

White American boyhood gained importance during what was widely
regarded as a "masculinity crisis" at the turn of the century. According
to new theories, unruly behavior in boys was critical to growing good
American men. These so-called boyologists argued that only unruly boys
could become independent of the female-run home and school and grow
into healthy manhood. The new boyhood was about male homosociality
and a rejection of effeminacy as pathological. The boyish masculinity that
such experts described was in a binary relationship with adult masculinity, and the more adult masculinity became about work, self control, and
rationality, the more boyish masculinity became about play, liberation,
and passion.

Yet boys were also in a binary relationship with girls, making the equation more complicated. Girls were sometimes posited as opposites of boys,
in the name of gender, but also as interchangeable with them, in the name
of youth. Who served as the foil for the boy? The girl. But who was breaking down gender barriers for adult women? The girl. The tomboy again
served as a useful compromise: a girl who broke barriers, but only when
she was half boy. Boyhood was closed off to girls, but with the aid of the
already well-established tomboy girl, boyish traits associated with American character and masculinity were not.

Admired qualities such as independence of spirit were portrayed as
inherent to male bodies, but there was no obvious reason why girls could
not show a similar spirit. Adding to such perceptions, educators, psychologists, and youth organizers were now suggesting that particular recreations
previously associated with boys would improve girls' moral, physical,
and mental character as well.[4] Social leaders made their argument on the
grounds that white middle-class girls were innately domestic and maternal,
and thus a little roughing it would not ruin them but rather prevent them
from slipping into excessive femininity.[5] As masculinity became celebrated
in mass culture, both girls and boys considered certain aspects of masculinity as something they not only *could* but *should* embody.

This bold new boyhood was crafted as a repudiation of what many saw as the earlier feminization of American culture, and it was equally connected with emerging theories of racial evolution, civilization, and masculinity. As Romesburg notes, "White, middle-class boys' success in their 'struggle for manliness,' coupled with commitments to marriage and procreation in maturity, earned them stewardship of supposedly less worthy subjects" according to theories of white civilization. They had to become manly but never attracted to other men. Leading "boyworkers" emphasized the importance of male homosociality while equally vilifying both effeminacy and same-sex attraction.[6] Early Victorian character guides, such as Harvey Newcomb's *How to Be a Man* (1855), promoted self-restraint: "A well-bred boy, who knows what is becoming and proper, and carries it out in his behavior, is already a *gentleman.* But the mischievous, rude, unmannerly lad, who pays no regard to propriety of conduct, will never be a gentleman."[7] But this push toward gentility was itself class-based, and not universally shared. Many defended boys' behavior as natural and healthy, such as an 1856 editorial arguing that "boys will be boys. . . . They will feel, and think, and act like boys. They will skate on ice, ride down hill, be frivolous and jolly, play all sorts of antics, do a great many things which to the sobriety of age will look like folly. But what of that?"[8]

What changed so drastically in the Progressive Era was not that such rowdy behaviors were seen as natural so much as that they were seen as *necessary.* In this period, the "savagery" of boys was promoted as an integral component of Anglo-Saxon evolution—and that wildness would be most properly guided and nurtured through organizations such as the YMCA, Boy Scouts, summer camps, and sports teams. As Roosevelt, writing in *St. Nicholas Magazine* in 1900, put it to his young audience: "We have a right to expect of the American Boy . . . that he shall turn out to be a good American man. Now, the chances are strong that he won't be much of a man unless he is a good deal of a boy."[9]

In the midst of this celebration of boys, many girls must have noted that, given their experiences at school and home and the behaviors of older girls—New Women—in the popular press, they were not so different from boys in many respects. But this similarity with boys was at odds with the evolutionary theory positing that gender traits moved *farther* apart as civilization advanced. The tomboy, a cultural figure before the celebration of boyhood, had long allowed a girl to claim some of boys' activities and traits, but only as a social outlier. Tomboys do not travel in packs. But now familiar tomboy traits could serve as an entry point, and girls did start to claim them en masse with the help of adults who saw a need for outdoor recreation for girls as well as boys.

The Masculinity Crisis and the Raising of Boys

Concerns over the raising of boys arose as part of what many at the time identified as a "crisis" of masculinity.[10] Whether or not masculinity was truly in crisis (or indeed if it is ever *out* of crisis) is of less importance than the fact that American mass culture rallied around the belief that manhood—and attached to it, the future of the white civilization—was in peril. Gender scholars argue that the masculinity crisis stemmed from many sources, including the perceived "closing" of the West, increased urbanization and industrialized labor, and cultural unease over the New Woman and woman suffrage. But the solution, according to much prescriptive literature, was plain: raise boys to be real boys and the crisis will pass.

When the middle class came into existence, in early nineteenth-century urban centers, True Manhood, with its hallmark characteristics of self-control and willpower, was as central to the antebellum middle-class construction of respectability as True Womanhood. After the Civil War, however, gender and class norms had to adjust to the new economy. The rate of self-employed middle-class men dropped nearly in half between 1870 and 1910, and more young men were entering office work with no clear path to management positions. At the same time, middle-class white women were visibly gaining opportunities as office workers, clerks in the newly invented department store, nurses, and educators. In other words, traditional sources of male power and status were disappearing just as young women were gaining new ones. Young women and men were not in competition, because gender divisions of labor remained even if some professions (such as teaching) were feminized, but in popular culture they were pitted against each other just the same.[11]

So many dramatic changes in lifestyle and economy, combined with a drop in white birth rates and an almost paranoid insistence that white children increasingly exhibited poor health, convinced many Americans that the scientists had it right: civilization was sapping men and women of strength because they were no longer physically challenged.[12] Yet they believed men needed to be strong in order to lead, and women to bear healthy children. At stake was white civilization itself.

The term "masculinity" largely dislodged the use of "manhood" at the turn of the century. This small but critical shift in rhetoric created space for a youthful masculinity attributed to Anglo-American boys. Manhood was achieved through adulthood, which was signified by particular life achievements (property, marriage, fatherhood). Masculinity, by contrast, had to be constantly reenacted. The sociologist Michael Kimmel posits that "*manhood* had been understood to define an inner quality, the capacity for autonomy and responsibility, and had historically been seen as the opposite of *childhood*. Becoming a man was not taken for granted; at some point the grown-up boy would demonstrate that he had become a man and put away childish things."[13] Shifting from manhood to masculinity opened cultural space to address the budding masculinity of boys.

Theories of youthful masculinity emerged from a sweeping fear of "racial degeneration"—that is, not simply a falling off of white birthrates, but rampant neurasthenia caused by modern innovations such as "luxury, over-heated houses, rapid transportation," which weakened character and willpower.[14] George Beard, the neurologist who "discovered" neurasthenia, a diagnosis that ran rampant in the postbellum period, stressed that Victorian social mores were especially destructive to men. Male neurasthenics were effeminate, overly intellectual, and feeble. Self-restraint and compliance were detrimental to the nervous system of adult men, just as modern passions and intellectual work overtaxed the system of girls once they reached menarche.[15] Expanding on the theory that bodies possess only a limited amount of nerve force, Beard hypothesized that neurasthenics were essentially highly evolved "undercharged batteries." Neurasthenia was an illness of the nervous system, not a mental illness. It could not be willed away. The only way to stop the epidemic was to find new ways to replicate the old ways of forging true manliness and womanliness through the tribulations faced daily in the historical past. As Gail Bederman adroitly summarizes, "Only white male bodies had the capacity to be truly civilized. Yet, at the same time, civilization destroyed white male bodies. How could powerful, civilized manhood be saved?"[16]

Beginning in the 1890s, Theodore Roosevelt brought manhood, masculinity, boys, and boyhood together in popular culture as no one else could.[17] Convinced of the imminent decline of white civilization,

Roosevelt promoted the importance of the "manly" man in maintaining white sovereignty in a world of competing races and nation-states. His obsession with masculinity and white race suicide spurred him to link masculinity to a conquering, white adult male body and bind it to white America's racial and cultural survival. His principal image was that of a self-made *male* rather than a self-made man. He did not represent the ability of an independent man to create his own fortune, which was Roosevelt's by birth, but his ability to transform his pale, skinny, asthmatic self into a burly man's man whose chief pleasures were hunting, soldiering, roughing it, and hanging out with other men like himself.[18] Along those lines, he became one of the most effective and consistent proponents of boyhood masculinity: the belief that boys have an innate version of masculinity that must be fostered if they are to grow into strong, American men. Working from the theories of Herbert Spencer and the psychologist G. Stanley Hall, he amplified fears over the effeminizing effects of modern urban life, and, as Bederman puts it, "exhorted the American race to embrace a manly, strenuous imperialism, in the cause of higher civilization."[19]

Not surprisingly, what constituted a "real boy" had to be clarified again and again. Roosevelt readily stepped up to the plate, laying out a list of requirements: "He must not be a coward or a weakling, a bully, a shirk, or a prig. He must work hard and play hard. He must be clean-minded and clean-lived, and able to hold his own under all circumstances and against all comers." He charged that a boy's first priority must to be play hard and have fun if he is to be of any use to his country when he matures: "It is only on these conditions that he will grow into the kind of American man of whom America can be really proud." Although, he added, a boy must not be "a goody-goody boy"—one of those effeminate, Little Lord Fauntleroy types that were the driving the boyologists crazy—"but just a plain good boy."[20] Roosevelt clarified his meaning by invoking characteristics promoted in popular fiction: "The best boys I know—the best men I know—are good at their studies or their business, fearless and stalwart, hated and feared by all that is wicked and depraved, incapable of submitting to wrong-doing, and equally incapable of being aught but tender to the weak and helpless." Roosevelt and others emphasized over and over that the truly ideal boy would be, as Dr. Lilburn Merrill, an expert on juvenile delinquency, put it in 1907, "rollicking, hilarious, tamed or untamed," with a "big, tender, loving heart" and explosive energy. Only through exertion in athletics and outdoor living, Roosevelt and the boyologists emphasized, could citified boys fulfill their manly promise.[21]

The authentic boy promoted by Roosevelt and others resembled the "bad boy" of earlier fiction: mischievous, big-hearted, and untamed. He was the hope for the continued evolution of American citizens. According to national newspapers in July 1902, Roosevelt's maxim was that "manliness of character is the true patriotism that every American ought to have."[22] But girls and women were patriots, too; did they also have a claim to manliness? Wives and mothers could express patriotism through their husbands and sons, but what about America's white daughters? Many native-born girls identified with the same "manly" ideals, even when the prescriptions they received from cultural leaders addressed them only as future mothers.

Roosevelt cast childbearing and marriage as a "woman's duty to the state" and her expression of patriotism.[23] In 1905, when Roosevelt addressed the National Congress of Mothers (a positive eugenics organization), he asserted that while men perpetuated the authentic American character, women made America possible through fecundity and domestic stability. According to him, America needed women in the home to reach its full potential: "No piled-up wealth, no splendor of material growth, no brilliance of artistic development, will permanently avail any people unless its home life is healthy." For this, the average woman must be a "good wife, a good mother, able and willing to perform the first and greatest duty of womanhood, able and willing to bear, and to bring up as they should be brought up, healthy children, sound in body, mind, and character, and numerous enough so that the race shall increase and not decrease."[24] Although Roosevelt frequently gave recipes for shaping the "real" boy into an ideal American, his only suggestion for raising girls was for parents to "teach boys and girls alike that they are not to look forward to lives spent in avoiding difficulties, but to lives spent in overcoming difficulties."[25] In other words, boys will grow into citizens, and girls can be raised much like boys until they grow into the mothers of citizens.

Again and again he implied that imperialism and pronatalism were two sides of the same coin used to purchase white dominance in a rapidly changing world: one side to be spent abroad, the other at home; one side on military endeavors (men), and the other on childbearing (women) and rearing (boys). Roosevelt became known for his imperialist vision of the "white man's burden" to civilize the world, but he was no less concerned about white racial superiority at home.[26]

Roosevelt's concept of masculinity had been shaped by his youthful struggles with poor health, and his reverence for the hard-working frontiersmen and soldiers of yore suggests a boy who grew up on juvenile adventure fiction. One historian argues that for Roosevelt, masculinity was "constructed, not around an adult desire to seduce the other sex, but around an infantile need to reconstruct and reassure his own."[27] And yet girls read dime novels along with their brothers; they, too, thrilled to the heroic imagery and sought to embody it.[28]

Roosevelt's rhetoric so actively linked masculinity with white Americanism that the two became inseparable in popular discourse at the turn of the century. And by not addressing a role for girls, Roosevelt unintentionally left boyhood masculinity open to them in the name of patriotism. Manhood (a state of maturity) had left no room for females as subjects, but masculinity did, because it did not explicitly hinge on the body but on behavior expected of that body.[29] Because masculinity had to be constantly reenacted, its attainment was always in question, suggesting that gender was not necessarily innate, but could be performed. For white American females, the equation presented a quandary. If masculinity meant an assertion of self, then femininity, as its binary opposite, was a denial of self—which put American females in a strange position since they were challenging exactly that norm in the guise of the New Woman.[30] And yet aspects that many presumed to be feminine, such as passivity, were in the process of being strategically disowned by modern females. Was femininity synonymous with a female body regardless of a woman's behavior? Not according to Roosevelt, who rigorously equated true femininity with motherhood.[31]

Roosevelt also linked masculinity to patriotism. In 1902 he declared that "manliness of character is the true patriotism that every American ought to have."[32] But men and boys were not the only ones encountering descriptions of the ideal American youth as self-reliant, physical, good-natured, and unpretentious, or assertions that manliness was synonymous with patriotism. Many white native-born girls caught the same fever, even when the prescriptions they received from cultural leaders addressed them only as future mothers.

Boyology

An idealized boyhood was promoted by self-described "boyologists" who drew on new theories of adolescence to emphasize that the future of both the white race and the nation hinged on the character of its boys. They created the Boy Scouts, YMCA chapters, summer camps, and organized sports leagues to supplement the old sources of authority, which had been family, church, and school. They theorized that only intensive physical and intellectual training under exclusively male supervision would save boys from modern, feminized culture.[33] Henry William Gibson, a frequent lecturer at YMCA gatherings, coined the term "boyologist" at the turn of the century. The frontispiece of his book *Boyology; or, Boy Analysis*—drawn from twenty years of talks he had been giving on the topic nationwide—neatly summarizes the mentality of the entire endeavor by featuring a wholesome, white adolescent boy above the line "Boy-stuff is the only stuff in the world from which men can be made." The objective of the boyologists was to train white middle-class parents in how to raise sons best suited to take their proper place in the world order.[34]

Boyologists promoted character building through organized athletics and recreation. Just as physicians continued to portray puberty as a time of vulnerability in girls, the boyologists—many of them psychologists—now posited adolescence as of particular concern for boys. Indeed, they depicted adolescence as the time when boys must leave their communities to bond with each other and develop, before returning as men.[35] Relying heavily on the theory of recapitulation, they asserted that boys must be allowed to transgress civil norms in order to keep evolving into real men. In their hands, American boyhood became more than a repudiation of earlier Victorian efforts to make boys suitable for parlors and schools; it became a biological imperative.

Until age twelve, the boy is, in Gibson's words, "more a little beast."[36] He was following the three adolescent stages described by William Byron Forbush in his 1901 book *The Boy Problem*: "twelve to sixteen, sixteen to eighteen and eighteen to twenty-four," which could be called "the stages of ferment, crisis and reconstruction."[37] Rife with fear and uneasy with socialization, he asserts, a healthy boy will join a gang. Reversing earlier child-rearing guides that blamed criminal sons on lax mothers, Gibson suggested that overly involved mothers who did not encourage gang membership would produce delinquents. Because—and here he quotes Forbush—"This gang instinct is absolutely necessary for the proper social education of every boy. There is no other way . . . whereby he must be saved from narrowness of mind, selfishness and self-conceit."[38]

Between 1900 and 1920 boyologists worked in an echo chamber of sorts. They cited and quoted each other, endorsed and wrote introductions to each other's books, and reinforced each other's efforts to find solutions. The same names appear again and again in the boyology literature: Roosevelt, Merrill, the psychologist G. Stanley Hall, and the youth organizers Luther Gulick, Ernest Thompson Seton, Forbush, and Gibson. Not all of them would call themselves "boyologists," but they worked together to support each other's theories as fact.

If medical experts wrung their hands over female puberty, when it came to boys the central concern was adolescence. In a 1902 summary of a wide range of contemporary studies of childhood, the anthropologist Alexander Chamberlain noted with wonder: "In many respects this lengthening of the period of growth or adolescence in man is one of the most remarkable phenomena of his existence—intra-uterine life, infancy, childhood, youth, seem all to have increased in duration, for the shaping of the human being, and the complicated environment accompanying modern civilisation tends to lengthen more and more the period of immaturity"[39] Concepts regarding the length and purpose of adolescence, or the "epoch of development" between childhood and adulthood, first introduced by reformers in the 1870s but eventually analyzed by medical doctors, psychologists, and others, had become accepted as common wisdom by the turn of the century. "Adolescence," a term in use since the Middle Ages, took on new meaning in the forty years spanning the turn of the twentieth century.[40]

In 1904 G. Stanley Hall thoroughly defined and shaped this new meaning in his two-volume study *Adolescence: Its Psychology and Relations to Physiology, Anthropology, Sociology, Sex, Crime, Religion and Education.*[41] And, with over 1,400 pages, it lived up to the subtitle—at least in terms of boys. Focusing now on adolescence rather than on teaching parents and educators how to raise children scientifically, Hall argued that what he called the "sturm und drang" (storm and stress) of adolescence was critical for boys' continued ascent up the evolutionary ladder.

It is arguable that few American actually read Hall's magnum opus, but his work was omnipresent in the articulations of youth educators and organizers, and Hall himself spoke directly to the public in lectures as well as magazine and newspaper articles. For example, in 1901 he waxed lyrical at a meeting of the federated women's clubs of Massachusetts: "We see the gradual development of the child into manhood, exemplifying in each successive life experience, the growth of the race. He is, indeed, the epitome of the race. His rudimentary and undeveloped instincts show the ripple marks of the great sea of life as the tracing of the rock speaks plainly to the geologist of the ebb and flow of the ocean in past ages." Addressing contemporary fears about perceived weaknesses—particularly effeminacy—Hall asserted that boys must have their "animal spirits" nurtured if the race was to continue evolving. "Above all, . . . suppress the tendency of too great interference, and let nature work her will on the boy."[42]

Hall took recapitulation theory into adolescence. All children spend time on the bottom steps of the evolutionary hill, but only the more advanced humans keep ascending. Hall and his contemporaries posited that since white males ascend further than women and nonwhites, it is also more important that they experience a protracted adolescence to reach perfection. Thus boys must go through an untamed, animalistic period—which white boys will leave at the appropriate time, while their "colored" counterparts remain. White girls, too, leave those primitive steps, and ascend a bit further alongside their brothers. White boys' time on these shared steps with white girls is made evident by their greater emotionality. But when white girls reach menarche they stop ascending, as their life force becomes consumed by developing their reproductive capacities. Their brothers continue on to the cool-headed rationality of the fully developed white male. Thus adolescence was both inscribed with whiteness and constructed as requisite for virile masculinity, and white middle-class perspectives, needs, and ways of living shaped what came to be seen as normal adolescent behaviors.[43]

Recapitulation theory provided an evolutionary explanation for why so many (white, male) scientists had observed that children of all races and genders appeared equally promising before puberty and yet reached vastly different outcomes as adults. In his analysis of child development studies at the end of the nineteenth century, Chamberlain concluded with anti-intellectual scorn: "It would appear then that the young negro is quite as capable as the white child of being crammed with Latin and Greek and the rest of the manifold curriculum of the day."[44] Yet although Chamberlain himself notes that the truncated "development" of African American youth might be more related to poverty and lack of opportunity than evolution, he continues to emphasize recapitulation theory as the more scientific explanation. Within the culture of fearful white supremacy that dominated the period, recapitulation theory was a seductive explanation for why white boys and men remained king.

At the same time that adolescence reached theoretical definition, it also gained an important cultural role. Adolescence came to symbolize the challenge of moving from childhood (dependent, sexless, communal identity) to adulthood (individuality, agency, and sexuality).[45] For both boys and girls, it came to symbolize the loss of freedom that attended aging into gender norms. Although (white) men continued to enjoy far more political, economic, and legal liberties than women, manhood itself was cast as being absent of the joys of boyhood and stifled by responsibility and duty in a world where men rarely enjoyed the autonomy supposedly dominant in earlier time periods. Such a struggle parallels what had long been the subtext of tomboy stories.

Boys are men under construction, the boyologists emphasized. To become "real men"—to achieve full masculinity—they must first enact the boy version of masculinity, and that involves boys spending most of their time with other boys, apart from both adults and females of all ages. In describing boyish masculinity, the boyologists used particular terms over and over: savage, mischievous, "semi-criminal," passionate, social, emotional, physical, aggressive. Boys are, in their rendering, homosocial and loyal above all else.

The boyologists most frequently likened boys to animals or Native Americans, and sometimes to both at the same time. Merrill asserted in 1907 that in their natural state "boys are animals. . . . There is a nomadic tramp instinct in every fellow. An undomesticated boy can shoulder a blanket and with a can of sardines and some rolls, turn his back on civilization with as much good grace and enthusiasm as can an Indian. God has tuned his soul into harmony with the swimming hole, the mountains, and the green fields." The problem, Merrill argued, was that "we frequently fail with boys because we present them to conditions which do not harmonize with the masculinity of their nature. We devote much time to trying to effeminize boy nature." Civilized life was sapping the life and strength from boys. Men could only grow strong from a barely tamed boyhood, full of well-intentioned but thoughtless mischief, joyful (and often life-threatening) play, and a certain amount of vicious competition. If there was a "boy problem" at all, it stemmed from adults trying to tame the boy into manhood too soon.[46]

Although popular reminiscences of "natural" boyhood tended to look toward rural life for the origins of ideas about boys as untamed and ungovernable, historical evidence suggests that it developed out of a "boy culture"—a culture created by boys themselves—that arose organically in daily urban life. There was little need for a new boyhood for rural boys; little had changed in their world. Boys on homesteads and farms still worked alongside their fathers and other adult men, as well as performing particular chores within the household. Outside of school, they rarely had the ability to gather with other boys their own age for daily play. By contrast, boys in towns and cities grew up largely apart from grown men and enjoyed significant time outside of the domestic spaces. They saw their fathers leave home all day to earn wages or salaries, daily joining a world apart from the family. Boys could see that this was their future as well, but for now they existed in a world of boys. Once away from the eyes of the boss or schoolteacher, it was a world without adult intervention. They created homosocial boy cultures that typically celebrated aggression and physical assertion and avoided duties and restrictions. It was a "defiant, physical, pack-minded boy culture," that was increasingly supported by youth organizers, psychologists, and popular literature for boys.[47]

Violence, considered off-limits in the lives of most middle-class men except as spectators, served as the glue of boy culture. Boys were particularly physical in their bonding: fighting and wrestling for fun, but also ganging up to goad other boys into unwilling fights. And, Anthony Rotundo notes, "If boys posed a danger to one another, they were downright lethal to small animals."[48] Killing small animals, by rural and urban boys alike, was treated as natural expression of boy identity. By the turn of the twentieth century, boys' tendency toward playful violence was given cultural sanction through the boyologist literature, but also through promotion of rough sports and outdoor recreation, such as hunting. Yet the boyhood masculinity advocated by boyologists was the stuff of play, not a show of virility. It was grounded in disorderly conduct combined with a romantic code that sanctioned their behavior as prerogative of youth.

Young people heard the boyologists, but not all of them were boys. Outside of extreme violence, girls appropriated many similar behaviors as their right—including physical fighting. Many girls considered fighting an expected part of girl culture, even into adolescence. The 1872 diary of the irrepressible Alice Stone Blackwell is filled with comments such as "At recess, during the game, Annie Phips and I got to fighting, a real wrestling match, and the girls joined hands and formed a ring round us, watching our evolutions with interest, and Mary Fifield called out that *she* bet on me."[49] In other words, all of the girls participated by egging on the fighters. According to many girls' private writings, adult ideas of what was proper meant nearly as little in the world of girl culture as in boy culture. Sophie Ruskay, who grew up Brooklyn at the turn of the century, later recalled, "We knew it to be a boy's world, but we didn't seem to mind it too much. We shared the life of the street unhampered by our parents."[50]

America promoted little mothers more than it celebrated tomboys, but girls did not necessarily put too much stock in adult prescriptions. In *Made to Play House,* Miriam Formanek-Brunell explores the rise of the doll-making industry and finds that dolls and playing house were promoted for a variety of reasons in this period. "Businessmen urged 'little mothers' to shop for the doll babies they loved," but for many female entrepreneurs dolls were equally about teaching health and hygiene and even "social hygiene"—the need for mothers to clean up society's morals. But she also notes that, regardless of what adults believed about teaching girls household skills, girls in the antebellum period preferred the outdoors and girls of the Gilded Age preferred bikes and roller skates. Just as not all boys wanted to play sports, not all girls wanted to play house. But through the figure of the tomboy girls found their rough play sanctioned, while boys more interested in quiet pursuits were depicted as effeminate. There was a place in girls' lives to play house, but there was an equal need to play outside of it.[51]

Roosevelt's own daughter Ethel followed the classic tomboy trajectory. Ten years old when she moved into the White House, she gained a reputation as a tomboy who spent all of her free time out of doors, preferably riding. She played pranks with her brothers well into her teens, but by the time she left the residence, at seventeen, she had reportedly become a "sweet, young woman with a very successful social career ahead of her."[52] Roosevelt and his followers were not opposed to girls emulating boys, just women emulating men. Roosevelt proclaimed that if the average girl became "twisted so that she prefers a sterile pseudo-intellectuality to that great and beautiful development of character" that comes with childbearing, American civilization would not survive.[53]

And many girls, still focusing on the middle-class belief in self-improvement rather than the impending sacrifices of motherhood, did not see a limit to their personal potential. Girls' diaries are rife with ambition. How should girls express patriotism when middle-class girlhood was not about selflessness but about cultivation of self?[54] These girls, after all, were not the "delinquent daughters" that many critics saw as undermining urban life, but rather the bright, white future in danger of being dimmed by the excesses of modern life.[55] Educators and doctors focused on girls began proclaiming that too much domesticity could be unhealthy and lead to passive, cowed, dull girls (and thus mothers). In the eyes of many (but not all) progressives, these girls—unlike their cohorts of color, poverty, or foreign birth—could be improved by a bit of boyish behavior.[56] Whiteness, class, and age allowed them to "transcend" the negative aspects of femininity and—at least until marriage—express national character in sanctioned boyish pursuits.

Some girls themselves noted with dismay that as they aged out of young childhood they lost freedoms while their brothers gained them. The custom had long been to raise very young children as gender-neutral. Boys and girls under six years old were still dressed virtually alike in plain, loose frocks. But upon reaching boyhood and girlhood—leaving the shared world of childhood—boys gained freedom through trousers while girls lost freedom through ever more fitted and restrictive clothing.[57] The changes in clothing laid bare the heart of the struggle: boyhood meant freedom, and girlhood meant its opposite. More frightening still, womanhood meant an even greater confinement than girlhood. Since the early nineteenth century, their brothers' worlds seemed to resemble the outward end of the telescope, while their own tapered down at the other end, to view the world at a distance. The Progressive Era, with its tomboys and New Women, appeared to be upending that reality. Now girls could behave like boys, and women like girls.

The boyologists did not agree at all; boyhood was for boys only. Indeed, a US census report stating that "one-third of school-aged girls wished they were boys" disturbed Hall profoundly. Hall referred to the mid-adolescence of girls as "the *backfisch* stage"; *backfisch* was a German term of the Wilhelmine period (1890–1915) for a girl who embodied innocence and purity like the tomboy, but was innately feminine, romantic, and conventional.[58] It literally meant a fish too big to throw back but too small to eat. Hall argued that the *backfisch* stage was unique to advanced cultures and must be prolonged as long as possible for evolution to continue to progress.[59]

But within *Adolescence,* Hall largely overlooks girls except when discussing their reproductive futures. For Hall, just as for Roosevelt and so many other social leaders of the period, girls were most worth discussing as vessels of future civilization; he was interested in exploring the contours of female adolescence primarily as it pertained to reproduction. When he raises the topic of adolescent girls, Hall begins, like the physicians before him, with the dangers of female puberty. He states that one of the "gravest dangers is the persistent ignoring by feminists of the prime importance" of establishing regular periods in girls, to which "everything else should for a few years be secondary."[60] Because Hall firmly believed that "nature demands that every girl should be educated primarily to become a wife and mother," he emphasizes the physical well-being of girls over all other concerns. He promotes exercise but echoes the earlier work by Edward Clarke and others, asserting that ambitious girls would endanger their reproductive capabilities unless adults intervened.[61] Yet regardless of the emphasis on reproductive capacity, girls must also remain sexually unawakened into their early twenties, because sexual awareness halted girls' evolutionary ascent.[62]

Despite his privileging of boys, Hall was truly worried that social emphasis on male superiority would lead to a loss of self-esteem for girls. He argued that a sense of inferiority would turn girls away from their true femininity. Indeed, such ideas coalesced later in the theories of Alfred Adler, who postulated that "children attentively observe the inequalities between women and men and come to associate femininity with a lack of power," and thus "all types of inferiority thereby become feminized." Both neurotic girls and boys "become overly masculine (aggressive, sadistic, and so on) in order to compensate for feelings of inferiority." Adler considered that tomboyism could been seen as an example of "masculine protest," but also believed that tomboys were too widely exhibited to signal actual neurosis.[63]

Indeed, to tomboy proponents tomboyism *prevented* neurosis. Many Americans believed that the modern girl was "adrift in a rapidly changing modern world, bereft of the guidance she needed to understand both it and the changes taking place in her adolescent body and soul."[64] This thinking suggested that girls must to be redirected to the natural world. Meanwhile, the popular press projected images of girls enjoying athletics and outdoor sports. Through the repetition of such images, the ideal girl was becoming ever more similar to the formerly singular tomboy.[65]

Rekindling the Domestic Fire

In 1902 Ernest Thompson Seton organized a camp for "Woodcraft Indians," a boy-centered response to cultural fears about fading American character. He designed the camp to reenact the challenges of the frontier so neatly laid out by Frederick Jackson Turner in 1893. Troubled by 1890 population statistics suggesting that "a frontier line of settlement" could no longer be mapped on the continental United States, Turner concluded that a great age was coming to an end. Wilderness, according to what has become known as Turner's "Frontier Thesis," takes the European immigrant "from the railroad car and puts him in a birch canoe. It strips off the garments of civilization and arrays him in the hunting shirt and the moccasin."[66] Claiming that westward expansion into the frontier had created the archetypal American, Turner emphasized that the loss of the frontier threatened the character of the nation.

Seton took such sentiments to heart, literally putting moccasin-shod boys into canoes in the name of creating character. First he founded a series of camps centered on playing Indian—that is, the mythological Indian, the noble part of the savage left after the genocide of Native Americans had stripped away threats to the mythology. He introduced his ideas to the public in a series of articles in the *Ladies' Home Journal* in 1902, titled "Ernest Thompson Seton's Boys," where he states his purpose in teaching boys to be like "Injuns." He notes that his boyhood self had wished for such guidance, adding, "That does not mean I wanted to be a cruel savage, but rather I wanted to know how to live in the woods, as he does. And enjoy and understand the plants and living creatures that are found there." Seton focused on the Sioux, the fierce warriors destroyed in the Plains Indian Wars, as the symbolic Indian.[67] The popular nature writer John Burroughs "visited one of Seton's camps in 1906, and immediately wrote to Theodore Roosevelt: 'Seton has got hold of a big thing with his boys' Indian Camp. . . . All the boy's wild energy and love of devilry are turned into new channels, and he is taught woodcraft and natural history and Indian-lore."[68] Eventually, in 1907, Seton helped to create the American version of the Boy Scouts, modeled on both the British Boy Scouts (focused on citizenship) and the Woodcraft Indians (focused on character).

Girls demanded their own version of Boy Scouts and Woodcraft Indians. And—to put it far more simply than this contentious movement actually evolved—they got them: the Camp Fire Girls (1910 as a camp; 1912 as an organization) Girl Guides (1912; renamed Girl Scouts as a national organization in 1913), Girl Pioneers (1912), and Woodcraft Girls (1915).[69] Hundreds of camps for girls sprang up around the nation, sponsored by religious groups, ethnic societies, and political clubs, although private camps for middle-class girls dominated New England girlhood. And although the original organizations appealed directly to white middle-class girls, African American, working-class, and ethnic organizations quickly organized Girl Scout troops in various cities.[70] Voicing conservative reassurances about the innately domestic and maternal nature of (white middle-class) girls on the one hand, and feminist urgings for female self-actualization on the other, leaders asserted that returning youth to nature promoted their self-development. Girls' organizations allowed adults to implicitly address the cultural conflict over the need for its females to be submissive as women and yet assertive as Americans. The white girl as a symbol of submissive purity was now challenged by the image of the strong, forthright, self-sufficient girl as the American ideal.[71]

Luther and Charlotte Gulick established the Camp Fire Girls as an antidote to the prevailing "girl problem," which referred to fears that girls were growing up in shallow urban worlds, losing sight of the true meaning of womanliness, and getting lost in a maze of novels, dance-halls, and that new phenomenon, dating.[72] In 1907 the Gulicks established a model of what would become the Camp Fire Girls. Working with Seton and James West of the Boy Scouts, as well as the ubiquitous Hall, they borrowed most of their ideas from the Boys Scouts, using many of the same frontier skills, survival techniques, and outdoor games. Yet if boys joined Scouts to become independent citizens, the aim of the Camp Fire Girls was to reignite domestic and maternal interest, fostering girls as helpmeets. Just as the Boy Scouts took boys into the woods to cultivate virility, the Camp Fire Girls put girls in the woods to cultivate domesticity.

The fire was a central symbol for the club because it could be used to connect girls to both frontier conditions and domestic labor. Luther

FIGURE 6: In this 1909 photograph, Camp Fire Girls reconnect with their inherent domesticity as they tend pots while dressed as "Indians" over the iconic campfire. Courtesy Ames Historical Center, Ames, Iowa.

Gulick stressed tradition: "The bearing and rearing of children has always been the first duty of most women, and that must always continue to be. This involves service, constant service, self-forgetfulness, and always service. I suggest that the fire be taken as the symbol of the girls' movement, the domestic fire—not the wild fire."[73] But Charlotte Gulick focused less on the selflessness of womanhood than on the thrill of mastering outdoor living: "I wanted them to think and discover by living in this primitive way, how this part of woman's work can be simplified, and the drudgery turned into a stimulating exercise of talent." For Mrs. Gulick contended that "woman's work is inherently far more fascinating than man's," and that modern technology and life ways were stripping it of meaning.[74]

One of the chief devices the Camp Fire Girls used to "reconnect" its members with their "natural" domestic spirit was to dress them as mythical Indian girls of yore. Camp Fire girls made their own fringed ceremonial gowns along the lines of Native American garb and decorated them with beads they won through acquiring new skills.[75] The trope of the Indian princess was baked into American mythology. From the story of Pocahontas (a nickname that newspapers now claimed translated to "tomboy"), to the native heroines of James Fenimore Cooper, to romantic paintings of the Native American woman as a beautiful, tragic symbol of the past, Americans were happy to embrace her as a model for their daughters.[76]

This was, of course, an act of white cultural imperialism. A mere two decades after a century-long genocide of indigenous peoples, the dominant culture was in the midst of refashioning the Indian as worth emulating rather than assimilating or destroying. With fewer real indigenous people to muck up the scenario, these white girls could impersonate Indian princesses, a creation of white culture. Likewise, white anti-modern feminists now celebrated indigenous women as "powerful women whose traditions embodied ideal gender relations."[77] But in spiritually reconnecting with supposedly lost and noble ghosts of American culture, the girls conversely emphasized what made them other than Indian: their intractable whiteness. They could, to paraphrase the historian Philip Deloria, play Indian without becoming Indian.[78]

Such a philosophy expanded on the theory that American wilderness had produced in its citizens a natural gentility of wholesome simplicity. Charlotte Gulick declared that girls should "express the poetry of the life about them in the work of their hands, with nature as their guide and inspiration." She was proud that the girls, "paddling their own canoes, carrying their own packs, building their own fires and cooking their own meals," were coming "to find a joy in this life that luxury and idleness could never give." Her chief worry about modern girls was not that they would discard their central roles of wife and mother as adult women, but that modernity would leave them ill equipped to perform those roles.[79] She believed that outdoor activities were withheld from girls because of wrongheaded notions that girls are intrinsically sedentary and materialistic. The Camp Fire organization pushed a sentimental kind of female independence that ultimately embraced middle-class gender roles.

The Girls Scouts, under the leadership of founder Juliette Gordon Low, subtly went in the other direction. The Girls Scouts supposedly began with a premise similar to that of the Camp Fire Girls, namely that girls deserved their own organization like the Boy Scouts. But Low did not come to her project like the Gulicks, rooted in evolutionary theories and the work of boyologists. While in England, Low, a bored, wealthy widow, became friends with Robert Baden-Powell, who founded the British Boy Scouts in 1907. Baden-Powell himself *was* strongly influenced by Ernest Thompson Seton, whose Woodcraft Indians and writings about boys were central to the philosophies of American boyologists. Baden-Powell looked to the Woodcraft Indians and to Daniel Carter Beard's Sons of Daniel Boone (founded in 1905) to create a similar organization for British boys, only with less emphasis on the frontier and more on the importance of national service. So when Low imported the project for girls to her hometown of Savannah, Georgia, she also approached it from the angle of emphasizing citizenship and service, with a frontier culture component. The Girl Scouts was less obviously tied to the recapitulation and frontier theories than the Camp Fire Girls.

The result was that the Girl Scouts became an organization more about building up girls as citizens than the Camp Fire Girls, which strove to inculcate greater pride in women as helpmeets. This became abundantly clear when American girls themselves elected to change their title from Girl Guides, used by their British corollary and initially their title in the United States, to Girl Scouts. Supposedly American girls identified with the word "scout" as a character of the frontier. But the Boy Scout founders, who used the word "scout" to signal military service, strongly objected. They preferred "guides" because girls were supposed to help men, not lead.[80] By 1917 James West, the president (or Chief Scout Executive, as he was officially called) of the Boy Scouts of America, was so incensed that he charged that the name Girl Scouts "trivialized" and "sissified" the word "scout" and demanded that Low's organization cease to use the term. He claimed that boys were quitting the Scouts over embarrassment that girls could also be Scouts.[81] One Boy Scout leader warned: "When you allow the Girl Scouts to organize you might as well say good-bye to Boy Scouts, because of all things that boys cherish is the fact that they are boys . . . , and the most diabolical accusation you can make against a boy is to call him a sissy." As the historian Susan Miller explicates, they feared that enjoying the same activities as girls would turn them into something other than boys, and "this was abject terror at losing one's identity."[82] Thereafter, the Boy Scouts threw their approval behind the more traditional Camp Fire Girls. Luther Gulick concurred with their assessment, stating baldly that "to copy the Boy Scout movement would be utterly and fundamentally evil, and would probably produce ultimately a moral and psychological involution. . . . We hate manly women and womanly men."[83]

In truth, the organizers of the Boy Scouts and other outdoor clubs had conflicted feelings about girls enjoying equal play, much as society had long both admired and reviled tomboys. On the one hand, they feared girls would taint scouting activities with effeminacy or damage the fragile egos of adolescent boys, but they also identified with girls' desire to engage in many of the same activities. After all, they, too, saw camping and fishing as far more interesting than sewing and cleaning. It all came down to nuances. In 1918 Boy Scout executives noted that Roosevelt himself had once said that "the fact that girls liked to do certain things was the best reason why he, as a boy, would not like to do them." But at the same time Roosevelt repeatedly voiced support for the Girl Scouts and encouraged his own daughter to play as the equal of her brothers.[84] And, although aware that Hall advocated separate-sex middle schools in an effort to protect boys' egos, organizers of girls' camps frequently quoted Hall's work as central to their own. Progressives saw the self-reliance expressed through camps as a positive development for the culture, as long as such play did not undermine the cultivation of masculinity in young men.[85]

But while outdoor organizations focused on emotionally elevating domestic labor, the girls actually participating and observing likely drew different conclusions. Many of their experiences in camp only proved once again that girls could compete with boys when given equal opportunities—girls such as thirteen-year-old Frances Pass, a Camp Fire girl, who crowed in her diary: "Game against the boys 7–8 in our favor. We won!!! We are going to keep up the good work as long as I'm captain."[86] Girls' diaries of the period consistently reinforce that girls believed they enjoyed wide future choices beyond domestic life. Many, indeed, were repelled by domestic life, such as Marion Taylor, also thirteen, who confided to her diary: "My ambitions are daily reaching higher . . . *I'm* not going to be a 'wifie' and household drudge! But I'm going to have the College education!"[87] And others, like ten-year-old Mildred Cornish and her sister, felt freedom to take pleasure in boys' entertainment, such as the cartoon "Peck's Bad Boy," simply because they liked it.[88] More than one girl recorded wishing to be a boy because "they had so much freedom and dared to do such exciting things."[89] Few diaries suggest that their writers were particularly easy to mold, despite their constant worries about their characters.

For the girls, a hearty show of American independence (which the culture defined as masculine) was perhaps the most celebrated cultural truth of their lives. As Susan Miller notes, "When girls wielded pioneer tools—which included rod, reel, and rifle, as well as pickaxes and hatchets—they were handling instruments that were almost universally equated with the hardy masculinity of the American sportsman."[90] They undoubtedly learned that they were just as good at outdoor pastimes as their brothers.

The existence of two ultimately successful national organizations for girls speaks to several gender transformations within the culture: along with boys, girls began to be treated as future citizens and not simply as future mothers of future citizens. And certain traits that were still tied to masculinity were now clearly sanctioned for girls (if not adult women), including leadership, self-sufficiency, physical exertion, ambition, competition, and (to a point) physical aggression.

Indeed, the Gulicks' philosophy was truly the tomboy tale writ large. They knew that the world was opening for girls, but they anticipated that girls would choose domestic life if raised in contact with nature. The aim of the Girl Scouts was quite a bit more feminist; the organization's literature asserted the importance of careers and listed books on famous women as suggested reading. Alongside books about such figures as Joan of Arc, Louisa May Alcott, and Mary Lyon, Low recommended Jeannette Gilder's 1901 best-seller *The Autobiography of a Tomboy*.[91] The belief that tomboys made the best women, just as untamed boys made the best men, appears to have been largely accepted by the first decade of the new century. Newspapers and magazines regularly carried stories of audacious tomboys, with exchangeable (and forgettable) titles such as "Tomboy Delia" and "The Way of Hetty the Tomboy."[92] And most leading feminists were now claiming tomboy girlhoods. As more and more American girls behaved like tomboys in the tales, the more tomboy tales appeared in the world of print. And the more tomboy tales appeared, the more mainstream the tomboy and her activities became. The tomboy of the late nineteenth century was becoming the all-American girl of the twentieth.

6

The American Girl

In 1898 a *Harper's Bazaar* article announced "the passing of the tomboy." The author declared that "tomboy has become an antiquarian's word," and added, "The spirit of the time is embodied in the girl who is to be the woman ruling the destiny of man in the first quarter of the coming century. The passing of the tomboy is complete."[1] Two of these supposed truths would continue to take shape over the next two decades: that the nineteenth-century tomboy was becoming simply the "American girl," and thus that the term "tomboy" was obsolete.

But this American girl was significantly different than tomboys of yore in two particular and telling ways: the American girl, unlike the tomboy, did not resist conventionality or maturity, and she was not a misfit. As educators, youth organizers, and physicians promoted the importance of outdoor life in growing strong future mothers as well as virile men, the hallmark traits of the nineteenth-century tomboy—fishing, hunting, sledding, and so forth—became signs of healthy girlhood, and a predilection for such activities now confirmed a girl's worth. The tomboy of earlier days had played alone or led others into trouble, but the American girl enjoyed tomboy games surrounded by like-minded friends, male and female. As a mainstream girl rather than an outlier, the American girl claimed freedom and independence as her right by virtue of youth, and she was allowed to do so because of her race and class. She reveled in the freedoms and opportunities brought by greater wealth and technology, but did not challenge white middle-class conventions of gender and sexuality so much as expand her own rights within those conventions.

This assimilation of tomboy characteristics into the American girl happened just when the American girl became a national symbol and central to consumer culture. The historian Martha Banta contends that "the phrase 'the American Girl' was neither mere fiction, abstract theory, nor fraudulent fact. Solidly backed by images that flowed quickly across the visual horizon of the American public, this complex composite of types was available for use by anyone who wished to use it for whatever reasons—commercial, personal, aesthetic, political."[2] Commercial use was already at its height, with images of the American girl used to advertise consumer goods from magazines to soda pop.[3] In the process of selling, these images also asserted an idealized American cultural norm easily signified. The American girl is consistently fair-skinned, wholesome, and laughing, usually wearing a shirtwaist and narrow white or dark skirt, frequently standing outside in the sunshine or wind, and often riding a bicycle or rowing a canoe. She is also clearly Anglo-Saxon, Protestant, native-born, and upper class, and yet, through print culture, promoted as representative of the values of the entire nation.[4]

The American girl gained dimension through her ubiquity in advertising and print culture, but particular book series for girls reinforced the normalcy of adventurous American girls claiming ambitions and freedoms. In advertising, this prevailing girl, with her candid gaze and air of self-reliance, expressed the spirit of earlier tomboys: ever ready for good, clean fun, or to fight wholeheartedly on behalf of her convictions. Slim but rounded, with her hair up (like an adult) but falling from its pins, she mixed signifiers of maturity and youth, appearing somewhere between adolescence and young womanhood. The stubborn resentment against growing up, innate in the tomboy, had shifted to a more positive stance: the American girl did not disparage maturity but rather celebrated youth.

The American Girl in Series Novels

Long before mystery-solving Nancy Drew, one of the twentieth century's most familiar heroines, there were the *Motor Girls* (1910), *Camp Fire Girls* (1912), *Outdoor Girls* (1913), *Ruth Fielding* (1913), and *Girls of Central High* (1914). These were formulaic novels of "ordinary" girls solving mysteries and catching criminals while playing with cars, planes, and boats, or camping, hiking, and playing sports. Their favorite pastimes, as well as their daring personalities, would have marked them as tomboys in earlier times, but now such heroines signified the kind of girlhood to which American girls felt entitled or, at the least, to which they should aspire.

For both male and female adolescent readers, early twentieth-century series novels played a critical role in modeling social expectations and normative behavior. They suggested how young women and men *should* relate to one another in their newly sex-integrated culture. The series essentially function as interlacing social stories, describing to readers—many of whom would never attend college—the social interactions found in higher education. The protagonists are uniformly white, Protestant, and financially privileged, and therefore enjoy copious leisure time. Cars, boats, and planes serve them as entertainment devices and give them a certain amount of freedom from adult control. Yet within their own company of similarly privileged adolescents, they operate as examples of normal and idealized American youth. The heroine and hero are particularly idealized, with admiring students at every turn confirming that they are, indeed, effortless arbiters of that increasingly important quality: popularity. Long before films and television, series novels—along with magazines—played a significant role in defining youthful understandings of how to look and be an adolescent in America.

The central heroine exhibits some tomboy ways but differs sharply in others. As we have seen, tomboys, both in fiction and in common understanding, are singular; they are defined by *not* being like other girls. The central heroine of series fiction, by contrast, is the personification of all that a good American girl could hope to be. She is always at the center of a pack of girls who exhibit a spectrum of gendered behavior, from ultragirly to rascally boyish. The heroine of the series novel is thus a point of moderation between greater extremes. She is as courageous, frank, loyal, smart, outspoken, and devoted to physical fun as any earlier tomboy. And, like all tomboy characters before her, she dismisses superficial social values. But she is not a figure of resistance. Instead she asserts a new kind of conventional girlhood that normalizes girls taking actions and having ambitions similar to male peers. The all-American girl heroine, as one novel describes her, has a "sane and sensible way of looking at almost every mysterious happening."[5] Even in her zeal for sports she does not lose her head, reminding a friend, "It will do us good to be beaten occasionally. . . . You begin to think that you must be on the winning side all the time."[6] She is not a "funny tomboy."[7] She is brave enough to act like the tomboy, but too much of a good girl to serve as a source of humor.

Nearly all of the series read by American adolescents were produced by the publishing empire known as the Stratemeyer Syndicate, established in 1906. Series novels were the brainchild of Edward Stratemeyer, who had earned his writing chops through crafting dime novels for firms such as Beadle and Adams.[8] Indeed, Stratemeyer himself drafted or outlined many of the stories up until his death in 1930 (after which the syndicate continued using the blueprints he had laid), and it shows in the uniformity of the characters and plot development. Literally all of the stories are powered by the interactions of the adolescent protagonists as they try to solve simple mysteries.

These were among the first books marketed specifically for adolescents, and they won over their youthful audiences by showing the protagonists acting with little or no adult oversight. Indeed, this is exactly what angered many adults: series books downplayed the influence of family and emphasized the importance of adolescent social worlds. In these books adolescents are in charge, and even beloved teachers tend to have more influence over the kids than their parents.[9]

Stratemeyer had his first commercial success with *The Rover Boys* in 1899. Having honed his skills in formula publishing, he responded not by simply writing Rover sequels, but by creating a syndicate to produce similar series. The Stratemeyer Syndicate published the series books through a few different houses and used a small number of pseudonyms to stand in for dozens of real writers. Thus it became the covert entity responsible for churning out inexpensively printed, hardbound juvenile book series that did not appear at first glance to be formula fiction.[10]

Stratemeyer set up a tight outline for the books, including details on the number of pages (roughly 225), how chapters would end, the time period (contemporary) and setting, and cover price (under market value for an independently authored book).[11] The stories were intended to be entertaining but also didactic, so that they might avoid the adult disapproval that undercut dime novel consumption.[12] His didacticism was clearly not intended to shape readers' characters so much as to attract their pocket money. Thus, although his books depicted how readers might improve themselves morally, physically, and socially, they also reflected back a freedom and agency that youth wanted to see, and validated what adolescents already found appealing. For example, several of his series endorsed female athletics and outdoor recreation, contributing to a perception of popular support for such activities and thus reinforcing their acceptance in the culture. But he also pushed the envelope. For example, now that girls were camping under adult supervision in real life, Stratemeyer put out books featuring girls camping independently and solving mysteries.

Although Stratemeyer himself did not believe in such modernisms as women working in offices, he promoted them in the syndicate's books to win over female readers who were drawn to tales that empowered them as thinkers, actors, and leaders.[13] His ambivalence toward the modernizing of young women's public roles, along with his depiction of adolescents living virtually free of adult supervision, contributed to locating the books precariously between proper middle-class conventions and daring adolescent fantasies. And while Stratemeyer produced far more series for boys than for girls, Nancy Drew, whom he introduced shortly before his death in 1930, became his most popular and enduring lead character. He knew how to captivate girl readers.

Despite Stratemeyer's efforts, many adults responded to the books much as their parents had to dime novels. Boy Scout leaders were particularly inflamed by the literature because of its methods of production. In 1914 the Boy Scouts' chief librarian, Franklin Mathiews, described the effects on young readers: "As some boys read such books, their imaginations are literally 'blown-out' and they go into life as terribly crippled as though by some material explosion they had lost a hand or foot."[14] But despite such hyperbolic views, the series only multiplied—by 1920 there were almost seventy different ones—and became ever more ubiquitous.

The first series for girls, *The Motor Girls,* which was modeled on the enormously successful *Motor Boys,* must have struck nearly as much fear in the hearts of parents as it sparked fantasies in its readers. The first book, published in 1910, is an action-romance novel involving a group of wealthy adolescent boys and girls racing each other in sleek roadsters, crashing or nearly crashing on numerous occasions, and flirting madly.[15] Perhaps tellingly, the second novel in the series, *The Motor Girls on a Tour,* tones down the romance and focuses more on the independent spirit of the girls, as do subsequent girls' series. When the four heroines decide that they must go on a car trip, they immediately question whether or not to invite the boys. It is not hard to understand why such scenarios had the potential to alarm parents. Girls unchaperoned on a motor trip? Girls traveling with boys? Girls deciding on their own if they should? The book depicts unprecedented freedoms for middle- and upper-class youth.

The girls are quick to dismiss the idea of bringing along boys, with Cora (the leader) arguing, "If we had boys along . . . they would claim the glory of every spill, every skid, every upset and every 'busted tire.' We want some little glory ourselves."[16] They are not worried about propriety. Quite to the contrary, they want to solve their own problems—"claim the glory" of meeting disasters that no doubt put fear in the hearts of most Americans who, after all, were just gaining access to cars through the newly available Model T (1908). The Motor Girls are clearly budding New Women of the technical age. Regardless of their wishes, the boys show up uninvited, and so begins a long adventure rife with collisions, evil characters, and engine-tampering, true to the spirit of earlier dime novels and story papers.

Through such books girl readers, regardless of their life experience, could enjoy modern opportunities and unlikely freedoms. Series novels asserted that girls should participate in the world outside of family, and that their adolescent relationships and concerns were real and important. Through series such as the *Camp Fire Girls* and the *Outdoor Girls* they could vicariously rough it while bonding with other heroic girls. Girls showed their appreciation for such messages with their continued purchases, and series for girls proliferated in response.

The books repeatedly stress the importance of girls fulfilling their potential not as future mothers, but as individual beings. The girls of the series novels are, indeed, the personification of the American girl Alexis de Tocqueville had described nearly a century before: independent and self-regulated, trusted with a shocking level of freedom yet facing severe penalties should she take them further than intended. The heroines in these books, unlike those in earlier fiction, do not discuss impending adulthood. They function as if their only existence is in girlhood; they do not see themselves, nor are they depicted, as future women. They do not resist or complain about approaching maturity, like the tomboys of yore; they simply ignore that they will need to change. And yet, as the literary scholar Nancy Tillman Romalov notes, girls' adventure novels were a "a genre often at odds with itself, replete with contradictory impulses and convoluted narrative strategies," striving constantly to reconcile such freedoms within the patriarchal order.[17] In order to be both exciting and realistic, the novels bounced back and forth between girls on the loose and girls affirming responsibilities to school and family.

In the *Camp Fire* series, the earlier Victorian emphasis of girls sharing a spiritual bond shaped by separate spheres and homosocial relationships had clearly shifted into girls bonding over a shared pride. The series principally explores changing notions of female relationships and abilities, as few male friends appear in these novels. Again and again, the protagonists of the *Camp Fire* series marvel at how much better Camp Fire girls are than "ordinary girls" because they have found something more meaningful than superficial urban social life. Camp Fire girls principally come to the rescue of other girls—wholesome girls who face ruin because of the death or illness of a father or mother and their female inability to earn enough money to save themselves.[18]

The *Camp Fire* series was not sanctioned by the camp's organizers, perhaps because it emphasized the daring of the girls without pushing domestic ideology.[19] But Stratemeyer had his writers borrow liberally from Camp Fire guides, repeating their mottos and rules, undoubtedly to appeal to real Camp Fire girls as well as the many girls who longed to join.[20] Again the stories left behind adult guidance, and usually depicted a group of unsupervised girls on their own in the woods (or later, in town), solving mysteries or confronting social injustice. In the 1914 novel *A Camp Fire Girl's First Council Fire,* for example, a Camp Fire gathering serves as a utopian oasis for two abused runaway girls. Bessie, the blonde runaway who serves as the central character, "had never heard of the Camp Fire Girls, and the great movement they had begun, meant to do for American girls what the Boy Scout movement had begun so well for their brothers."[21] With her is Zara, the ambiguously dark runaway whose victimization at the hands of an evil farmer sets the story in motion.

Escaping through the woods, the runaways are struck dumb when they come upon a group of girls and their peer leader, Wanaka, sitting around a campfire with their hair down and dressed in ceremonial beaded robes like Native Americans. Upon seeing the two girls, Wanaka calls out, "Girls, launch the canoes! We have two guests here who haven't had any breakfast, and they're simply starving to death!" Bessie notes that most girls would fuss, "but these girls were different. They didn't talk; they did things."[22]

Upon hearing their story, Wanaka organizes the Camp Fire girls to take on the farmer, assuring Bessie and Zara, "You know that's what we are here for—to help people, and to love them and serve them."[23] Yet regardless of her language of service, Wanaka is also claiming girls' right to fight for social justice. The Camp Fire girls confront the village men, Zara is vindicated, and Bessie joins the troop.

Despite the repeated emphasis on selflessness, a female pride infuses even the earliest novels in the series and serves as the bottom note to all exploits. Assertion of female equality with males is often explicit, for within each story there is a scene that pits boys and girls against each another, with the girls ultimately impressing and surprising the boys. In another 1914 *Camp Fire* book, the ubiquitous Wanaka remarks, "Women have been taking handicaps from men too long. They got so that they think they can't do anything as well as a man. This Camp Fire movement is going to show you that that's all over and done with."[24] Wanaka is suggesting that the Camp Fire experience was forging a new kind of girlhood—an independent one that will change the relationship between the sexes.

Stories of unsupervised girls going on fanciful adventures did not present readers with a realistic template for life, but did allow them to fantasize themselves as drivers of action. Readers could choose for themselves what they wished to emulate, appropriate, or discard.[25] Romalov, who read countless letters from readers to publishers, notes that turn-of-the-century girls "showed a penchant for not only relating life to fiction but also for behaving like fictional characters." Scores of girls wrote to publishers about their communal (clubs, book sharing) and personal (self-recognition) responses to the heroines of book series.[26] Girls entertained the possibility of certain freedoms, based on reading material and this discourse of youth culture that sidestepped adult authority.

One of the notable traits of tomboys in earlier fiction is that they usually have a male sidekick, and he is often a sissy boy, as if to balance out the gender transgressions of the tomboy. By contrast, the American girl does not have a close male friend, but her group of girl friends has a parallel group of male friends. Just as girl characters serve as foils for boys in the books targeted to boys, the boys in the girls' books play the same role. Boyfriends tend to be athletes (captain of the football team is popular) and blandly agreeable, with few defining characteristics. The pack of boys, meanwhile, usually has one boy who is a bit snide, and another who is lazy or likes to eat, but for the most part they are two-dimensional, interchangeable characters. Although there are male characters with a streak of effeminacy who serve as figures of fun, the male friends are presented as solidly masculine, without a trace of the gender flexibility seen among the girls.

With the advent of the *Outdoor Girls* series, the novels began promoting equal and platonic friendships between groups of girls and boys. Betty (the lead heroine), Mollie, Grace, and Amy start a "camping and tramping club" in their hometown of Deepdale, New York, and so their families dub them the Outdoor Girls. They have adventures side by side with a group of four boys: Allen, Frank, Roy, and Will (Grace's brother). Sometimes the two groups merge to hang out in one large group, but they reflexively return to the smaller ones they belong to by gender. Aside from a few secret romantic longings, the boys and girls interact as equal and platonic friends. They are not genderless so much as equally integral to their little society.

Although one would be hard pressed to find any characters in the series novels who are fully developed, the female characters in the books targeted to girls demonstrate more depth and nuance than the male characters, even when filling formulaic roles. Betty is marked as the central heroine because she is the leader; she is fearless and instinctively knows what to do in every situation. Mollie is volatile, Amy is shy and quiet, and Grace is tall, thin, and fashionable. Betty owns the best of the earlier tomboy characteristics, while Mollie owns the ones most problematic, such as a quick temper.

A passage in the 1916 novel *The Outdoor Girls on Pine Island*, by Laura Lee Hope (a pseudonym shared by several writers, most notably those who penned the long-lived *Bobbsey Twins* series), is a good example of both the banality of the books and how they present sex-integrated society. The episode opens with the four heroines lolling around a campsite with the boys, complaining of the heat. When one of the boys remembers that they brought fishing gear, Mollie jumps up and is "all action, now that there was some definite point in view":

> She called to the others, speaking quickly.
> "We are going to catch some fish," she announced eagerly. "Or at least we are going to try to. . . . It is strange that I didn't remember before . . . about the wonderful fishing pool about a mile away."
> "A mile!" groaned Grace. "Do you mean to say that we have to walk a mile in this blazing heat?"
> "Nobody *has* to," Mollie retorted. "It's only a question of wanting to. I'm going if I have to go alone."
> "Oh, come on, Grace, be a sport," Frank coaxed."[27]

Grace gives in and reluctantly walks the mile with her friends. Once they arrive, two of the girls demand that the boys bait their hooks and one frets about damage to her shoes, before they all begin competing to see who can catch the biggest fish. In other words, they fuss like girls and rely on boys even in the midst of otherwise independent behavior.

Such a dull exchange hardly seems like an ideal way to hook new readers, but banality was apparently part of the charm of such books. The series novels typically open before any action, often with a gathering of bored youth (possibly reflecting the state of many of their readers). The lead heroine inevitably displays what would have been seen earlier as tomboy characteristics, such as candor, lack of sentiment, enthusiasm for physical challenge, and so forth. But again the central heroine's behavior is normalized by depictions of fussy, feminine girls to one side, and sloppy, boyish ones on the other. Thus the more assertive Mollie is juxtaposed with languid Grace. In earlier times Grace might have demurred in the name of feminine disinterest, but here Frank's comment asserts that such femininity is no longer admirable, and participation is central to popularity and inclusion. Yet regardless of their gender performance, *all* of the heroines presume themselves to be the equal of boys in terms of intelligence, bravery, and loyalty. Furthermore, these four heroines of the *Outdoor Girls* series travel extensively, often walking twenty miles in a day, camping alone, and dressing in uniforms reminiscent of soldiers. The fact that the girls are allowed to develop such skills was a sign that girlhood and gender boundaries were changing, even when positioned alongside conventional messages about the importance of marriage and family.[28]

Many series novels, but particularly *The Girls of Central High,* assert that healthy girls are as competitive as boys when it comes to athletics. This was a sharp move away from earlier depictions, when supporters had insisted that girls' sports were by nature cooperative, not competitive. The central heroine of the series, Laura Belding, is flanked on one side by the mischievous tomboyish character, Bobby (Clara) Hargrew, and on the other by the languid, fashionable girl, Jess Morse. To create an athletic association for the girls of Central High, Laura drafts every girl into the venture. In the first book, *The Girls of Central High; or, Rivals for All Honors* (1914), when a male friend asks Laura if it is true that the girls are "really going in for athletics," she replies tartly, "We are. Why shouldn't we? It isn't fair for you boys to have all the fun."[29] But it was not simply a matter of fun: according to the books, athletics made for better girls.

Athletics teach girls to learn self-control—exactly what tomboys struggled with in earlier domestic fictions. The narrator breaks in with comments endorsing the value of female athletics throughout, such as assuring readers that once a girl "has learned to repress her hysterical excitement and play quietly instead of boisterously," she "has learned to control her emotions. . . . Indeed, she has gained, without doubt, a balance of mind and character that will work for good not only to herself, but to others."[30] This echoes opinions abounding in the prescriptive literature of the time. For example, one journalist, Christine Herrick, in 1902 asserted in *Outdoor Magazine* that most girls are self-centered, manipulative, and overly emotional, and thus athletics teach the "average" girl "respect for others, and for herself, logic, proportion, accuracy, self-control, patience, conscientiousness, honor, moderation, and the ability to make the best of what bodily powers she possesses." Sports teach her "fairness and squareness."[31]

Sports also lead a girl away from foolish rites of femininity in which she might otherwise become ensnared. The narrator of one of the Central High novels observes, "It was much more healthful and much more wise for them to take part in sports and exercises calculated to build up muscle and mind, than to parade the streets in couples, or cliques, or to attend picture shows, or to idle their time through the big stores in emulation of the adult 'shopping fiend.'"[32]

The third book in the series, *The Girls of Central High at Basketball* (1914), depicts basketball as the center of the girls' lives with the blessings of their parents. The first few chapters set the characters and outline the benefits of basketball. One girl's beloved father states: "Loyalty. That's the kernel—loyalty. If your athletics and games don't teach you that, you might as well give 'em up. . . . The feminine sex is not naturally loyal."[33]

The central heroine is allowed the positive boyish traits, while the more boyish girl in these books is a puckish character whose chief role is to entertain. Thus even though Laura expresses many tomboy traits, Bobby is marked as the tomboy because of her love of pranks and general immaturity. The series begins with Bobby setting up a magnifying glass in her father's store window as a sly joke, which backfires when the sun causes the paper in the window display to catch fire. Laura saves the day, when all the adult men around her are dithering about what to do, by lowering the awning and blocking out the sun to put out the fire. Within two chapters, incorrigible Bobby, hamming it up for the other girls, ends up accused of starting a fire in the principal's office.[34]

Again, Laura is the loyal and courageous friend, who sticks up for Bobby against all of the others.

The nondomestic ambitions found in former tomboys were fully supported in most of these books, but in none more overtly than the *Ruth Fielding* series. Ruth, the central heroine of thirty novels published between 1913 and 1934, was clearly the prototype for Nancy Drew, complete with two girlfriends, one of whom is sloppy and boyish and the other daft and feminine. But while Nancy Drew is a rather opaque and utterly poised character who gives little sense of her worries or ambitions, Ruth Fielding openly ruminates on how she feels about conventional domestic life versus her own self-development.

Importantly, Ruth makes no apologies for her ambitions. Early in the series, for example, she is adamant about going to college. Perhaps more remarkable, in a later novel (1922) Ruth decides that she and her boyfriend, Tom, are still too young for marriage and that "she wanted to live her own life and establish herself in the great career she had got into almost by chance."[35] Love and domestic bliss were all very well—after a girl had her adventures and tested her mettle.

This attitude, of course, harkened back to sentiments expressed long before in story papers by authors such as Winnie Woodfern, and in juvenile fiction by independent authors such as Louisa May Alcott, among others. Indeed the ground for such series was broken first by the story papers and dime novels, as well as series novels by independent authors. But the juvenile series novels of the early twentieth century were an altogether different phenomenon. Wanting girls to develop to their full potential before marriage was not a new sentiment, but putting it in the mouth of a mainstream character was wholly modern.

When the United States entered World War I in 1917, the books began openly celebrating girls preparing to go into service as soldiers, even though there was no actual way for women to do so. In Irene Elliott Benson's *Camp Fire Girls Mountaineering; or, Overcoming all Obstacles* (1918), for example, the girls give up Indian dress for military uniforms. They were supposedly training to become nurses, but they drill as if they are going to the battlefront: "The girls actually drilled with guns, and they would shoot those guns with all the grim fatality of so many boys." Still, preparedness was in the air, and "the girls voted to a—a—girl (I almost said man, for they were as brave as men in many respects) to take up military drill and tactics two hours a week as part of their curriculum," the narrator recounts.[36] The narrator's "slip" suggests it is admirable, not scandalous, for girls to be mistaken for young men in certain instances.

Despite the fact that the nation was in thrall to a pronatalist, positive eugenics agenda that elevated childbearing and rearing as the highest potential a girl could reach, the series books emphasize the ambitions of girls living up to their present, rather than their future, potential. Marriage was frequently noted as something to be embraced eventually, but only after the girl explored the world on her own. Indeed, after the protagonist Ruth Fielding fell out of popularity upon getting married, the Stratemeyer Syndicate decided that heroines must remain adolescent and unmarried (if not entirely uncoupled).[37]

Consumerism and the "Passing of the Tomboy"

The American public also found the tomboy predilections of the adventure-loving American girl illustrated in images at every turn in popular culture during the late 1890s and early 1900s. In 1897 Edward Bok, editor of *Ladies' Home Journal,* warned that "it is a very fine line which divides unconventionality in a girl's deportment from a certain license and freedom of action, which is so fraught with danger—a very, very fine line." But every month of that year his own magazine published images of girls engaged in outdoor or athletic activities. It became typical for the magazine to feature girls' activities out of doors, giving them advice such as "how to dress, what sorts of sanitary problems might arise, what food to take, how to pitch a tent."[38] The doubt expressed by Bok—that girls could enjoy "freedom of action" without courting danger—was largely drowned out by a proliferation of images in the media, which in turn normalized the agency he found worrisome.

By the turn of the century, the equation of outdoors, adolescent girls, and consumer products was hard to escape in popular culture. These images coincided with articulations that "tomboy" was a term passing out of usage, as is suggested in the 1898 editorial described at the beginning of this chapter. Lines were becoming blurred. Tomboys still dressed like other young women, and prescriptive literature urged young women to act like tomboys. Meanwhile, popular culture increasingly asserted that the healthiest American girls had been called tomboys in the past, and questioned why the term was still useful.

The new technology of personal cameras played a symbolic role in pop-ularizing the outdoor American girl. In *On the Trail: An Outdoor Book for Girls* (1915), Lina and Adelia Belle Beard devote a chapter to discussing the importance of using a camera in nature, noting that "you will be only half-equipped if you go without a camera and note-book."[39] As Roland Barthes once observed, cameras are "clocks for seeing." Thus through photographs women could retain reminders of their girlhood dreams, and put them aside when turning to adult responsibilities.[40] The camera was a modern form of magic, much like the girl herself, able to capture a moment at its passing.

Kodak launched an ad campaign depicting American girls on the go—traveling, camping, romping—with cameras to document the moment. The campaign helped turn such girls into symbols of modern life. With their poufy topknots, confident demeanor, and outdoor predilections, these girls echo a visual stereotype first made popular by the illustrator Charles Dana Gibson in *Life* magazine, and later by Harrison Fisher and Howard Chandler Christy.[41] Nearly every model wears an ankle-length white skirt topped by a blouson white shirtwaist, with a loosened string tie, all of which was clothing associated with college girls and the new middle-class occupations for women, such as office work and teaching. Although there are exceptions, the young women are usually depicted alone, either taking a picture or posing for one. The girls in these advertisements tend to revel in innocent outdoor pleasures; sometimes they are demure, but also just as likely to gaze assertively at the viewer. Submission, one of the most celebrated and elaborately explained female virtues of earlier periods, plays no part.[42]

But as the literary scholar Peter Stoneley cautions, "consumerism was and is an especially effective means of discipline and control precisely because it seems to liberate and empower."[43] Kodak's advertising campaign illustrates this principle by featuring fresh-faced laughing girls as a tender symbol of the new freedoms allowed through modern technology, while also suggesting that the freedoms documented by the camera would be fleeting. The advertisements came out at the height of the suffrage move-ment, and more and more girls were going to college or taking modern jobs in department stores or offices. The clothing of the young women suggested that the middle class was now a social class in which young women now enjoyed unprecedented liberties (much like elite girls before them). Kodak joined a much larger marketing movement that presented, as the historian Carolyn Kitch points out, "outdoor life—true leisure in an industrial era—as proof of social status."[44] Real freedom, according to these ads, was about personal choice and leisure time. The liberty taken up wholeheartedly by the girl at the center of each frame suggests that young women could now follow their own inclinations openly, but the moment must be captured, for it will pass.

For example, one Kodak ad from around 1908 features a slightly disheveled young woman sitting on a hillside, with her profile to the viewer and a cheerful knowing grin aimed beyond the frame. She sits on the ground, slouched comfortably over a camera delicately balanced in the cradle of her hands, in the safety of her lap. Her manner and haphazardly upswept hair suggest a girl who has just sat down to catch her breath after running. "To every out-door hobby," the caption beneath her promises, "to every delight of nature, to the very spirit of Spring itself, there is an added charm for those who KODAK." She is not rough, but she is unselfconscious and messy—caught up in the joy of the moment and unconcerned with

FIGURE 7: In this Kodak ad, a disheveled and happy young woman relaxes on a hillside, her delighted attention on something outside of the frame. Vivid and relaxed, this girl suggests a modern version of young womanhood with social life at its center. Courtesy Sallie Bingham Collection, Duke University.

guarding her self-presentation. She is inward-looking, and in that sense beyond social constraints.

An advertisement from around 1910 presents an unusually assertive girl who turns her camera on the viewer. She is the one in charge, and her bold gaze acknowledges her daring. It is all in good fun, and she takes pictures knowing that time is fleeting. The caption below reads: "On the bright days I Kodak; on the rainy days I print these velox postals—that makes all the days bright." Other ads suggest a similar spirit of fleeting fun, depicting single women traveling, sightseeing, or enjoying the outdoors. One advertisement features a young woman perched on the narrow edge of her suitcase, consumed by examining her camera. She appears to be traveling solo, but with a camera a woman can travel alone without being entirely alone—the camera will remember for her. Kodak promoted the idea of a modern young woman in charge of herself—moving as a single human being across space and time, responsible for her own actions and protection—something not allowed to respectable girls of earlier periods.

All out-doors invites your Kodak.

Let Kodak keep a picture record of your every outing. There's a new pleasure in every phase of photography—pleasure in the taking, pleasure in the finishing, but most of all, pleasure in possessing pictures of the places and people that you are interested in.

KODAKS, $5.00 to $100.00.   BROWNIES (they work like Kodaks), $1.00 to $12.00.

EASTMAN KODAK COMPANY,

ROCHESTER, N. Y., *The Kodak City.*

FIGURE 8: This ad shows a young woman looking straight at the viewer with her camera aimed, demonstrating that she can see as well as be seen. Courtesy Sallie Bingham Collection, Duke University.

The advertisements are devoid of domestic symbolism; none of them depicts a woman taking a picture of her modern kitchen or evidence of her cake-baking prowess. Even the ads featuring young children did not include an adult. Kodak chose to celebrate youth, not motherhood. Focusing on idealized, relaxed young women, the ads underline the impermanence of this moment. A young woman might revel in her freedoms for a time. Once she is married and mothering, these pictures will remain to remind her of her time in the sun.

One of the ads most suggestive of the feminist freedoms suggested by the campaign shows a young woman paddling her own canoe underneath the line "Oh for a camera!" Grinning saucily in her white shirtwaist over skirts filling the canoe, she is young and carefree, and she wields her own paddle. Her laughter invites the viewer in on the fun. The ad underlines the importance of youth and memory: Young women, your time is now. Seize it with a camera. Kodak's campaign centered on the idea that such a figure represented modernity, but also that young womanhood was a time of freedom and self-assertion that would pass and needed marking.

The girls in these ads look like tomboys of earlier periods, who nearly always dressed in skirts and were marked as tomboys mostly by their

FIGURE 9: In this 1908 Kodak ad a lively, laughing young woman paddles her own canoe, and one gets the sense from the caption that she has a friend nearby, sharing her sense of fun and the desire to document youthful adventures. Courtesy Sallie Bingham Collection, Duke University.

untidiness and enjoyment of physical sports. Now, what thrilled the tomboy is simply expected of healthy girls. The fun-loving, rapscallion adolescent is the American girl, able to sell consumer products with her smile.

Kodak's advertising campaign capitalized on the many changes in the lives of America's young female citizens. College and professional training were becoming more common, middle-class as well as working-class girls came to expect adolescence as a time of freedom to explore romantic relationships and work lives, and technology promised to change daily life at a pace never before seen, transforming household labor in ways that they hoped would set them free. Many of girls' barriers to the freedom and autonomy enjoyed by boys seemed to be disappearing.

According to the author of the 1898 *Harper's Bazaar* editorial quoted at the beginning of this chapter, the "modern young girl-on-wheels" owes her new freedoms to the tomboys of yore, as she "moves joyously, gracefully, fair to see, along the pathway blazed for her through the jungles of conservatism by the pioneer tomboy of the past." The author credits outdoor life and athletics, the activities promoted by the series novels, with the creation of the American girl: "The girl of the period far surpasses her predecessor in staying power. All this outdoor life means vigor, grace, and buoyancy. It is a fine thing to watch a girl athlete. She is bewitching."[45]

The author accurately observes that the earlier tomboy designation sprang from past gender norms that were far too rigid for children and youth. Because society is becoming more realistic about girls, there is no longer any need for a label suggesting that sedentary girls were the norm and active girls the aberration. But the author also celebrates tomboys as a beloved relic of the past because society at the time refused to recognize girl's physicality and sense of fun as equally intrinsic to girls as to boys. The writer notes: "Once in a while you may meet ladies of fifty or seventy or ninety, gracious and silver-haired, young-hearted, and with a lively interest in the thoughts and pursuits of all girl-kind, who will tell you in sweet voices that they were called 'great tomboys' when they were little girls. And if they recount to you their maddest, merriest pranks, their wildest and most daring adventures, you will find that these were commonplace."[46] Most girls were tomboys in the past, too—but that reality went against the social conventions of the period.

Beginning with this editorial in 1898 (widely reprinted in 1902), articles began appearing every few years questioning the validity of the term "tomboy," all the way up to the present day. It is not surprising that the public began to ask if the term was still useful. After all, what had made the tomboy stand out before now made her a popular and healthy girl, not a misfit. Did calling a girl a tomboy mean anything at all, when she was surrounded by other like-minded girls? "Tomboy" had long been a term to single out one girl for behaving differently, but now many girls were taking up tomboy pastimes.

Advertising overlapped with these editorials. For example, in 1901 a piece titled "The Tomboy: A Kind of Girl Who Became Extinct in the Last Century" appeared in newspapers from Oregon to North Carolina over a period of several months. It begins, "It's a far cry from the sampler-working maiden of a hundred years ago to the athletic girl of today. The girl of a hundred years ago did not dare to be original in thought or action, or if she did was at once stamped as eccentric and strong-minded." By claiming that the tomboy is a relic of the past, the writer emphasizes how much more advanced girls are in 1901. It flatters contemporary readers: girls in the past were passive—sewing maidens, fearful and cowed—but girls of the present are active agents of change and original thinking. In the past, if a girl "revolted from the cup and the ball . . . she was invariably set down as a 'regular tomboy.' That was a familiar term only a few years ago. Now one hardly ever hears it." Indeed, at the turn of the century, the writer asserts, "girls are encouraged to row and ride, to run and roam, in the interest of their own physical well being, and for the general advantage of the mothers of the future," for "such girls make the healthiest and happiest of women."[47]

This piece looked like an article, but it was not; it was an advertisement for a health tonic to regularize menstruation. In other words, the term "tomboy" was being used to sell the idea that contemporary attitudes toward young women were radically advanced from those of the short-sighted Victorians—that "tomboy" was a relic of the past because now Americans recognized that what had been hitherto ostracized was in truth the sign of a healthy young woman.

In fact, the tomboy label did persist, but its most obvious parameters changed while leaving the core identity intact. Focusing on boyish pastimes and activities had served to mask the most consistent difference between tomboys and other girls: a sense of one's core identity not suiting the dominant cultural narrative. In that sense, activities that had marked the tomboy were less important than her determination to resist others changing her spirit. The tomboy could never become mainstream because that identity hinged on her moving against the current.

We do know that, despite articles repeatedly questioning the validity of the term, its use continued to flourish in the consumer world. Even the most casual glance through period newspapers reveals the tomboy used as a style, a type, and a role. Mary Pickford was rocketing to early cinematic stardom for her tomboy roles, and she is only the most well remembered of many other popular actresses called tomboys for their work on stage and in nickelodeon and silent films.[48] In 1909 Mabel Normand, one of the most prominent actresses in silent films, played the lead in *The Tomboy* and reprised that role in 1912 in *Tomboy Bessie*. From 1910 to 1915 the British director Cecil Hepworth put out a film series featuring "Tilly the Tomboy" as she engaged in various adventures.[49] In 1919 "Tomboy Taylor," a comic strip that ran through the 1920s, debuted in newspapers from the *Pawtucket Times* in Rhode Island to the *Seattle Times*.[50] Stories of tomboys (real and fictional) increased in number, and hit songs like "My Tomboy Girl" (1905) and "Daddy's Little Tomboy Girl" (1908) found their way onto parlor pianos.[51] And at the same time, proponents of the modern playground movement became more vocal about the importance of raising girls as tomboys.[52]

But the parameters of what made a tomboy, and what was included in that label, changed at the turn of the century and beyond. Tomboys who had emerged as popular cultural figures in the 1860s, such as Jo March and Gypsy Breynton, had struggled mightily with volatile tempers and against their internal impulses and desires. They slowly and reluctantly relinquished the sense of self cultivated through girlhood freedoms in an effort to please elders and society by picking up the yoke of womanhood, with its attendant acceptance and even celebration of subordination to the rights and wills of men. But by the turn of the century, idealized American girls were no longer feeling the weight of those expectations, but rather the imperative to cultivate one's self in the service of middle-class, white motherhood. "Tomboy" became a positive term in the sense of self-assertive girls, and in the process all-American girls became interchangeable with earlier tomboys.

But the American girl, while she displayed a certain aura of "American independence," did not embody the tomboy's resistance to convention, and for that reason tomboys as a concept and an identity would persist in slightly different manifestations. Tomboys took on different shapes as attention to sexuality and the rise of consumerism altered both awareness and performance of self. "Tomboy" remained as a label to identify a girl with a spirit of resistance at the core of her identity. It was not enough to play sports, go camping, and fish—all traits earlier designated to set the tomboy apart. Now the tomboy came down to what had always been there: a sense of her as a misfit. A square peg of a girl who, for whatever reason, could not and would not be pounded into a round hole.

But the spirit of the 1898 article was correct even if the central argument was not: all-American girls did now embody the traits and enjoy pastimes hitherto associated with tomboys. Girls were now going to college, pursuing careers, playing sports, wearing the new mode of clothing called "sportswear," and expressing ambition with pride and community support. Things had changed for middle-class white girls, and for many, many other girls across the nation, particularly in urban areas.

The irony is that these articles appeared even as women were still fighting for the right to be treated as social, cultural, legal, and political equals. In other words, the tomboy, who once served as an assertion of modern progress, becomes the symbol of old-fashioned myopia. Writers evoke the tomboy to argue that girls and boys, men and women, are now so equal that "tomboy" has become a useless term. Male prerogatives and pastimes are now gender-neutral, so the term "tomboy" as a girl taking on the rights of boys makes no contemporary sense. Her supposed "passing" is used to make the present look more modern.

But without that spirit of rebellion, the American girl was not the tomboy. The need for a term for a girl who behaved with boyish freedoms had sprung naturally from binary gender norms that normal girls found impossible to fulfill. But even now, with the gender norms for youth relaxing, "tomboy" still persisted as a necessary term. There were still girls confused by and resisting the gender restrictions assigned to them, even in this supposedly more liberal culture. Allison Miller notes in her study of early twentieth-century self-described tomboys that many of them "had believed that their similarity to boys extended right to their very bodies: they acknowledged that girl bodies and boy bodies were anatomically different, but they detected enough similarities that differences did not matter." Puberty was therefore particularly disorienting for these girls. For them, tomboy identity coincided with their understanding of the gendered body and sexuality. The American girl, with her easy acceptance of where she fit within the social world, would not serve as a suitable replacement.[53]

But this shift does complicate what "tomboy" would come to mean in the new twentieth century. There were, after all, more "tomboys" than ever in popular culture, but what the word described was changing. Many starlets called themselves tomboys or, conversely, denied that they were tomboys, as did female athletes. Female aviators readily embraced the tomboy label. Society women were in a universe all their own, slipping in and out of the term as it suited them. Meanwhile, newspapers frequently carried stories of former European queens and other royalty who had been tomboys as girls, as well as stories of tomboy criminals. "Tomboy" could still mean a boisterous young girl or an adolescent struggling to understand why her body defined her choices, but within the media it was becoming a term applied to adults as well, unlike the earlier "mannish woman," which was unambiguously derogatory.

In 1917 yet another article titled "Passing of the Tomboy" noted, "She is the girl they used to call a tomboy. They don't do it anymore." Out of her rough-and-tumble girlhood, she has emerged instead as "young Miss America," and the author emphasizes that it is not her social class or dress that sets her apart, but her manner. "She walks with confidence. Her front of self reliance has been known to merge into assertiveness." Yes, "she was the Tomboy of yesterday. What has happened to her? Oh nothing. She has just grown up. She can still kick higher than any young man of her acquaintance. But she doesn't." In fact, the author muses at the end, "something seems to have happened to the tomboy crop. Either the genus has unhappily ceased to exist or the characteristics have become so common that they have ceased to be distinguishing. Perhaps that is it."[54]

But the genus could not cease to exist, because both in real life and in commercial culture there was clearly still a need for girls behaving outside of expected behavior—especially as the New Woman flourished and evolved into the modern woman. Indeed, as time went on, tomboys increasingly served to explain the origins of forward-thinking women. The American girl now resembled the tomboy, but the tomboy as a cultural figure remained one of resistance and singular thinking that transcended sex.

7

Tomboys as Retrospective

Americans editorials began stating that there was no longer a need for the term "tomboy" as early as the 1890s and have continued to the present day, and yet the more the term is said to be "no longer needed," the more it is used in popular culture. This surprising paradox is accompanied by another one: grown women looking back claim they were tomboys in their youth, but girls rarely refer to themselves in the present as tomboys. At its heart, the word "tomboy" has consistently signified difference; tomboys were perceived as misfits who actively resisted their assigned gender roles. But as we've seen in the preceding chapters, there were varying ways that this difference has been (and arguably still is) interpreted and valued. The tomboy signifiers of sports, pranks, rowdy outdoor fun, and humor were ways to recognize the tomboy, but only as a surface behavior that hinted at the depths below. At its heart, tomboy identity was about feeling out of sync with the culture, in part because gender norms were too extreme to fit well with everyone, but also because for many girls femininity felt unnatural and undesirable. In other words, they were fine with being *girls,* just not passive, fearful, quiet, overly sensitive followers.

Diaries, memoirs, biographies, and autobiographical fiction suggest that the two paradoxes are linked. From the onset of its usage for boyish girls in the 1860s, "tomboy" was not a term that girls personally embraced, even as tomboys became empowering figures within print culture. Later, when the tomboy had been established as the American girl, and women tried to describe their girlhood, the term implied a difference they now admired. Analyzing how tomboys are presented in texts of "real" girls and adult women looking back on their girlhoods, it becomes clear that when used in the present tense, "tomboy" in this early period could be stifling, but when put into the past tense, it became liberating.

In their written records girls rarely referred to themselves as tomboys. Nearly all of them record joy in tomboyish play, so while a disgruntled adult or archrival may have occasionally called them out as tomboys, they clearly saw themselves as ordinary girls, not social outliers. And, like the tomboys of domestic fiction, they often expressed a jaundiced view of what lay ahead for them as adult women. Many expressed discomfort with the imperative to marry, some because marriage was disempowering to women and others because boys (other than brothers) were foreign in their lives. Passionate love for other girls was pretty much expected of these adolescent girls who had little contact with boys, and many expressed a deep love for or infatuation with other girls. If they did express dismay over being unlike others, it usually stemmed from being overwhelmed by their own emotions (a common phenomenon for adolescents, but each girl treated her own insecurities as unheard of among other girls). And most of them engaged in rowdy play along with the other girls, as one member of a larger group. In short, their view of appropriate girl behavior was far broader than anything depicted in print culture.

Perhaps responding to an external view of Victorian girlhood, retrospective pieces by women recounting girlhoods of the period, such as autobiographies, memoirs, and fictionalized autobiography, frequently use the term "tomboy" toward the beginning of the text. While the word may truly describe the misfit identity they felt as girls, it is also just as likely served as a mechanism for squaring memories of their active girlhoods with contemporary views of Victorian culture as narrow and repressive. But it is equally possible that as adults they could look back fondly on their tomboy girlhoods because the things that had made them feel like misfits as children had become celebrated by the time they recorded their memories.

Biographers of famous women growing up in that period are most fond of the term. They typically use tomboy origins to explain how their subject found the courage to resist convention and choose a life of public work over private marriage. These later biographies of such women are also where one is most likely to find tomboy identity tied to later adult lesbian identity, beginning in the late twentieth century, even though tomboy behavior or self-identity is not reliably expressive of a girl's sexual feelings.

In Their Own Words

In 1871, fourteen-year-old Minnie Thomas identified so deeply with America's beloved tomboy heroine from *Little Women* that she inked "The Journal Kept by Jo March" in large emphatic script across her diary. Thomas would grow up to be known as M. Carey Thomas, dean and later president of Bryn Mawr College, founder of the Bryn Mawr School for Girls, and a tireless advocate for equal standards of education regardless of gender. She also chose not to marry, and eventually became romantically involved with other women.[1] In other words, she not only identified with the archetypal tomboy heroine and expressed disdain for everything feminine, she also grew to fit the profile of the kind of great woman who would later harken back to a tomboy girlhood.

Her identification with Jo March is not surprising; Thomas's diary is exactly the kind that Jo would have kept—full of curiosity, pranks, love of family, and disavowals of feminine absurdities. For example, there was the time she decided to try her hand at anatomy after reading John Henry Pepper's *The Boy's Playbook of Science* (1869). After convincing her cousin Bessie that they needed a skeleton to observe, they went through the grisly work of obtaining one from an unfortunate mouse. Things went awry, and the hard-won skeleton ended up smashed before it could be properly examined. Thomas noted that when Bessie recounted the story to her Quaker father, "he looked very grave and said 'thee is losing all thy feminine traits, I [am] afraid.'" Thomas concluded dryly, "I haven't got any to lose as I greatly prefer cutting up mice to sewing worsted."[2] If anyone would embrace the tomboy identity, one would expect it to be a girl like Minnie Thomas.

Yet in her journal Thomas rejected "tomboy" alongside "ladylike." Both terms were judgments used to curb girls' behavior. Thomas also disagreed with the narrow set of behaviors considered appropriate for adolescent girls: "Girls never can have any fun. They can't play or else everybody thinks they're tomboys, and I haven't had one nice game since I came home, and I am nearly fifteen, and each year I have less fun and am more grown up. . . . I ain't good and I ain't bad, I ain't a *tomboy* nor I ain't *ladylike,* and I'm everything that's disagreeable, and I do want a little excitement."[3]

Thomas was pushing hard against the walls of conventional womanhood closing in on her. Why did being a girl place her in such a narrow space between female masculinity and ultra-femininity? She longed to stretch her wings intellectually, physically, and emotionally. Thomas stridently proclaimed her views in a school oratory address: "If a girl gets tired of doing nothing and joins in some of her brothers' games, jumps a few fences, climbs a few trees, she is called, oh horrible name, a 'tomboy.' She is not allowed to hunt. She is told that such expressions as 'jolly' are 'shocking' and 'unladylike.' If she whistles, she is reminded, 'Whistling girls and crowing hens never come to good ends.'"[4] Thomas found such constrictions intolerable. She wanted to have *fun* and she wanted to go to college to become a doctor. Thomas identified with Jo March but rejected the tomboy label because it suggested that many of her favorite pursuits belonged to boys and must be outgrown.

Thomas presents a vivid illustration of the uneven relationship between tomboys in print culture and girls' experiences. "Tomboy" suggested that outdoor play was natural to boys, and therefore unnatural for girls, even though we know from diaries that tree climbing, jumping fences, and hunting were activities that girls had undertaken long before the tomboy label became popular.[5] Thomas resisted the term because, despite its increasingly positive gloss in the world of print, "tomboy" at its core suggested that her sense of self was aberrant.

As cultural phenomena journals and diaries have their own history, from work logs and commonplace books to what we now think of as private spaces for introspection. For American girls, diary keeping took off in the nineteenth century, with middle-class parents and educators encouraging it as a form of self-cultivation.[6] Sometimes such diaries also became a site of exchange between the girl and a parent or teacher.[7] Many times girls used them as a kind of written performance for parents, teachers, and themselves. Indeed, some seem to have served as records for the family as well as the girl. One unnamed Mississippi girl in 1877, for example, recorded events of her days selling watermelons or cutting sugar cane between the pages of an old ledger used by other members of the family.[8] In the postbellum period, many girls also began using diaries more as they do today, as safe spaces for working out emotions and expressing grand ambitions. For all of these reasons, while diaries are our only means of hearing from the girls themselves, they are highly imperfect historical sources for uncovering a view of girl culture.

Regardless of their drawbacks and differences, however, their diaries and journals make it clear that these young women did not resemble the girls of didactic fiction. And girls themselves could sniff out unrealistic female characters. In 1870, for example, sixteen-year-old Julia Newberry wrote, "I have just been reading 'Lucy Howard's Journal' by Mrs. Sigourny [i.e., Lydia Huntley Sigourney], it presents such a contrast to mine. Her life was so quiet, day after day, year in & year out. . . . She had evidently a great deal of book knowledge, but seems lacking in what young girls almost always possesses, namely, fun, humour, sarcasm & enthusiasm. I don't think any young girl ever wrote such a journal." The details of Lucy Howard's fictional diary were, in fact, lifted from Sigourney's own diary; it was the serious, sedate quality of Lucy's personality that made her an obvious fabrication to Newberry's mind.[9]

Although these girls sometimes complained about pressures to be lady-like, they were far more likely to fret about their perceived failure to be "good." In their private writings they did all of the things that the published world claimed of tomboys, but since they typically engaged in such activities as part of girl culture, they did not see their behavior as having anything to do with boys. Girls recorded the endless pleasures of sledding, hunting, fishing, playing ball, playing pranks, reading popular fiction, and dreaming of fame—alongside the more expected details of visiting, being sick, going to school, and eating. Real girls were far more eager to downplay singularity, and not comfortable adopting a term thrust upon them by adults.

Alice Stone Blackwell never claimed to be a tomboy, but her lively personal journals reveal a youthful female society that reveled in physical fights, passionate crushes on other girls, and elaborate pranks. Alice was the only child of the famous abolitionist and women's rights advocates Henry Blackwell and Lucy Stone (and niece of several other prominent Blackwell women), and thus we have to assume that she grew up with a completely different sense of gender parameters than most other girls. Yet according to her finely detailed daily record, Blackwell was rarely at the margins of her girl world, but at the center—and well surrounded.

Blackwell frequently recounts "duels" and other colorful fights and pranks with classmates at the all-girls Harris Grammar School in the Dorchester section of Boston. For example, in February 1872 she notes: "A battle royal took place at recess between us girls, each having taken the name of some English or American General of the Revolution. Those who had muffs used them as weapons; Sadie had none; she was Burgoyne; Hattie Burditt was Howe; I was Clinton, to be on their side; Maggie Whitton was Washington. The fight ended with a general stampede at the end of recess."[10] In print culture such behaviors would be beyond the pale, but duels and battles are simply Blackwell's girl culture. She never apologizes for her behavior or suggests that she is not a proper girl—nor does she report being scolded by adults for rough behavior.

Although depictions of boys actively shaped depictions of girls as their opposites, girls tended to engage in activities all along the gender spectrum. According to diaries and memoirs alike, girls' lives were a balance of inside and outside, work and play, public ambition and domestic consumption. The emphasis in public culture on the differences between boys and girls left out an important detail: girls enjoyed both sedentary indoor games and rowdy outdoor games; they valued intellectual stimulation and education but *also* entertainment afforded by parties, shopping, and callers. In this sense, girls had more gender freedom than their brothers, who were expected to eschew anything related to girls in their ongoing effort to enact masculinity. In her study of elite white southern girls of the antebellum period, Anya Jabour notes that girls' ability to enjoy both inside and outside pursuits was what set them apart from male and enslaved playmates, and gave them a way to enjoy the pastimes of youth while also preparing for their adult racial and gender roles.[11] The same could be said about girls in other periods and parts of the country. Messages throughout the culture told them that society preferred docile girls, but when it came down to daily real life, they saw rowdy behavior as an expression of youth. Their parents may have scolded them for being overly exuberant, but there is little evidence of that in the diaries.

Quite the opposite, in fact; both diaries and letters suggest that most families expected them to play outdoors. In 1865 sixteen-year-old Jeannette Gilder's brother Richard wrote: "Dear Wench— . . . What are your winter sports? What about ice and snow and skates[?]."[12] Likewise, in 1875 Marion Boyd Allen spent blissfully active days at her family's summer lodgings in New Hampshire: "I rowed for as much as a mile down the lake. As soon as we came in from rowing went out in a yacht and sailed for a long time. In evening went pickerel fishing, but we only caught one pickerel."[13] Girls' fathers, brothers, and uncles readily took them into the woods for hunting and fishing, and included them in games.

If girls did not comment in their diaries about the struggle to sit still, they did fret about their inability to be "good" and learn greater self-control, particularly the need to suppress anger. Part of this may be that many girls approached diary keeping in the way described by Annie Ware Winsor in 1882: "to help me remember my faults, and my convictions upon all important matters."[14] Common was the sentiment expressed by Lucy Breckinridge: "My good qualities, if I have any, are so hidden by the bad ones that I am afraid Ma has nothing to comfort her about me."[15] Charlotte Forten Grimké, the daughter of an African American abolitionist couple, wrote upon turning seventeen: "My birthday—How much I feel to-day my own utter significance. It is true the years of my life are few. But have I improved them as I should have done? No! I feel grieved and ashamed to think how very little I know of what is really good and useful."[16] But while girls almost uniformly express angst over their inability to govern their thoughts and feelings, they tend to record events like "went sledding" and "fished all day" without any need to label it. Indeed, like another diarist, Kathie Gray, they reveled in the strength of their "tomboy muscles," or, like Grimké, proudly put on bloomers and climbed the tallest tree.[17]

But if few diarists called themselves tomboys, they certainly complained about the prospect of becoming a lady. Eleanor Agnes Lee confided to her journal in 1854, "What a different creature I am this year. In one year I have learnt & experienced a great deal. I feel differently too; young as I am I must sit up & talk & walk as a young lady and be constantly greeted with ladies do this & that & think so all as if I was twenty."[18] When Kathie Gray returned to town life in 1877, she groused, "Preston [Ohio] is quite a little city and one must keep so proper and not romp much or you'll be called a Tomboy. It's awful how ladylike a thirteen year old girl must be!"[19]

Alongside entries about adorable babies and saintly mothers, diarists were consistently dubious about marriage. Despite frequently admiring their parents, the subordination required by marriage struck most diarists as distinctly worrisome. Lucy Breckinridge bitterly noted in 1862, "A woman's life after she is married, unless there is an immense amount of love, is nothing but suffering and hard work. I never saw a wife and mother who could spend a day of unalloyed happiness and ease."[20] In 1882 seventeen-year-old Annie Ware Winsor was similarly skeptical about the supposed advantages of marriage: "I think not withstanding all the talk about the incompleteness of an unmarried woman, it is the unmarried man who is most incomplete. He needs more than we realize. . . . A woman unmarried can, much more easily than a man, find her way into a home or make one for herself." Later she remarked, "How infinitely better a loving helpful life without a mate—free to think and feel and do—not cramped."[21] Young Louisa May Alcott wrote of her mother, "I often think what a hard life she has had since she married,—so full of wondering and all sorts of worry!"[22] And after studying the writings of St. Paul in Sunday school, Kathie Gray declared, "Journal I have got to be an old maid!! Yes, —sad as that will be I've made up my mind this afternoon." Indeed, she and her friend Sunny were so certain of their conviction that they took time to write it into their family Bibles. Gray declared that only a "Namby Pamby" would suffer to follow the commands of St. Paul.[23]

Several girls also struggled with the social imperative of heterosexual unions taking precedence over the deep love they had for female friends, and some of them took it further, and pondered if they were really meant to be male. Lucy Breckinridge declared, "I wish I was a man! I would make a wife so happy. She should never repent having married me." Throughout her diary of 1862–64, Breckinridge careens from flirtation or near-engagement with one man to another, even as she declares her distaste for marriage. In 1864 she confessed, "Jennie Caldwell and I are really in love with each other. I wish I could love Mr. Bassett as I love her. There was a mistake made about me by Mother Nature. She gave me a man's heart. I fall so desperately in love with girls and do not care a straw for gentleman."[24] Likewise, Frances Willard fell deeply in love with her friend Mary Bannister, only to watch Bannister marry Willard's brother Oliver. Soon she and her entire family were pulled into her despair over Willard's inability to love her male suitor as much as her friend. Abjectly, she wrote, "I know—no other woman of whom I ever heard would feel as I do," and later resigned herself to being "tormented with the abnormal love & longing of a woman for a woman."[25]

Although few took the socially prescribed emotional shift as hard as Willard did, such deep love for another girl is echoed with joy or pain in countless journals and diaries, from the 1872 diaries of Alice Blackwell of Massachusetts and May Williams of New Orleans, to Marion Taylor of Los Angeles in 1913. Crushes on other girls seem to have been expected among the white middle class and elites—until a mature girl failed to embrace heterosexuality, and then her love for other girls had the potential to become pathological.

It is not until the 1880s that girls appear to have adopted the tomboy label for themselves, demonstrating that some girls now saw "tomboy" as a moniker worth earning. In chapter 4 we met fourteen-year-old Emma Sonedecker, who in 1880 wrote to an Ohio newspaper that after she got her hair shingled, "Pa calls me his little 'tom boy,' but I am quite proud of that name."[26] Emma had plenty of like-minded company. Less than a decade after Minnie Thomas disavowed the term as punitive, girls like Emma were embracing it. Indeed, beginning in the 1880s the United States became fairly overrun with self-proclaimed tomboys both on and off the printed page. And now *adults* were encouraging tomboy behavior. For example, Lurline Hatton Warner wrote to the *Southern Cultivator* in 1887, "I am a Tom-boy, or at least mother and father say so; and father says he is glad of it."[27] By the turn of the century, popular culture had reached a conclusion: it was indeed a good thing for a girl to act a bit like a boy.

Looking Back at Girlhood

In the late nineteenth century, biographies of famous American women came into vogue. These sources, though based in truth, depicted a different sense of how girls saw their less-than-feminine activities. In memoirs and autobiographies, the subject is acutely aware of her differences from other girls and sees herself as having a more boyish sensibility. In biographies, writers employ the tomboy identity to explain how the subject came to transcend the perspectives of most women. In autobiographies and memoirs, the authors recall tomboy girlhoods as a way to assert that they were different from other girls from the outset because they possessed a more masculine spirit.

Our Famous Women, a compilation of female biographies written by well-known female authors, provides a comprehensive example of the kinds of tomboy girlhoods attached to famous women. Lucy Larcom writes of Clara Barton, founder of the American Red Cross, as the product of an untamed country childhood. The young Barton was "blessed with outdoor freedom and indoor comfort and peace, such as . . . going through wild snow-drifts or summer sunshine two miles to school, playing on the hillsides, wading in the brooks, or scampering across her father's fields on any untamed pony she could find."[28] Lucia Gilbert Runkle credits the mother of Elizabeth and Emily Blackwell, pioneering female doctors, with putting them on their unconventional path by promoting tomboys as ideal girls. Runkle describes Elizabeth Blackwell as masculine in body as well as ambition, much to the pride of her family. Blackwell's brother brags that "when Elizabeth chooses she is more than a match for the best of us at wrestling or at lifting, and carries us about as she likes."[29]

Readers who chafed at the inferiority accorded to girls might take solace in the lifelong struggle of the celebrated activist Elizabeth Cady Stanton with her conservative father. Upon the death of her only brother, her father mourned, "O my daughter, I wish you were a boy!" Young Elizabeth answered, "Then I will be a boy, and will do all my brother did." Stanton would go on to strive to be as much like a boy as possible to give her father something of what he had lost in his son. But her triumphs in school and sports, which would have brought pride to her father were she a boy, proved time and again to be either useless or shameful in his eyes because of her sex.[30] Stanton lived a tomboy girlhood, but her biographical sketch, by fellow suffragette Laura Curtis Bullard, suggests that her most boyish behavior simply led to her father reemphasizing the inescapability of girlhood, with all of the limitations that implied.

Other sketches in the book reinforce that the transition from a free tomboy life to adult womanhood could be devastating. Kate Sanborn makes the adolescent despair of Frances Willard fundamental to her lifelong sense of self by including a telling passage from Willard's adolescent diary:

> This is my seventeenth birthday and the oath of my martyrdom. Mother insists that I shall have my hair done up woman fashion, and my dress made to trail like hers. She says she shall never forgive herself for letting me run wild so long. We had a great time over it all, and here I sit like another Sampson shorn of my strength . . . . [M]y feet are entangled in the skirt of my new gown. I can never jump over a fence again so long as I live. As for chasing the sheep down in the shady pasture it's out of the question, and to climb to my eagles'-nest seat in the big burr-oak would ruin this new frock beyond repair. Altogether, I recognize the fact that my occupation's gone.[31]

In most of these sketches and memoirs the authors repeat the message: tomboys make the most admirable grown women, but the transition to womanhood is painful, and the young woman takes to the required path with a sense of loss.

If we look to the available journals and diaries of some of these same women as girls, we see that they do not package up their experiences under the label of tomboy or suggest they are particularly boyish. They simply record their daily lives. In her teens, Frances Willard was convinced she would never marry, and decided she must attend college. In her early twenties, as I noted earlier, she writes extensively about her passionate love for her best friend (and soon-to-be sister-in-law), Mary Bannister.[32] But she does not associate her ambitions or her romantic attraction with being masculine, even though as a girl she went by "Frank," cut her hair short, and embraced a tomboy persona.[33]

Tomboy pasts were frequently used to explain the success of female entertainers. James Parton, for example, has the legendary actress Charlotte Cushman—who gained international fame by her serious performances of male characters—enter his biographical collection *Daughters of Genius* by declaring, "I was born a tomboy." Parton hastens to explain that "tomboy" meant "she was a vigorous, strong-limbed courageous girl, who might have been the mother of heroes if it had not been her fortune to be a heroine herself."[34]

The sculptor Harriet Hosmer was a particular darling of 1880s print culture, as much for her tomboy swagger as her success as an artist. According to a multitude of newspaper accounts, Hosmer's physician father encouraged her to cavort with abandon in the countryside in order that she might survive the many diseases common to nineteenth-century children. By the late 1880s, stories of young Hosmer jumping trains, riding bareback, and shooting became public lore.[35] Jeannette Gilder, in her 1901 best-seller *The Autobiography of a Tomboy,* recalled her girlhood fascination with Hosmer upon reading a sketch about her in a periodical: "I was enchanted . . . both by the portrait and the biography. The former represented her with short, curly hair, parted on the side, a turn-down collar, and floating tie. My mind was made up instantly. I too would be a sculptor, and wear short hair, and turn-down collar and floating tie."[36]

Sexuality often hovered in the background of these stories, though readers may have overlooked the signs simply because "lesbian" was not an identity, or even a coherent concept, for most Americans, despite the fact that medicine was in the process of codifying it as deviant (in a binary with heterosexual as "normal"). Many of these famous tomboys—particularly Hosmer and Cushman—lived openly with female partners. If there was ambiguity regarding their sexual passions, it was on the part of the viewer, not the viewed. Because they were internationally celebrated artists, they were held to an entirely different standard than other women.

Their tomboy girlhoods were celebrated in the American public press as a precursor to greatness, not condemned as proof that boyish girls grow up to be mannish women who never marry. As numerous articles on Hosmer and Cushman attest, the work of these women was often eclipsed by a fascination with their gender performance.[37]

Similarly, we saw in chapter 2 that when the writer Louise Chandler Moulton interviewed Louisa May Alcott (for her biography in *Our Famous Women*), Alcott essentially hinted that she considered her tomboy identity an extension of her sense that, because of her attraction to other women, she truly had a man's soul, "put by some freak of nature into a woman's body."[38] Although sexuality would not be a trait associated with tomboy identity until the early twentieth century, this undoubtedly had to do with a lack of conversation about hetero- and homosexuality until that period. From Winnie Woodfern to Frances Willard, particular attraction to girls underlined narratives of girls with tomboyish traits. Even at this time when passionate love for other girls was the norm in white middle-class girl culture, extremely strong homosexual feelings suggested—at least to some—that gender was not determined by the body.

Women writing about themselves routinely claimed tomboy girlhoods to show that their dashing identities extended all the way from childhood.[39] For example, in 1887 the writer and activist Jessie Benton Frémont wrote of her girlhood self, "I was called 'Tom-boy,' and never had an untorn dress. . . . So I understood boy-nature and knew that . . . the natural outcome of strength and will and courage and fun would come out all right when it settled into working channels."[40] Married to the western explorer John Frémont, and daughter of Missouri senator Thomas Hart Benton, Frémont used her tomboy identity to emphasize her own connection to "untamed" western culture. Also connecting wilderness to gender transgression, the scandalous Civil War–era actress and poet Adah Isaacs Menken crafted tales that essentially read like the story of her boyhood on the Texas frontier.[41] In *The Woman in Battle* (1876), Cuban-born Loreta Janeta Velazquez implies that her girlhood bravery and preference for boys' clothes enabled her to later comfortably pass as a male soldier in the Civil War.[42]

Other memoirists, too, readily turn to the tomboy identity as a way to explain their feelings of being singular. Sarah Rice, the daughter of a minister in turn-of-the-century Alabama, recalled, "I was a tomboy. I could climb any tree my brothers would climb; I could ride a horse, mule, cow;

plow; all those things." She describes her ability to play the boy role with a glee: "I learned how to plow. I asked my brother Albert to teach me, even though Papa didn't want his girls to plow." Perhaps more surprising is her brother's participation: "Albert and I would switch. We'd be down in the bottom, and Albert would put on my dress and do the hoeing, and I would put on his pants and plow. All anybody standing on the hill would see would be the pants plowing and the dress hoeing."[43] For Rice as well as many other adult women looking back, their girlhood tomboy identity suggested that they had always felt an internal equality with males. Yet it is unlikely that Rice in that girlhood moment would have felt so certain.

Absorbing the shift in tomboyism from uncouth to particularly and idealistically American, Laura Ingalls Wilder's long-unpublished memoir, *Pioneer Girl,* depicts a girlhood in 1870s Wisconsin and Minnesota that included playing games with the boys. Like the diarists, she played with boys alongside other girls because that was simply how girls played. Wilder writes of her ten-year-old self playing games in Walnut Grove, Minnesota, in 1877:

> Being, as my sister Mary said, a tomboy, I led the girls into the boys' games. We played Anti-over, Pullaway, Prisoner's Base and handball. Only one boy in the school could run faster than me and not always he could do it. When the boys saw how well we could play, in an hour of triumph, they took us into their baseball game and we played that the rest of the summer, much to the scandle [*sic*] of . . . [the] big girls, being ladies.[44]

Wilder readily accepted the label "tomboy" given by her older sister, and ran with it. She took pride in her athletic ability, but she served as a leader to the other girls, not an outlier. For Laura and her friends, age determined when ladyhood must begin; until then, they could play alongside boys in so-called boys' games (which is not the same as saying they could play "like" boys, which was clearly less acceptable).

In 1901 the literary critic and editor Jeannette Gilder published her memoir of growing up in New Jersey in the 1860s, *The Autobiography of a Tomboy,* to great commercial success. Her memoir stands out because she did not harken back to that identity to explain how she became a public figure; she clearly still saw herself a tomboy as an adult. As a girl she had identified with boys to the point of seeing little difference between them and herself. The body differences could be dismissed, since they were somewhat hypothetical, being hidden by clothes. Letters between herself and her brother (who refers to her as "brother Jen"), suggest that among the boys—her brothers and cousins—she was seen as an honorary boy.[45]

Gilder begins her autobiography by raising the question that has bothered the public since "tomboy" first began to be applied exclusively to girls in the 1860s: Why exactly *are* energetic girls called tomboys? "I never quite understood why a girl who climbed trees, clung to the tail-end of carts, and otherwise deported herself as a well-conditioned girl should not, was called a tomboy. I always seemed to me that, if she was anything she should not be, it was a tomgirl." Tomgirl, of course, would suggest that such behaviors belonged to girls as well as boys. But Gilder shrugs off the point as soon as she makes it: "I did not care what they called me, so long as they let me alone; but that they were loath to do. My relations and friends of the family predicted all sorts of dreadful ends for me, and talked in my presence about the awful fate awaiting whistling girls and crowing hens."[46] Disarmingly self-deprecating about her tomboy antics, she is equally playful about femininity in others. She pokes fun at herself and the horrified response of her relatives, but also at her hyperfeminine cousin Frances, of whom she mockingly asserts, "[We] never dared tell her the naked truth, for fear that she would faint."[47] In Gilder's autobiography, girls and boys behave as they do, and then adults label them. The labels are an adult means of controlling the young, and they do not work particularly well.

As in classic tomboy tales, Gilder asserts that older women present the most resistance to her trespasses into male territory. In an early scene in her sequel to the *Autobiography*, she argues that she must begin earning a living by citing cross-dressing Hosmer, the famous Civil War surgeon Mary Walker, and the French artist Rosa Bonheur as respectable female professionals.[48] Her aunt blanches in horror and retorts, "Not one of the women you mention proves your argument, for they one and all admit that a woman has no right to go out into the world to work, by making themselves look as much like men as possible." Gilder emphasizes her outsider tomboy status by reinforcing that her family's view of her desire to work was the "only one held in those days," adding, "Girls were not supposed to occupy themselves with anything but sewing and housekeeping. Anything like independence was shocking, to be deplored." But the fact that Gilder paid no heed says a lot about how she and her generation were beginning to revise their understanding of women's place in the public world.[49] And indeed, it made her autobiographies enormously attractive to contemporary readers.

Although she never suggests that she longed to be a boy, she aspired to the physical toughness she associated with boys. In the *Autobiography* she notes, "My hands were as hard as any boy's, of which I was very proud; but the fly in my ointment was that I hadn't a broken little finger. . . . There wasn't a boy in the village who hadn't a crooked finger, and I felt rather humiliated that all mine should be straight."[50] And frustrated by her much-admired long, curling hair, she writes, "I longed for the freedom of short hair, like a boy's, that wouldn't catch . . . in the trees I climbed." Her nurse and mother both burst into tears when she comes home with her hair chopped short. But Gilder remembers thinking at the time that she looked "a great deal nicer" and proudly held her head up at her school's commencement ceremony, where people responded by groaning, covering their eyes, and pretending to faint. Thus, with good humor throughout, Gilder portrays her tomboy self as beloved by her community for the very acts they also deplore.[51]

The autobiography ends abruptly with the death of Gilder's father, and she concludes simply: "I got a position in an office a few weeks later and began work. The Tomboy's play days were over."[52] But fans and her publisher thought otherwise. *The Autobiography of a Tomboy* proved so popular that Gilder produced a sequel, *The Tomboy at Work,* in 1904, though in this case the title is misleading. The second book is largely devoid of the playful gender commentary that enriched the first. She had ended her first book honestly: she really could not be a tomboy any more, now that she worked for a living. Tomboys were playful creatures. In *The Tomboy at Work,* family financial need forces her to stop resisting the system.

In the 1930s and 1940s, two particular texts helped to solidify the image of late nineteenth-century white girls as either repressed little Victorians who conformed or lovable tomboys who refused to relinquish their sense of self. The heroines of the *Little House* books (1932–1947) and *Caddie Woodlawn* (1935) were prank-playing, adventurous tomboys who could not, or would not, surrender their boyishness to please their frustrated mothers, much to the delight of their indulgent fathers. The instant commercial success of the books owed something to the popular notion that the Victorian era was so backward and restrictive that most girls spent their lives indoors sewing, too trussed up in corsets to play games and too domesticated to have adventures. The heroines, Laura and Caddie, are set apart from these other girls. In fact, readers identified passionately with these two characters in part because they were progressive enough to resist misguided gender norms. These were the kind of girls from whom sprang modern American girlhood, for how could the modern girl possibly come from the female foils surrounding these tomboy heroines?

Laura Ingalls Wilder's eight *Little House* books, juvenile fiction based on her then-unpublished memoir *Pioneer Girl*, arguably give the most comprehensive depiction of nineteenth-century pioneer girlhood available, and perhaps the most detailed recording of the daily domestic life in the late nineteenth century available anywhere. Indeed, Wilder's books play a large cultural role in shaping our images of nineteenth-century expectations for girls. Rose Wilder Lane, Wilder's daughter and an internationally recognized author, gave strong characters and narrative shape to her mother's memoir. Lane essentially wrote her mother into a tomboy without including the term in any of the books. But the books' covers and copyright notices list Wilder alone as the author—and given their extensive and exact details about domestic production, farming technology, food, stories, entertainment, and songs, the public largely accepts that the books accurately represent the social mores of the period.[53] But, of course, Lane and Wilder wrote the books for audiences in the years between 1932 and 1943, after female aviators, athletes, and celebrities were regularly and affectionately called tomboys in the press. Wilder's book helped to solidify the impression that the tomboy had remarkably modern sensibilities compared to the Victorian girls around her.

The *Little House* books are rich in details that captivate readers, but it is the character of Laura Ingalls who pulls the reader in, much like Jo March in *Little Women*. Although writing Laura into the classic tomboy may have been true to Wilder's girlhood personality, the familiar and beloved tomboy trope also provided the personable central heroine needed to ground the series. As a whole, the *Little House* books suggest that nineteenth-century culture replicated nonsensical gender norms for females, and that strong, assertive girls like Laura were the ones who took the culture into the twentieth century. Laura has all the earmarks of classic tomboy heroines: she hates sewing and sitting, her curiosity gets her into all kinds of trouble, she is often cross and selfish, and she complains about constrictive female clothing. Young female readers can identify with Laura for many reasons, but the books are constructed so that she alone does not buy into the gender-restrictive nonsense of the world around her, even while trying hard to meet her parents' expectations. Thus she is a tomboy because she is unusual. She is not like the other girls around her, who are comfortable with gender expectations while Laura clearly is not. Laura, though never described with that word, is a tomboy because she is not—*can not* be—the typical girl.

By giving her fictional doppelgänger a tomboy spirit, Wilder reinforces the notion that nineteenth-century girls were raised as little ladies, even though her own memoir suggests that tomboy behavior was in fact typical of many girls. In *Pioneer Girl,* Wilder makes it clear that while she was the ringleader, she had plenty of female company in her games, and she played baseball alongside the boys well into her teens.[54] The memoir suggests that she was lively but not unusual; just another spirited girl who might be called a "tomboy" by her dismissive older sister. But in her fictional rendering, the girls around her are sedate, well-behaved, and demure—*except* for Laura, the girl with a modern heart. In *Pioneer Girl,* she is the leader of a gang of girls who tear up the prairies when they can get away from endless chores. In the novels, she is set apart for those same behaviors.

Throughout the novels, Wilder principally uses the figures of Ma and Laura's older sister Mary to emphasize the senseless restrictions faced by girls in the past. Ma is stalwart and steady, but also an unyielding proponent of Victorian respectability. Scolding Laura for not sleeping in her steel corset (like Mary), Ma brags about how Pa could span her waist with his hands when they were married.[55] But what use was this nod to high-fashion vanity in a world of grasshopper scourges and crippling poverty? Ma insists that keeping up a show of civility matters, even through winters of near-starvation, hours of cooking for boarders, and endlessly sweeping a dirt floor on a treeless prairie. But Laura dislikes sitting still and sewing sheets and samplers, and rebels against parental pressure to be good (although she readily capitulates out of competition with goody-two-shoes Mary). She would rather get dirty than be "ladylike" and loves adventure more than she fears it. And because Laura, like Jo March, struggles to behave while still refusing to subscribe to wrongheaded Victorian sentiment, she reinforces the notion that there is a long history of society oppressing the true nature of girls.

It is not simply Laura's athletic ability and disdain for female clothing that make her modern, but also her internal sense of self. She does not self-flagellate over her less feminine feelings of anger and a desire for retaliation. When Mary and Laura first encounter Laura's longtime enemy Nellie Oleson in *On the Banks of Plum Creek,* Mary (of course) says, "My goodness . . . I couldn't be as mean as that Nellie Oleson." And Laura thinks to herself, "I could. I could be meaner than she is to us, if Ma and Pa would let me."[56] Laura, for all her obedience and ultimate self-sacrifice (she earns much of the money that sends Mary, who became blind after a bout of scarlet fever, to college), suggests that her opinion is powerful and her will is formidable. She sees clearly, no matter how hard she also tries to meet expectations.

And this is what gives the nineteenth-century tomboy her contemporary appeal: she is cognizant of the myopia of her own time. Like the reader, she sees the ridiculousness of Victorian mores, and she refuses to embrace them even as she struggles to please her parents. She is ahead of her time even if she is bound by the rules of her time.

But it is arguable that the fictional biography *Caddie Woodlawn* (1935), by Carol Ryrie Brink, did the most to solidify the images of nineteenth-century girls as uncritical and submissive, with the exception of the tomboy. Brink, already a successful juvenile author, fictionalized her grandmother's life growing up in rural Wisconsin in the early 1860s by employing the structure of the well-established tomboy tale. Caddie is a lively twelve-year-old girl forced to give up her boyish freedoms and embrace womanly responsibilities (namely decorum) at the onset of adolescence. If writers such as Alcott and Wilder hinted at the internal gender struggles tomboys faced with maturity, Brink makes it central to Caddie's story.

The novel begins by echoing the tomboy origins often lurking in biographies of public female figures: after Caddie nearly dies as a young child, her parents allow her to roam free with the boys in an effort to regain her strength. Brink's story buttresses the image, but not the reality, of how little girls were raised. But there is clearly a cultural need to continue believing that depiction, despite evidence to the contrary.

Caddie's outdoor life produces a robust, adventurous, joyful girl who, in the course of the novel, is forced to give up her core identity because she is outgrowing tomboy freedoms. The tug of war between Caddie and her mother, the enforcer of femininity, culminates when Caddie is singled out for punishment for playing a prank alongside her brothers. Her brother tries to share the blame, but the mother replies, "No, Tom, I cannot blame *you* so much." Tom is a boy, so he clearly cannot help it. However, she declares, "That a *daughter* of mine should so far forget herself . . . that she should be such a hoyden as to neglect her proper duties as a lady! Shame to her! Shame! No punishment that I can invent would be sufficient for her." Caddie is "stung by [the] injustice" and resolves to run away to her friends, the Santee Sioux (who inexplicably trust Caddie, despite the fact that the novel takes place when the real Santee Sioux were engaged in a horrific struggle with the white settlers of the region).[57]

Alone as she plans her escape, Caddie fumes that when the Indians take her in she will "never have to grow into that hateful thing which Mother was always talking about—a lady. A lady with fine airs and mincing walk who was afraid to go out into the sun without a hat or a sunshade! A lady, who had made samplers and wore stays and was falsely polite no matter how she felt!" Caddie's complaints echo Jo March's protest: "I hate to think I've got to grow up and be Miss March, and wear long gowns, and look as prim as a China aster!"[58]

Brink works within the classic tomboy structure, but Caddie does not naturally age out of her ways like the tomboy heroines of newspaper fiction. Nor is she like Jo, who is exhorted to learn self-control as form of self-cultivation. Caddie must change out of duty to society; her work is external. Trying to ease the conflict between mother and daughter, her father comments, "It's a strange thing, but somehow we expect more of girls than of boys. It is the sisters and wives and mothers, you know, Caddie, who keep the world sweet and beautiful." Caddie is not particularly interested in sweet or beautiful, but she will do anything to please her doting father. Brink's tomboy tale goes from reveling in one girl's sense of fun to reinforcing why girls have to leave it behind: "A woman's work is something fine and noble to grow up to, and it is just as important as a man's." And, of course, the supportive Papa rejects the Victorian femininity that Caddie fears (with good reason): "I don't want you to be the silly, affected person with fine clothes and manners whom folks sometimes call a lady. . . . I want you to be a woman with a wise and understanding heart, healthy in body and honest in mind."[59] The problem is that performing that vaunted femininity will require a certain level of civility even in the midst of rural pioneer life, as Laura's and Caddie's mothers both know.

Although *Caddie Woodlawn* and the *Little House* books were biographies reframed through fictional structures, they nonetheless provide a window on the cultural role that late nineteenth-century tomboys came to play in the early twentieth century. These tomboys as young adolescents served to show that even in the high Victorian period, the kernel of the modern girl lived in the tomboy who embraced candor, fun, and physicality, regardless of convention. Twentieth-century readers could see their world as remarkably advanced because the stories they told of past girls reinforced an image that was largely fictional. But the tomboy identity only proved useful to real girls and women if it served as a story of origins. In this time before widening acceptance of female masculinity as simply another expression available to those with female bodies, to be a tomboy in the present tense was to allow someone else to assert that a girl's most comfortable sense of self was in fact unnatural.

In the lives of real girls and the women remembering their childhoods in the nineteenth century, "tomboy" is a source of strength only in the past tense. Tomboy behavior proved useful as a means of looking back and finding spirited, likeable girls in a vast landscape of subdued ones. But in the present tense, it was nearly always seen as constrictive—a means of asserting feminine subordination as innate to a female body in a way that most girls either did not recognize or rejected outright. What was a term of empowerment on the published page proved time and again to be a means of limiting girls' self-expression.

Coda

I once overheard a conversation between a couple sitting beside me at a bar. "She's such a tomboy," the man concluded after telling a story about a young woman leaving for college. "That term doesn't exist anymore," his female companion scolded. "It's completely outdated."

Eavesdroppers should not interrupt, so I restrained myself from leaning over to offer counter-examples easily found on the Internet, such as wiki-sites on "How to be a tomboy" and "How to dress like a tomboy," or reviews of Instagram accounts that are "doing tomboy style right," as well as the "tomboy jeans" sold by every major jean manufacturer. I could have brought up my recent experience as a parent enduring my son's (endless) tee-ball games. Although about a quarter of the team was female, parents referred to only one particular girl as "the tomboy"—apparently because she was a crackerjack player and wore gender-neutral clothing, unlike her female peers happily rounding bases in sparkly skirts. I could have talked about Ella, my son's friend, who adores pink and sparkles as well as backward baseball hats. She is routinely called a tomboy not only because she is tougher than the boys but, perhaps more importantly, because she does not give credibility to the notion of her sex shaping her identity.

And truthfully, I agreed with the woman at the bar: one would think that progress in gender politics would relegate tomboys in all forms to the dustbins of history. After all, what is considered appropriate behavior for girls has expanded exponentially since the term first gained a positive gloss in the post–Civil War period. Despite a binary marked clearly in pink and blue, many Americans recognize that gender is indeed a spectrum—or rather a path along which all of us walk, this way and that, stopping where comfortable given our particular place, time, and inclinations.

Yet many modern girls and women do indeed continue to identify with the term as concepts of gender expand. If tomboys are supposedly outliers because they are more rough, ambitious, and physical, and less sentimental, than most girls, that would suggest that few women began their lives as tomboys. Yet in 1977 psychologists discovered that while few girls would claim to be tomboys at that moment, 51 percent of American adult women happily claimed having been tomboys in their youth.[1] In 1998 another study found that "46 percent of senior citizens, 69 percent of baby boomers and 77 percent of Gen-X women reported having been tomboys."[2] The fact that numbers of self-identified tomboys went up as the age of the women went down confirms that, despite more progressive and flexible ideas of gender, the term "tomboy" continues to gain rather than lose cultural efficacy.

The conflicting sense of the tomboy concept as both useful and outdated is what I address here. If tomboy traits became part of the American girl at the turn of the twentieth century, then who are we still calling tomboys? What does the term mean? Does the present concept of tomboy share similarities with the figure that emerged from new girlhood in the late nineteenth century? My interest is not in haphazardly tracing the entire arc from end to end—for if there are important nuances of detail in the sixty years I have covered, there are surely many more in the century that followed, as the work of other tomboy scholars demonstrates.

In much in the same vein as early twentieth-century articles like the 1917 piece "Passing of the Tomboy,"' in 2015 the online *New York Times* ran an article titled "Where Have All the Tomboys Gone?" The author, Marisa Meltzer, begins by noting the success of the best-selling graphic memoir *Tomboy*, by Liz Prince, but then proclaims that "the word used for its title—and the phase of female life it denotes, even the idea that it is a phase at all—is increasingly falling out of fashion in an era when Caitlyn Jenner is more likely to be a topic of conversation on the playground than Caddie Woodlawn." Meltzer quotes bloggers, parents, educators, and feminists who largely agree that the term sounds oh-so-twentieth-century. Or as, the third-wave feminist Jennifer Baumgardner puts it, "It feels retro, this affirmative way of talking about a girl who likes boy things, as if boy things were better." Likewise, Wendy McClure, an editor of children's books, suggests that perhaps "tomboy is one of those adaptive terms, something once used to describe any girl who just happened to want to wear dungarees and climb a tree. Now that those things have been more accepted as part of normal girl behavior, we don't need it anymore." Her hopeful suggestion sounds eerily like the ending of the 1917 article: "Something seems to have happened to the tomboy crop. Either the genus has unhappily ceased to exist or the characteristics have become so common that they have ceased to be distinguishing."[3]

"Dungarees" might itself be an outdated term, but for hundreds of readers who rapidly posted responses to Meltzer's article, "tomboy" is firmly enmeshed in the culture whether one approves of it or not. The piece struck such a nerve that the sheer volume of responses compelled the *Times* to post a follow-up piece four days later, highlighting a selection of comments that ran the gamut from celebration to disgust.

The notion that "transgender" or "gender queer" could replace "tomboy" aroused particular ire. EAP from Bozeman, Montana, scoffed, "This is ridiculous. I am a Tomboy. It is/was my identity growing up. It was my personal space in a family of five girls and no boys." Sara of Boston recalled, "I remember how cool I felt to be called a tomboy, and it was sweet and sassy and not at all masculine, but very powerful." Respondents who self-identified with the term stressed how it had given them a particular sense of power not available to more conventional girls. Memi from Canada proclaimed, "I was a tomboy because I was (and am) a boyish kind of girl and woman. . . . Did I think of myself as a boy? Never. I loved being a girl. I just didn't love what the world wanted that to mean." She reflected, "I'm glad that girls today are empowered enough to be exactly what they want to be, and maybe to them 'tomboy' is a label they no longer need. But to me growing up when I did, it was my badge of honor and I wore it with blazing glory. At 65, I still think of myself like that, and I still think it's hot."[4]

For readers like Memi, being a tomboy was not about being a boy, but about being a *girl*—or woman—who finds conventional femininity alien and female masculinity comfortable. In her 2016 memoir, *You'll Grow Out of It,* the comedian Jessi Klein observes that she knew she had to grow out of her tomboy ways in adolescence or become an outcast, but prescribed female markers repelled her: "The tent poles of femininity as I observed them—high heels, eye makeup, Diet Coke, smiling, etc.—all seemed to be focused on the external. In any case, they felt completely foreign to me."[5] Even with much effort, tomboy identity was not something Klein could entirely outgrow; it was her norm.

For some of Meltzer's respondents, being a tomboy is also about feeling neither boy nor girl. Or, as one fourteen-year-old girl posted on the website Tomboy Stories in 2016, "Physically I am a girl. Though emotionally I don't feel like one. I am not transgender. I am just a tomboy."[6] For such girls and women, tomboy is an identity all its own. Meltzer's article suggests that the term "tomboy" is pejorative because it associates healthy physicality with boys, and outdated because of the currency of "transgender." But "tomboy" can easily be viewed the other way around: as a way for a girl to claim her body while simultaneously denying that it is the sole source of her identity. It means asserting an internal sense of self that is not entirely gender-neutral but overrides external forces of gender. In April 2017 an op-ed in the *New York Times,* titled "My Daughter Is Not Transgender. She's a Tomboy," sets out to reclaim the term. The mother, Lisa Selin Davis, explains, "She is not gender nonconforming. She is gender *role* nonconforming." Ironically, according to Davis, adults are thrown off by her daughter not identifying as a boy, but rather as a girl who likes a style more akin to the boys around her. Again, readers commented (1,513 times) with reactions all over the map, but there was one new common thread: seeing tomboys as transgender means erasing a beloved *female* identity.[7]

Allison Miller explores the conundrum of compulsory synchronization of gender, sexuality, and the body in her beautifully nuanced 2012 dissertation, "Boyhood for Girls: American Tomboys and the Transformation of Eroticism, 1900–1940." She directly addresses the question of who remains left to be called a tomboy when the old tomboy markers were taken up by the frank and athletic all-American girl. Counter to suggestions that progress rendered "tomboy" outdated, Miller argues that changing social and sexual attitudes presented tomboys with a new set of challenges rather than greater liberation. In large part because tomboyism was (and is) still treated as a stage to be outgrown, the internal stresses actually became more acute for self-identified tomboys. "What adolescent tomboys had trouble with was how it all was supposed to feel," Miller contends. "Becoming a normal girl meant changing one's behavior, but it also entailed shifting one's affective relationships with others. The transformation was both outward and inward."[8] Now that adolescent girls were expected to socialize in order to date, and date in order to marry (and most women could not afford to stay single), tomboys found themselves under greater pressure than ever to adopt evaluations of body differences that had largely eluded them. They knew that boy bodies were, on the whole, physically stronger, but they could not see how they were better, or even particularly different outside of the most obvious difference, and that was hidden under clothing, and therefore conjectural.

To explore how former tomboys understood the space they inhabited on the gender-and-sexuality matrix, Miller uses interviews conducted between 1935 and 1937 by Agnes Landis, a research fellow at the New York State Psychiatric Institute and Hospital and wife of Carney Landis, an eminent psychologist who directed the study.[9] Landis interviewed 294 anonymous female subjects about their early and current sexual experience and proclivities, focusing particular attention on what she saw as instances of "masculine protest," the term coined by the psychologist Alfred Adler.[10] The questions she asked them tended to be loaded: "Have you ever feared that your sex parts might be different from those of other women?" "Did you ever consciously want very much to be a boy?" "What do men have that you would especially like to have?"[11] Subjects responded in a wide variety of ways. A Romanian Jewish woman stated that as a child she had wanted to be a boy because she "fell in with boys so completely I never thought of myself as different," adding, "Mothers used to yell at me. Boys thought of me as a boy and one of them." But she also reported that now, at age twenty-four, she felt "perfectly content to be a girl."[12] Likewise, another woman answered that she was a complete tomboy until she started going out with boys at seventeen, and then "it all changed." She also confessed that she envied feminine girls more than men because they so easily expressed what escaped her.[13] Another self-professed tomboy admitted to wanting to be a boy simply because it would have been easier than struggles over skirts and hair ribbons.[14] Miller notes that in their interviews, "women of all classes and educational backgrounds could speak knowingly of developing 'complexes,' seeking sexual 'adjustment' and fighting 'fixations.'"[15] That the subjects were so well versed in the terminology suggests not only that popular psychology saturated the culture, but that these women hungered for a means of reconciling their sense of difference.

They clearly wrestled not only with their confusion, but with the meaning of that confusion. Miller writes that as girls, these tomboys "had a sense of affinity with boys and boyishness that included their girl bodies. . . . [T]hey proved willing to ignore or downplay anatomical distinctions between themselves and boys"—which is not the same as wishing to be male. Many of the adult women were still deeply troubled by the idea that bodies were supposed to synchronize with gender expression and sexual pleasure in particular and, indeed, inexplicable ways. In an effort to explain what they saw as defects within themselves, many of them returned to memories of their childhood confusion over body and gender differences. Some former tomboys reported that while they knew that bodies were sexed differently, they "shrugged off gender dichotomies. Boys had penises and girls did not; tomboys simply did not care. Why should they? They could do everything boys could. If anything, these girls saw themselves as more different from other girls than from boys."[16] And indeed, adopting tomboy identity disrupted the gender binary that created their confusion. Having a hybrid gender created a triad of identity that allowed instincts, rather than bodies, to guide gender definition in ways that allowed for greater possibilities and complexities.

Carney Landis asserted in the conclusion of the resulting text, *Sex in Development,* that charting connections between sexuality and normality proved too complicated to simplify because sexuality is socially embedded.[17] That statement is given a more lyrical and personal gloss by Hilary Mullins, whose powerful personal essay "Evolution of a Tomboy" alleges that it was her tomboy identity that shaped her sexuality. "In the beginning, it had nothing to do with liking girls," Mullins recollects. "In fact, in the beginning, being a tomboy was not about whom I liked at all; it was about *what* I liked: climbing trees, building forts, playing any kind of game that involved throwing or hitting a ball." For Miller and her younger sister, being a tomboy in rural Vermont meant playing out of doors, daring each other into dangerous stunts, and "wading uphill through knee-deep snow, dragging the long wooden toboggan ourselves, leaping on at the top with a pounding, running start, and hurtling down, whooping in the whip-white blur of it, holding on with crusty mittens."[18]

Her sense of being neither girl nor boy intensified when surrounded by peers. "I was the class tomboy—a girl, but different, my identity split." Although she liked girls, and found them more "emotionally honest," overt femininity repelled her. But she also knew she was not like the boys either, and insists, "I didn't want to be one, even though I liked the things they did." But because male identity is assumed as enviable in ways that female is not, "they accused me of it at times anyway, marking the boundaries of their male terrain like spraying tomcats."[19]

Because she violated male privilege by not understanding herself as primarily female, the boys turned her into a means of proving their masculinity to each other. Eventually, her cousin raped her—and then her brother, then another brother, then all of their friends. "Looking back, it seems to me that the stakes were high for them, that those sex games were nearly as compulsory for these boys as ball games during recess were for the boys in my class. All of them had to prove their budding manhood to the other boys or else, and in this dirty little game, a female body was the field on which to demonstrate it."[20]

Although Mullins was initially attracted to men, as an adult she consciously decided to be with other women—not because her tomboyism predetermined her sexual attractions, but because her tomboy identity created conflict in her heterosexual relationships. "I was a tomboy from the very beginning . . . but I was not a lesbian. . . . [C]ontrary to the usual assumption that a girl becomes a tomboy because she is really, underneath it all, a lesbian, I have come to believe that I became lesbian because really, underneath it all, I was, and remain to this day, a tomboy." But as a lesbian, she found a way to be an adult tomboy with impunity. She concludes that the sexual abuse "taught me young and hard, about the bad bargain between boys and girls, men and women. It wasn't just that they weren't going to let me play ball—the fixing of the game went deeper than that": it was an "arrangement designed to rob me of my integrity and personhood simply because I was a girl in a world where boys had to prove they were men or else."[21]

Mullins's essay illustrates Judith/Jack Halberstam's contention that the popular embracing of the tomboy does not necessarily suggest that girls can enact masculinity without consequences. Halberstam notes that, however much "tomboyism remains comfortably linked to a stable sense of girl identity," it will be "punished . . . when it appears to be the sign of extreme male identification (taking a boy's name or refusing girl clothing of any type) and when it threatens to extend beyond childhood into adolescence."[22] In other words, acceptable tomboyism comes with particularly feminine limitations.

Yet if Mullins suffered from her subordinate position in a man's world, she did own a sanctioned term for crossing the binary, and one that gave her a fair amount of latitude compared with her male corollaries. Boys still do not have a positive term for embracing femininity. Responding online to Meltzer's *New York Times* article, Chester from New York City wrote, "The reality is that boyishness is considered the norm and aspirational, but girlishness is at best a 'norm' for girls and a strike against a boy." This double standard is undeniably true; females claiming boyish identity are not as threatening to the patriarchy as effeminate boys because their desire is largely seen as only natural, given the privileges of male identity. Boys claiming femininity, however, are a direct threat. Indeed, femininity in boys is pathologized at far higher rates. According to the journalist Ruth Padawer, "Boys are up to seven times as likely as girls to be referred to gender clinics for psychological evaluations. Sometimes the boys' violation is as mild as wanting a Barbie for Christmas. By comparison, most girls referred to gender clinics are far more extreme in their atypicality: they want boy names, boy pronouns and, sometimes, boy bodies."[23]

The central issue, according to tomboy scholars across the board, is that tomboyism remains a stage to outgrow. Although, to borrow Kathryn Bond Stockton's image of queer maturation, it is arguable that persistent tomboys simply grow in different ways—not upward to feminine adulthood, but outward, allowing their own sense of self to override gender imperatives. Several tomboy scholars have focused on the character of Frankie Addams, in Carson McCullers's *The Member of the Wedding*, the quintessential queer tomboy heroine. McCullers introduces the twelve-year-old Frankie: "This was the summer when for a long time she had not been a member. She belonged to no club and was a member of nothing in the world. Frankie had become an unjoined person who hung around in doorways, and she was afraid." Halberstam clarifies that "while childhood in general may qualify as a period of 'unbelonging,' for the boyish girl arriving on the doorstep of womanhood, her status as 'unjoined' marks her out for all manner of social violence and opprobrium."[24] Frankie grows sideways rather than up. She is a queer tomboy because she is advancing in age but cannot find herself—shape herself—into womanhood.

But if scholars give us a grim view of the tomboy's inability to find a safe space, the informal online collection of personal anecdotes on the website Tomboy Stories suggests that current tomboys robustly claim their identity as the right of girls and women regardless of the opinions of onlookers. Unlike the early tomboys examined in this study, these tomboys are of many races, ethnicities, ages, classes, and nations. Twenty-year-old Maysa from Afghanistan, for example, posted: "No one in my country accept tomboys and they hate tomboys. I faced many problems still now with all the people I could cut my hair this year and i am really glad of this! But still my parents don't know i am a tom . . . and they want me to marry :-(how can i tell them i am a tom?"[25] Many older women add tomboy stories asserting that their girlhood sense of self has remained intact, not the least bit influenced by the idea of growing out of tomboy traits.

Tomboys' sexuality comes with a big question mark, which is not surprising given the twentieth- and twenty-first century obsessions with treating sexuality as a totalizing identity. Frequently, lesbian tomboys will post on Tomboy Stories with the assumption that everyone knows tomboys are lesbians. Sarah writes, for example: "I am an 11 year old lesbian who is still in the closet. My mom always tells me i have to act feminine!" This association of lesbianism and tomboyism frustrates the many straight girls who are clearly on a mission to reclaim the term. Jess expresses rage over being sexualized because of her tomboy mien: "Everywhere I go, YOUR UGLY! LOOK OUT GIRLS, ITS A DYKE! I mean wtf? Not all tomboys are gay. I have a boyfriend." Likewise, Lyd writes: "I'm 18, and I am a tomboy. I am writing this post as an encouragement to my fellow STRAIGHT tomboys. I have always been a tomboy and for the most part I have been accepted." She notes that her mother has the most difficulty accepting her self-expression: "She doesn't want people to think I am gay . . . because I'm not gay." And then there is Margo, lost in the confusion of labels: "I can't figure out if I am lesbian, or if I am just me."[26]

A surprising number of tomboy storytellers suggest that hyperfemininity and tomboyism are similarly self-conscious gender performances rather than irreducible aspects of their core identity. Many confess that tomboy is a phase they have adopted after enjoying an earlier girly phase. Some continue to keep one foot in each camp; for example, Cody writes, "You could say I'm half tomboy, as for my liking to some girly things and some boyish things. I was very girly as a child." Another wrote in anonymously: "I've always been able to balance my girly and tomboy interests. I used to like dresses and dolls but I also played with my brother and his friends (sword fighting and wrestling) and liked it a lot better than playing with the girls my age." Faith clearly intends to claim rights to the entire spectrum, asserting, "Although i am a tomboy every one has a little bit of girly in them." Indeed, for some, being a tomboy is a deliberative choice. One such girl writes: "Hi my name is Amber and im 14 years old. I love being a tomboy. I just started. I was always girly and loved makeup. I decided to be a tomboy because im growing up and im not a little girl anymore." This last comment is ironic, because Amber determines that acting like a tomboy is more mature than acting feminine—the very opposite of how tomboyism has been posited for two centuries.[27]

Perhaps one of the most poignant stories comes from Krystal, who candidly concludes: "I'm starting to question what defines me precisely. I would say Im a pretty girl but also have a guys charm and approach and for some reason I feel like I identify mentally as something rather than just psychologically female or male. Can someone please help with a term to describe exactly how I feel as an individual?"[28]

The definition put forth by Rachel Simmons, whose work focuses on educating and empowering girls, may be the most workable for Krystal and many other girls of the past two centuries: "The tomboy is a girl who flouts the unwritten rules of girlhood and femininity, who seems to have an unnatural level of unselfconsciousness in the face of powerful gender norms, who freely and bravely take[s] on challenges and experiences and venture[s] into places girls don't go."[29] It is not that the tomboy in question is *masculine* in dress, pastimes, or bearing, but she resists the "unwritten rules of girlhood and femininity."

The central issue of tomboy identity is not its relationship to masculinity but to femininity. Tomboys are a way for girls to own their own identities in a world that reduces them to stock characters, not because they want to act like boys but because acting "like" girls feels like eerily like performing a script they cannot read. Jessi Klein, for example, claims to have clung to tomboy identity well into her thirties, when she came to accept that she had to make peace with femininity if she wanted to be taken seriously as an adult. She finally reaches her denouement: "This is when I learned one of the biggest secrets of being a woman, which is that much of the time, we don't feel like we're women at all."[30]

Tomboys come in more varieties than the depictions offered in the period between the Civil War and World War I, but they remain girls who identify with not belonging. Regardless of progress—or perhaps because of progress that never quite reaches the desired conclusion—the tomboy identity allows girls and women the pleasing paradox of being able to articulate discomfort with conformity through an easily recognized yet malleable concept. A concept, in fact, that each girl shapes herself.

Notes

Preface

1. These are the title characters of the following books and series: Laura Ingalls Wilder's *Little House* books (1932–1947), Carol Ryrie Brink's *Caddie Woodlawn* (1935), Louisa May Alcott's *Little Women* (1868), Madeleine L'Engle's *A Wrinkle in Time* (1962) and its sequels, Harper Lee's *To Kill a Mockingbird* (1960), and Mary Calhoun's *Katie John* books (1960–1980).
2. Higginbotham, *Righteous Discontent*, 14.

Introduction

1. "Long Live the Tomboy," *Daily People* (New York), May 14, 1911, 5. Though it appeared in a Socialist paper, this piece differed little in tone from similar articles in the *Boston Herald*, the *Kansas City Star*, and other newspapers across the country.
2. The term itself goes back to 1556, and is applied to rowdy girls by 1656, though not exclusively. *Oxford English Dictionary*, online edition, www.oed.com.
3. Besides my own experiences reading through newspapers and magazines, I am basing this statement on the results of a Google Ngram query, which graphs over time the number of occurrences of a given word in the Google compendium of sources. If one puts "tomboy" into the Ngram viewer, the line rises fairly consistently and takes a steep upward turn about the time of women's liberation in the early 1970s. Despite its usefulness, Google Ngrams are problematic in that the amount of print material expands over time, so one would expect *any* modern word to gain in usage. At the same time, the Ngram refutes the contention that "tomboy" drops in popularity.
4. Higgenbotham, *Righteous Discontent*, 187–200.
5. Painter, *History of White People*; M. F. Jacobson, *Whiteness of a Different Color*; Ignatiev, *How the Irish Became White*.
6. L. M. Simmons, *Crescent City Girls*, 4.
7. "Tomboy," definitions 1–2, *Oxford English Dictionary*, online edition, www.oed.com. "Tomboy" remains a term for prostitutes in other parts of the world, most notably Bangkok. In Uganda, "tommy boys" are a distinct lesbian identity; see Nagadya and Morgan, "Some Say I Am a Hermaphrodite."
8. Lloyd, *The Romp*. The earliest US production I have found is in Philadelphia; see advertisement, *Philadelphia Federal Gazette*, December 8, 1790, 2.
9. Abate discusses differences between the terms; see *Tomboys*, xiv.
10. *Boston Daily Evening Transcript*, May 8, 1835, 2.
11. Charlotte M. Yonge, *Womankind*, quoted in *Oxford English Dictionary*, online edition, s.v. "tomboyism."
12. Avery, *Behold the Child*, 171. Avery notes that tomboys tended to be American until the heyday of L. T. Meade, a tremendously successful commercial writer of girls' series fiction, in the early twentieth century. The Australian girl was essentially identical to

the American girl of the same period, but "tomboy" did not become a preferred term in literature until the twentieth century; see Woollacott, *To Try Her Fortune,* 157.

13. "A Tom-Boy's Terrible Love: Miss Duer, of Maryland, Indicted for Murdering Her Best Girl-Friend," *New Orleans Times-Picayune,* May 28, 1879, 2.
14. Cogan, *All-American Girl,* 3–14.
15. Stavney, "'Mothers of Tomorrow,'" 534.
16. Jiménez, *Replenished Ethnicity,* 6, 255.
17. Hart, "Black Codes," 36.
18. Abate, *Tomboys,* xxvi–viii.
19. Ruth Arnett, "Girls Need a Physical Education," *Chicago Defender,* December 10, 1921, 10.
20. Cahn, *Coming On Strong,* 229.
21. Wright, *Black Girlhood,* 10. For discussion of parents' and community efforts to establish an adolescent girlhood in the early twentieth century, see L. M. Simmons, *Crescent City Girls,* and Chatelain, *Southside Girls.*
22. Kaestle and Radway, "Framework for the History of Publishing and Reading," 7.
23. See Wright, *Black Girlhood;* L. M. Simmons, *Crescent City Girls;* Klapper, *Jewish Girls Coming of Age;* Sicherman, *Well-Read Lives.*
24. Macleod, *Age of the Child,* 5, 103–4.
25. Elliott, "Tomboys," 670.
26. Habegger, *Gender, Fantasy, and Realism,* 119.
27. Advertisements, *Tulsa World,* March 10, 1911, 10; and *San Diego Evening Tribune,* April 24, 1908, 3.
28. Connell, *Masculinities,* 71.
29. K. Brown, *Foul Bodies,* 88–89.
30. Saxton, *Being Good,* 13.
31. Catharine Sedgwick, *Mean and Ends, or Self-Training* (Boston: Marsh, Capen, Lyon & Webb, 1839), 29–30, quoted in M. Nash, *Women's Education,* 67.
32. Halberstam, *Female Masculinity,* 6.
33. Stockton, *Queer Child,* 1, 37.
34. A. Miller, "Boyhood for Girls," 22.
35. Stockton, *Queer Child,* 15.

1. Tomboys and the New Girlhood

1. "Our Daughters—Tom-boys," *Nashville Patriot,* May 25, 1858; this is the earliest instance I have found. In September 1858 *Graham's Illustrated Magazine* ran the piece under the same title (276–77) and named the source as the Nashville-based newspaper *Southern Homestead;* the article is signed L.V.F., which is almost certainly the southern writer and editor L. Virginia French, who was the literary editor of *Southern Homestead* at the time. Other reprintings include "Tom-boys," *Columbian Register* (New Haven, CT), January 15, 1859, 1; "Tom-boys," *Daily True Delta* (New Orleans), January 16, 1859, 2; "Tom-boys," *Norwich (CT) Aurora* January 22, 1859, 1; "Tom-boys," *Lowell (MA) Daily Citizen and News,* January 31, 1859, 1; "Our Daughters—Tom-Boys," *Washington (PA) Reporter,* March 30, 1859, 1; "The Tom-boy," *Southern Cultivator,* April 1859, 4; *The Sibyl: A Review of the Tastes, Errors and Fashions of Society,* July 15, 1859, 590.
2. "Our Daughters—Tom-boys."
3. Mitchell, *The New Girl,* 1. Historians differ on when they posit the beginning of new girlhood, largely based on how they define modern girlhood. Stephen Mintz asserts that girlhood began gaining new meaning in the early nineteenth-century North as a result

of economic opportunities and middle-class print culture; see *Huck's Raft,* 84–85. But if one considers girlhood a stage with its own styles, consumer goods, and girl culture, then one would agree with Jane Hunter, who in *How Young Ladies Became Girls* presents evidence suggesting that modern girlhood truly took root later in the century.

4. Hunter, *How Young Ladies Became Girls,* 11–37.
5. Linton, "The Girl of the Period," 2–3.
6. Abate, *Tomboys,* 29–31.
7. Avery, *Behold the Child,* 85; Avery, *Childhood's Pattern,* 15.
8. DeLuzio, *Female Adolescence,* 131–33.
9. Leslie, "Lucy Nelson," 149.
10. K. Brown, *Foul Bodies,* 247.
11. Leslie, "Lucy Nelson," 149.
12. Ibid., 159.
13. Corbett, "Homosexual Boyhood," 109.
14. Leslie, "Billy Bedlow," 274–75.
15. Ibid., 276–80.
16. Anon., "The Tom-Boy Who Was Changed into a Real Boy," [8]. The edition of *Aunt Oddamadodd: Little Miss Consequence* in which the poem appears is likely an American imprint of a British children's book put out in 1858 by Dean & Son of London. According-ing to Ian Dooley of the Cotson Children's Library at Princeton, Dean & Son put out a series of children's books inspired by *Der Struwwelpeter,* by the German author Heinrich Hoffman. These stories, often called "cautionary tales," tell of commonplace childhood mischief leading to tragedy for the naughty child. Dooley, "The Importance of Reading," May 5, 2014, https://blogs.princeton.edu/cotsen.
17. Rotundo, *American Manhood,* 31, 33, 34.
18. Emerson quoted in Hunter, *How Young Ladies Became Girls,* 177.
19. Tocqueville, *Democracy in America,* 684.
20. Ibid., 686.
21. Ibid., 685.
22. Ibid., 686–87.
23. Mrs. A. M. F. Annan, "Old Truth and the Trout-Fisher. A Country Story," part 1, *Godey's Lady's Book* 31 (November 1845): 207–15, quotations on 210, 213. Part 2 appeared in the December 1845 issue, 253–60.
24. A. F. Banes, "An Old Man's Yarn," *Godey's Lady's Book* 47 (July 1853): 70.
25. S. Annie Frost, "Anna Warrenton's Fortune," *Godey's Ladies' Book* 70 (February 1865): 158.
26. Zelizer, *Pricing the Priceless Child,* 57.
27. Reinier, *From Virtue to Character,* 2–5.
28. M. Ryan, *Cradle of the Middle Class,* 99–101.
29. Ibid., 100.
30. Bushnell, *Discourses on Christian Nurture,* 18.
31. DeLuzio, *Female Adolescence,* 46, 72. Ironically, the fact that poor and enslaved chil-dren could not have such a childhood served to reinforce the scientific argument rather than undermine it. Scientists depicted the shortening of a childhood for children of color as biological, as opposed to white children, whose childhood was developmental and intrinsically longer. White children who worked too hard at school or for wages had their character inappropriately stunted.
32. Mintz, *Huck's Raft,* 92, 137–38.
33. "Tomboy," definition 1, *Oxford English Dictionary,* online edition, www.oed.com.
34. Bernstein, *Racial Innocence,* 4, 6.
35. Degler, *At Odds,* 11–12.
36. Catharine Sedgwick, *Mean and Ends, or Self-Training* (Boston: Marsh, Capen, Lyon & Webb, 1839), 29–30, quoted in M. Nash, *Women's Education,* 67.

37. Hunter, *How Young Ladies Became Girls,* 14–15, 19.

38. Macleod, *American Childhood,* 7.

39. Willard, *How I Learned to Ride the Bicycle,* 15; Creevey, *Daughter of the Puritans,* 15–19, 270. Once one gets past the 1840s, and diaries that are largely records of weather and work, it is hard to find a diary of a girl or a memory of girlhood that does not have a significant commentary on the commonality of outdoor play.

40. MacLeod, *American Childhood,* 6.

41. Diary of Young Lady in Mississippi (1877–78), Manuscript Collection M-940, Louisiana Research Collection, Howard-Tilton Memorial Library, Tulane University, New Orleans; *Aunt Sally,* 26; Burton, *Memories of Childhood's Slavery Days,* 3.

42. Jabour, *Scarlett's Sisters,* 21.

43. Cremin, *Transformation of the School,* 127. There were, however, many states that attempted earlier means of promoting public education. For one example see Leloudis, *Schooling the New South.*

44. Fass, *Children of a New World,* 22.

45. Syrett, *American Child Bride,* 3–4.

46. Zboray, *A Fictive People,* 197.

47. Farnham, *Education of the Southern Belle,* 70–78.

48. Jabour, *Scarlett's Sisters,* 52.

49. Saxton, *Being Good,* 25.

50. Skemp, *Judith Sargent Murray,* 12. Society considered writing more important for boys, who would grow up to sign contracts; sewing was viewed as the corresponding skill for girls. See M. Nash, *Women's Education,* 74.

51. M. Nash, *Women's Education,* 61–63. Many southerners made the same argument, but their efforts were clearly more class-based. See Jabour, *Scarlett's Sisters,* 52.

52. Reinier, *From Virtue to Character,* 121–22. Integration of Massachusetts schools evolved over a battle to integrate Boston's schools, which began with African American parents suing for integration in 1849 (*Roberts v. City of Boston*). Many of the state's largest towns already had integrated schools by the 1840s.

53. Fass, *Children of a New World,* 23.

54. Reinier, *From Virtue to Character,* 103, 119, 104. Reinier notes that tax-supported schools for white children did make headway before the war in several states, including Virginia, Georgia, North Carolina, Alabama, Louisiana, and Kentucky. The most successful was in Charleston, South Carolina: "Extolled for elevating white labor and coalescing white supremacy in slave society, the public school system flourished in Charleston until the Civil War" (124). The most popular primers, the ubiquitous McGuffey Readers, were published in Cincinnati, but McGuffey himself was fully enmeshed in the Calvinist ethos that dominated print culture. See Westerhoff, *McGuffey and His Readers.*

55. Syrett, *American Child Bride,* 3–4.

56. Leloudis, *Schooling the New South,* 6–25.

57. McClelland, *Education of Women,* 129.

58. Radke-Moss, *Bright Epoch,* 5, quoting Julie Roy Jeffrey, *Frontier Women: "Civilizing" the West? 1840–1880,* rev. ed. (New York: Hill & Wang, 1998), 233.

59. Hunter, *How Young Ladies Became Girls,* 4.

60. Hunter, "Inscribing the Self," 55; Reinier, *From Virtue to Character,* 119, 122.

61. Quoted in M. Nash, *Women's Education,* 89.

62. Skemp, *Judith Sargent Murray,* 85; M. Nash, *Women's Education,* 77–89.

63. Hunter, *How Young Ladies Became Girls,* 169.

64. Ibid., 5.

65. D. A. Cohen, preface to Gibson, *"Hero Strong,"* vii; Merish, "Story Papers," 46–47.

66. D. A. Cohen, preface to *"Hero Strong,"* xxviii, xxiv.

67. D. A. Cohen, introduction to *"Hero Strong,"* 10–11. Looking at the Boston story papers *True Flag* and the *American Union,* Cohen points out several regular adolescent female authors: Louise E. Cutter (b. 1835), Ellen Louise Chandler (later Moulton; b. 1835), Virginia F. Townsend (b. 1836), and Clara Augusta Jones (b. 1835 or 1839), as well as Louisa May Alcott.
68. D. A. Cohen, "Making Hero Strong," 99, 117. "Female masculinity" is a direct reference to the work of Halberstam, *Female Masculinity.*
69. M. Gibson, "Hero Strong" in *"Hero Strong,"* 46.
70. D. A. Cohen, preface to *"Hero Strong,"* xxxviii.
71. M. Gibson, "The Good Angel of Georgian Eden's Life," in *"Hero Strong,"* 124.
72. D. A. Cohen, preface to *"Hero Strong,"* xiv.
73. Hunter, *How Young Ladies Became Girls,* chap. 2.
74. D. A. Cohen, preface to *"Hero Strong,"* viii. See also D. A. Cohen, "Winnie Woodfern Comes Out in Print," 371–72.
75. Mintz, *Huck's Raft,* 85.
76. Baym, introduction to *The Hidden Hand,* x–xi.
77. Southworth, *The Hidden Hand,* 40.
78. Baym, introduction to *The Hidden Hand,* xii–xiv.
79. Southworth, *The Hidden Hand,* 95, 154.
80. Habegger, *Gender, Fantasy, and Realism,* 181.
81. M. Ryan, *Cradle of the Middle Class,* 164.
82. Habegger, *Gender, Fantasy, and Realism,* 177.
83. "Bad boy" was the cultural title given to such male characters, alluding to Thomas Bailey Aldrich's ground-breaking memoir, *Story of a Bad Boy* (1869).
84. Southworth, *The Hidden Hand,* 437.
85. Baym, introduction to *The Hidden Hand,* xi.
86. Advertisement for *The Hidden Hand, Daily Confederation* (Montgomery, AL), November 9, 1859, 2. The play, starring the popular comic actress Joey Gougenheim as Capitola, appeared in cities as far north as Boston and as far south as New Orleans. "Burlesque" at this time indicated slang and social commentary, not overt nudity, as it would come to mean later. It also suggested working-class aesthetics. See Allen, *Horrible Prettiness,* 136.
87. For a sample review of *My Tomboy Girl* see "Melodrama Is Back at the Grand," *Los Angeles Herald,* February 18, 1907.
88. Habegger, *Gender, Fantasy, and Realism,* 181.
89. Sentilles, *Performing Menken,* 185, 206. Lotta Crabtree essentially presaged the "perky" tomboy of twentieth-century film. Examining tomboy characters, such as Gidget, in both television and film in the 1960s, Susan Douglas defines "perkiness" as "assertiveness masquerading as cuteness" that allowed tomboy characters to keep male approval while meeting their own goals. Douglas, *Where the Girls Are,* 108.
90. I have found only a few exceptions to this rule, the most consistent being the dime novel heroines, who may go through several serials before marrying the hero. Joan Jacobs Brumburg discusses changes in menses at the end of the nineteenth century in *The Body Project,* 4–7.
91. The American Sunday School Union and the American Tract Society (both based in the Northeast) excelled at producing these stories. For some examples see Anon., *The Gardener's Daughter* (Philadelphia: American Sunday School Union, 1828); Anon., *the Affectionate Daughter* (New York: American Tract Society, 1829).
92. Annie S. Frost, "Acting Charade: Wind-Fall," *Godey's Lady's Book* 78 (January 1869): 77; Judith K. De Ruyter, "The Story of Letty's Rings," *Godey's Lady's Book* 89 (October 1874): 340.
93. Several of the most prominent women activists of the century noted the painful shift to adulthood, citing both the constrictive clothing and the curtailed freedoms.

2. Tomboy Heroines in the Home

1. "Prize Essay Contest," *Seattle Daily Times,* January 21, 1906, 70.
2. Vallone, *Disciplines of Virtue,*119.
3. Phelps, *Gypsy Breynton,* 19.
4. Phelps, preface to *Gypsy Breynton,* n.p.
5. Phelps, *Gypsy Breynton,* 44–45.
6. Martha Finley's twenty-eight Elsie Dinsmore novels of Christian morality, family loyalty, and nineteenth-century racism enjoyed a lively following as they appeared sequentially from 1867 to 1905.
7. Sicherman, *Well-Read Lives,* 17–19.
8. Heilbrun, "Jo March: Male Model," 144.
9. Alcott quoted in Wadsworth, *In the Company of Books,* 48.
10. Townsend, *Written for Children,* 26–34.
11. Elizabeth Janeway, "Meg, Jo, Beth, Amy and Louisa," *New York Times Book Review,* September 29, 1968, 42.
12. LaPlante, *Marmee and Louisa,* chap. 9.
13. Sicherman, *Well-Read Lives,* 18.
14. Elbert, introduction to Alcott, *Work,* xiv–xvi; Elbert, introduction to Alcott, *Moods,* xii–xiii.
15. Brophy, "Sentimentality and Louisa May Alcott," 94–95.
16. Alcott, *Little Women,* 4.
17. Ibid., 5.
18. Ibid.
19. Willard, *How I Learned to Ride the Bicycle,* 15.
20. Alcott, *Little Women,* 5.
21. Brophy, "Sentimentality and Louisa May Alcott," 95.
22. Alcott, *Little Women,* 4–5.
23. Habegger, *Gender, Fantasy, and Realism,* 177–81.
24. Alcott, *Little Women,* 133.
25. Fetterley, "Alcott's Civil War," 379.
26. A. Miller, "Boyhood for Girls," 39.
27. Alcott quoted in Murray, *American Children's Literature,* 65.
28. Sicherman, *Well-Read Lives,* 31.
29. Ibid., 23.
30. Cynthia Ozick, "The Making of a Writer," *New York Times Book Review,* January 31, 1982, 24.
31. Louise Chandler Moulton, "Louisa May Alcott," in Phelps et al., *Our Famous Women,* 49.
32. Proehl, "Battling Girlhood," 59.
33. Ibid., 60–70.
34. Sicherman, *Well-Read Lives,* 28.
35. Barrett, "*Little Women* Forever," 91. In 1880 the two parts were combined and treated as one novel titled *Little Women.*
36. *New-York Daily Reformer* (Watertown), May 15, 1869, 2; "New Publications," *Albany (NY) Evening Journal,* August 16, 1869, 2.
37. Helen Church, "Recollections of Her Childhood," *New York Times,* March 25, 1899, 188; "From Boston," *Springfield (MA) Republican,* December 13, 1869, 2.
38. Sicherman, *Well-Read Lives,* 14.
39. "Little Women Heads Best Children's Books," *San Jose Evening News,* August 29, 1922, 5; "*Little Women* Leads Pool: Novel Rated Ahead of Bible for Influence on High School Pupils," *New York Times,* March 22, 1927, 7; Mann, "When the Alcott Books Were New," 85; Russ, "Not to Be Read on Sunday," 99.

40. Russ, "Not to Be Read on Sunday," 99.

41. Janeway, "Meg, Jo, Beth, Amy and Louisa," 42.

42. Quoted in Sicherman, *Well-Read Lives,* 28.

43. Alger, *Tattered Tom,* iv. The term "street Arab" seems to have been a late nineteenth-century way of "othering" homeless urban children and stems from images of nomadic Arabs. Jacob Riis addresses the topic of street Arabs in detail in chapter 17 of *How the Other Half Lives.*

44. Ibid., vii, 9–10, 16–17.

45. Alger, *Tattered Tom,* 71.

46. Ibid., 95.

47. Ibid., 200–201.

48. Ibid., 274.

49. "Book Notices," *New York Evening Post,* October 23, 1871, 2.

50. Mumford, *Hila Dart,* 5, 8.

51. Ibid., 34, 144.

52. Foster and Simons, *What Katy Read,* 122.

53. Coolidge, *What Katy Did,* 16, 17.

54. Ibid., 18–19.

55. Ibid., 11–12.

56. Ibid., 40–42.

57. Keith, *Take Up Thy Bed and Walk,* 5, 2–3.

58. Baker, *Running to Waste,* 8–10.

59. Ibid., 118, 191.

60. Ibid., 200–203, 244–45.

61. Rebecca's story later became popular as *Our Folks: A Play in Three Acts,* also by George Baker (Boston: G. M. Baker, 1879).

62. Vallone, *Disciplines of Virtue,* 120.

63. Fiedler, "Come Back to the Raft," 143.

64. M. A. Jacobson, *Being a Boy Again,* 1.

65. Aldrich, *Story of a Bad Boy,* 4.

66. Howells quoted in M. A. Jacobson, *Being a Boy Again,* 1.

67. Wadsworth, *In the Company of Books,* 81.

68. Edwin H. Cady was the first to clarify the difference in *The Road to Realism* (1956); see M. A. Jacobson, *Being a Boy Again,* 4.

69. Norris quoted in M. A. Jacobson, *Being a Boy Again,* 2.

70. Wadsworth, *In the Company of Books,* 82.

71. M. A. Jacobson, *Being a Boy Again,* 47.

72. Twain, *Tom Sawyer,* 21.

73. Ibid., 22.

74. William Dean Howells, *A Boys' Town* (1890), quoted in Avery, *Behold the Child,* 190.

75. The tomboy as horse-girl (and in British literature, growing into a horse-woman) has been a consistent favorite since the early nineteenth century. For a recent example see Klein, *You'll Grow Out of It,* 2–3.

76. *The Adventures of Huckleberry Finn* was first published in London in 1884, and in New York in 1885. Twain originally conceived of Huck Finn's story as a sequel to the commercially successful *Adventures of Tom Sawyer,* but lost interest in the story several times, prolonging its execution from 1873 to 1884.

77. Trites, *Twain, Alcott, and the Birth of the Adolescent Reform Novel,* 34.

78. Twain, *Tom Sawyer,* 64.

79. Macleod, *Building Character,* 54.

80. Aldrich, *Story of a Bad Boy,* 4.

81. Alcott, *Little Men,* 11.

82. Habegger, *Gender, Fantasy, and Realism,* 182.

3. Tomboy Heroines on the Manly Frontier

1. E. L. Wheeler, *Bob Woolf,* 3. *Bob Woolf* is a reprint of the original 1877 dime novel *Hurricane Nell: The Girl Dead Shot,* retitled with the name of the villain, Bob Woolf, in 1884 by Beadle & Adams. It was reprinted yet again under the original title in the 1890s as part of the Deadwood Dick Library, printed by M. J. Ivers in New York, 1899, and George Newnes of London, 1899. The cover illustration stayed intact, despite the title shift.
2. Sport referred not only to athletics, but to forms of male public fraternizing, such as gambling or attending the theater. See Gorn, *The Manly Art,* 68.
3. E. L. Wheeler, *Bob Woolf,* 7.
4. Ibid.
5. Denning, "Cheap Stories," 6; Cox, *Dime Novel Companion,* xv.
6. For one example among many analyzing the "frontier" as a process of cultures coming together and defining the frontier as different from the West as a geographical and mythical region, see Worster, "New West, True West."
7. Kimmel, *Manhood in America,* 61–62.
8. Greenberg, *Manifest Manhood,* 3.
9. West, "Reconstructing Race," 9.
10. Horsman, *Race and Manifest Destiny,* 158–86.
11. F. J. Turner, "Significance of the Frontier."
12. Indeed, the "dime novel" changed in size, shape, and price, and in the 1890s went from black and white to color, eventually coming close to resembling the "story papers" of fiction and verse intended for family reading. This completed a circle, as many of the stories appearing in dime novels were first serialized in earlier story papers. Denning, "Fire of the Dime Novel," 84.
13. Kasson, *Buffalo Bill's Wild West,* 15. See also "Western Essays," https://centerofthewest.org/learn.
14. Cox, *Dime Novel Companion,* xvii
15. Johannsen, *House of Beadle and Adams,* 4, 293–95.
16. Ansley, "'Girls-in-Breeches,'" 6.
17. Pearson, *Dime Novels,* 227.
18. "Juvenile Education," *New York Times,* July 25, 1882.
19. Pearson, *Dime Novels,* 227, 239, 253.
20. "She Wants to Be a Cowboy," *New York Times,* October 23, 1888, 6.
21. Diary, 1863–65, box 7, folder 1, Mary Sheldon Barnes Papers (MS 217), Sophia Smith Collection, Smith College, Northampton, MA; Bederman, *Manliness and Civilization,* 172–75.
22. Tompkins, *West of Everything,* 39.
23. Creevey, *Daughter of the Puritans,* 229, 256–57.
24. E. L. Wheeler, *Deadwood Dick on Deck,* 1–2.
25. Ibid., 7.
26. Elise, "Tomboys and Cowgirls," 149.
27. E. L. Wheeler, *Deadwood Dick on Deck,* 2.
28. Etulain, *Life and Legends of Calamity Jane;* McLaird, *Calamity Jane.*
29. The most famous *Calamity Jane* is probably the 1953 Warner Brothers musical, starring Doris Day. The movie inspired a stage musical of the same title, first produced in 1961, which continues to be performed; see www.ovrtur.com/show/119154.
30. McLaird, *Calamity Jane,* 98.
31. Her life was partially fictionalized in *The Rifle Queen: Annie Oakley of the Wild West Exhibition* (1887), and then later in plays, movies, and a television series.
32. Riley, *Life and Legacy of Annie Oakley,* 1–14, 202–4; Kasson, *Buffalo Bill's Wild West,* 80–81.

33. Riley, *Life and Legacy of Annie Oakley*, chap. 4.
34. Badger, *The Girl Rider*, 2.
35. Badger, *The Girl Cowboy Captain*, 5.
36. E. L. Wheeler, *Apollo Bill*, 4.
37. Katz, *The Black West*, xiii, 318–21.
38. Badger, *The Black Princess*, 17, 47.
39. Another example is Cheyenne Charlie in Old Scout, *Young Wild West's Luck*, 30–31.
40. Gleason, *Wistah*, 7.
41. Ibid.
42. Cox, *Dime Novel Companion*, xviii
43. E. L. Wheeler, *The Girl Sport*, 4.
44. E. L. Wheeler, *Bob Woolf*, 7.
45. Harbaugh, *Kit, the Girl Detective*, 2.
46. E. L. Wheeler, *Girl Sport*, 7.
47. E. L. Wheeler, *Bob Woolf*, 7.
48. E. L. Wheeler, *Deadwood Dick's Doom*, 8.
49. E. L. Wheeler, *Captain Crack-Shot*, 7.
50. E. L. Wheeler, *Deadwood Dick's Doom*, 15.
51. E. L. Wheeler, *Bonanza Bill*, 4.
52. Old Scout, *Prince of the Saddle*, 8.
53. Ibid., 14; *Young Wild West and the "Mixed Up" Mine*, 5.
54. Old Scout, *Prince of the Saddle*, 14–18.
55. Pearson, *Dime Novels*, 241.
56. Old Scout, *Young Wild West and the "Mixed Up" Mine*, 26; *Young Wild West's Luck*, 22.
57. Old Scout, *Young Wild West's Even Chance*, 3.
58. Old Scout, *Young Wild West's Luck*, 30.
59. E. L. Wheeler, *Calamity Jane Heroine of the Whoop-Up*, 2.
60. Old Scout, *Young Wild West: An Original Western Melodrama*, 2.
61. Old Scout, *Prince of the Saddle*, 8.

4. The Tomboy and the New Woman

1. *Boston Herald*, June 30, 1900, reprinted as "The New Species (from the *Boston Herald*)," *Dallas Morning News*, July 15, 1900, 18.
2. Patterson, *American New Woman Revisited*, 1.
3. H. L. Horowitz, *Wild Unrest*, 28.
4. Patterson, *American New Woman Revisited*, 2–3.
5. Matthews, *Rise of the New Woman*, 13.
6. Halberstam, *Female Masculinity*, 193.
7. Patterson, *American New Woman Revisited*, 5.
8. Carol A. Senf, introduction to Grand, *The Heavenly Twins*, xiii.
9. "The Woman of the Age: A Study in Character," *New Haven Daily Register*, March 15, 1885, 2; Edward Bok, "At Home with the Editor," *Ladies' Home Journal*, October 1894, 14, quoted in Patterson, *American New Woman Revisited*, 130.
10. Duffey, *What Women Should Know*, 34–35.
11. *Omaha World Herald*, April 6, 1888, 2.
12. Letter from Emma B. Sonedecker of Louisville, *Ohio Farmer*, September 18, 1880, 187.
13. Lurline Hatton Warner, "An Excellent Letter," *Southern Cultivator*, February 1887, 4.
14. "Trials of a Girl of Fourteen," *Courier-Journal* (Louisville, KY), October 2, 1887, 17; see also *Aberdeen (SD) Daily News*, March 14, 1888, 2; *San Jose Evening News*, January 13, 1888, 1.

15. "A Tom-boy Grows Up," *Cincinnati Daily Enquirer,* November 25, 1872, 7, reprinted in the *New Hampshire Sentinel* (Keene), December 26, 1872, 1.

16. Promoters of the play suggested that Swain's tomboy antics on stage were merely an extension of her true character. For example, in 1883 the New York *Truth,* an entertainment weekly, claimed that Swain had saved two people from drowning. Most astoundingly, the paper claimed that Swain had saved seven people just in the past season: "four in New Haven, two in Newport, and one in Brayport." According to the paper, saving drowning victims was a regular occurrence for the tomboy actress, who had been award the "medal of the Humane Society" for such acts three years before. See "Brave Carrie Swain: Cad, the Tomboy, Saves the Lives of Two Drowning Ladies," *Truth* (New York), August 19, 1883, 7.

17. Grinspan, "A Birthday Like None Other," 86; Syrett, "Statutory Marriage Ages," 105, 109; Schmidt, "'Rendered More Useful,'" 153–55.

18. Matthews, *Rise of the New Woman,* 77. As Matthews notes, "race suicide" was a term coined by the sociologist Edward A. Ross, but became a popular concept as one of Theodore Roosevelt's favorite dangers (38).

19. Kline, *Building a Better Race,* 1.

20. R. D. Cohen, "Child-Saving and Progressivism," 274.

21. Newman, *White Women's Rights,* 7.

22. Butsch, *Making of American Theater Audiences,* 66–68.

23. Matthews, *Rise of the New Woman,* 7.

24. Newman, *White Women's Rights,* 5.

25. Ibid., 6; Patterson, *American New Woman Revisited,* 5.

26. Goldin and Katz, "Putting the Co in Education," 1.

27. Patterson, *American New Woman Revisited,* 11. Patterson notes that a 1911 report by the Immigration Commission, which focused on 63 different colleges, found that 23.8 percent of the female students had immigrant parents and 0.3 percent had black parents (11). Given that populations of immigrants were concentrated in cities, typically in the North, and black families in rural areas, typically in the South, regional differences likely had a large impact on access to higher education, despite the commission's attempt to look nationwide.

28. "About Iowa: History of Leadership," www.uiowa.edu/about.

29. Goldin and Katz, "Putting the Co in Education," 3.

30. Nidiffer, "Crumbs from the Boy's Table."

31. This would change during and after the Second World War; see Bailey, *From Front Porch to Back Seat,* 32–42.

32. H. L. Horowitz, *Alma Mater,* 5–6, chap. 5.

33. Ibid., 4.

34. Matthews, *Rise of the New Woman,* 13.

35. Ibid., 11.

36. Smith-Rosenberg, *Disorderly Conduct,* 253.

37. Ibid., 186–87.

38. DeLuzio, *Female Adolescence,* 52, 58, 63; Smith-Rosenberg, *Disorderly Conduct,* 183.

39. On such fears in Germany see de Ras, *Body, Femininity and Nationalism,* 19; Ehrenpreis, "The Figure of the Backfisch," 480.

40. Cahn, *Coming On Strong,* 19. Cahn comments that twentieth-century female athletes subverted the idea that sports were intrinsically masculine, but tomboys and New Women had the same effect in the late nineteenth century.

41. DeLuzio, *Female Adolescence,* 51. *Sex in Education* evolved from a talk Clarke had recently given to the New England Women's Club in Boston, where the president of the club, Julia Ward Howe, had invited him to speak because of his earlier assertions that women should be allowed to study medicine. To the dismay of the club—and

particularly Howe, who would become one of his staunchest critics—Clarke proceeded to argue that higher education was structured for male physiology and therefore detrimental to female development. See DeLuzio, *Female Adolescence,* 56; Vertinsky, *Eternally Wounded Woman,* 52.

42. Rosenberg, *Beyond Separate Spheres,* 12.
43. Clarke, *Sex in Education,* 28, 19.
44. DeLuzio, *Female Adolescence,* 52.
45. Clarke, *Sex in Education,* 12, 30, 82.
46. DeLuzio, *Female Adolescence,* 57, 69.
47. *Popular Science Monthly* was founded in 1872 in part as a forum for Spencer's ideas. DeLuzio, *Female Adolescence,* 59; Vertinsky, *Eternally Wounded Woman,* 47.
48. DeLuzio, *Female Adolescence,* 58; Herbert Spencer, "The Psychology of the Sexes," *Popular Science Monthly* 4 (November 1873): 32. Darwin reinforced the theories of the French biologist Jean-Baptiste Lamarck, and Spencer took his ideas from Darwin. Vertinsky, *Eternally Wounded Woman,* 47–48.
49. A. B. Blackwell, *The Sexes throughout Nature,* 155–56. Antoinette Brown Blackwell was the first female Protestant minister in the United States.
50. DeLuzio, *Female Adolescence,* 9.
51. Leavitt, *Brought to Bed,* 14–19.
52. Henry Maudsley, "Sex in Mind and Education," *Popular Science Monthly* 5 (June 1874): 199–200. Maudsley also argued that female brains were as different from male brains as were their respective bodies, which became the basis of Clarke's next text, *The Building of a Brain* (1874); see Hamlin, *From Eve to Evolution,* 79.
53. Brumberg, *The Body Project,* 7. The article she describes is A. F. A. King, "A New Basis for Uterine Pathology," *American Journal of Obstetrics and Diseases of Women* 8 (August 1875): 237–56.
54. Brumberg, *The Body Project,* 9.
55. DeLuzio, *Female Adolescence,* 9.
56. Brumberg, *The Body Project,* 10, 11.
57. A. B. Blackwell, *The Sexes throughout Nature,* 161.
58. Clarke, *Sex in Education,* 89.
59. T.H.W., "Women and Men. The Athletic Girl," *Harper's Bazaar,* December 8, 1888, 830.
60. S. Weir Mitchell quoted in H. L. Horowitz, *Wild Unrest,* 130.
61. Brumberg, *The Body Project,* 21; Banta, *Imaging American Women,* 2, 88.
62. Bittel, *Mary Putnam Jacobi,* 11; Leavitt, *Brought to Bed,* 68, 71–73.
63. Brackett, *Education of American Girls,* 19.
64. Jacobi, "Mental Action and Physical Health," 259, 262–63, 301.
65. Ibid., 304.
66. "The Grown-Up Tomboy," *Kansas City Times,* October 30, 1886, 6.
67. Cahn, *Coming On Strong,* 217; Hult and Trekell, *A Century of Women's Basketball,* 22; Park, "Sport, Gender and Society," 84–85.
68. McCrone, "Play Up! Play Up! and Play the Game," 129.
69. Gilder, *Autobiography of a Tomboy,* 287–89.
70. "Athletics, 1865–1945," *Vassar Encyclopedia,* https://vcencyclopedia.vassar.edu.
71. Warner, *When the Girls Came Out to Play,* 220.
72. "How Woman's College Girls Play Ball," *Cleveland Plain Dealer,* May 7, 1896, 5.
73. Nutt, "Swinging for the Fences," 35.
74. Hult and Trekell, *A Century of Women's Basketball,* 23; Grundy and Shackelford, *Shattering the Glass,* 13.
75. Hult and Trekell, *A Century of Women's Basketball,* 25, 41.
76. Grundy and Shackelford, *Shattering the Glass,* 19.

77. "Basket Ball Game between Sophomores and Freshmen of Smith College," *St. Louis Republic,* November 25, 1894, 20; "Basket-Ball a Fad," *Daily Inter Ocean* (Chicago), December 30, 1894, 24.
78. Hult and Trekell, *A Century of Women's Basketball,* 41.
79. Quoted in Cahn, *Coming On Strong,* 85.
80. Elise Nelson, "Girls at Basketball: They Want to Play in Public for the Sake of the Gate Receipts," *Trenton Evening Times,* April 4, 1897, 9.
81. "Basket Ball Adepts: Substitute for Football Played by Society Women," *Birmingham Age-Herald,* January 12, 1896, 9.
82. "Girls Pulled Hair: Football Tactics Employed in Game of Basket-Ball," *Daily Inter Ocean* (Chicago), April 4, 1896, 6.
83. "Causes of the Growth of Women's Feet," *Daily Inter Ocean,* June 20, 1896.
84. Park, "Sport, Gender and Society," 86; Hult and Trekell, *A Century of Women's Basketball,* 22–23; Berenson, "Significance of Basketball for Women," 23; Dudley A. Sargent, "Are Athletics Making Girls Masculine? A Practical Answer to a Question Every Girl Asks," *Ladies' Home Journal,* March 1912, 72.
85. McCabe, *American Girl at College,* 15.
86. Kate Masterson, "Fair Athletes at the Training Table," *Los Angeles Herald,* May 1, 1898, 26.
87. Willis, "'Heaven Defend Me,'" 53.
88. Nelson, "Introduction: Who We Might Become," xii.
89. "The Influence of the Bicycle on Character," *Daily Illinois State Register,* May 24, 1896, 9.
90. Larrabee, "Women and Cycling," 90.
91. "Beauty on Bicycle: Craze for the Wheel among New York Women," *Boston Herald,* May 6, 1894, 13.
92. "Short Skirts May Result from the Bicycle Craze," *Evening Star* (Washington, DC), November, 16, 1895, 16.
93. Ibid.
94. Larrabee, "Women and Cycling," 95.
95. Galsworthy quoted ibid., 96–97.
96. Kitch, *Girl on the Magazine Cover,* 30–31.
97. "Spoil the Servants: Wheels Make Men and Women Alike Decrease in Value," *Cleveland Plain Dealer,* Sept 26, 1897, 27.
98. "*Fin de Siecle* Young Lady and the Bicycle," *Boston Herald,* October 22, 1893, 32.
99. "Gay Girls in Bloomers," *Knoxville Daily Journal,* July 21, 1895, 12.
100. Willard, *How I Learned to Ride the Bicycle,* 73–74. Willard's short book was originally published in 1895 as *A Wheel Within a Wheel.*
101. Nelson, "Introduction: Who We Might Become," xii–xiii.
102. "To Protect Herself All Wheel Women Should Carry Revolvers," *Daily Oklahoman,* May 12, 1898, 2.
103. Stanley, *Raising More Hell,* 167–69.
104. "The Bicycle Girls," *Saginaw (MI) News,* July 14, 1896, 4.
105. Smith-Rosenberg, *Disorderly Conduct,* 175.
106. "American Girls as Models," *Kansas City Times,* November 17, 1888, 4. The London source is the political paper *Truth,* November 15, 1888, 863.
107. "The American Tomboy: She Often Becomes a Woman Men Admire and Worship," *San Francisco Call,* August 2, 1891, 16.
108. "Statue of a Tomboy Will Be at the Fair for California," *Daily Inter Ocean* (Chicago), January 26, 1893, 9.
109. "California Girls: Their Various Qualities Defined," *San Francisco Chronicle,* August 25, 1889, 8.
110. Higginbotham, *Righteous Discontent,* 187–88; Giddings, *When and Where I Enter,* chap. 6.
111. "Woman's Beauty," *Evening Star* (Washington, DC), May 4, 1895, 16.

5. Boyhood for Girls

1. "Boys," *Commercial Advertiser* (New York), March 31, 1874, 1.
2. Romesburg, "Tightrope of Normalcy," 418.
3. Fiedler, "Come Back to the Raft," 144.
4. S. A. Miller, *Growing Girls,* 1–19.
5. Ibid., 5.
6. Romesburg, "Tightrope of Normalcy," 418, 433.
7. H. Newcomb, *How to Be a Man,* 10.
8. "Madcap Boys," *Daily Illinois State Journal* (Springfield), April 3, 1856, 2.
9. Roosevelt, "American Boy," 155.
10. Hoganson, *Fighting for American Manhood,* 29.
11. Bederman, *Manliness and Civilization,* 11–12.
12. Some of the unease over masculinity also had to do with a widespread belief in the Lamarckian theory at the heart of evolution: if a quality is not used, it will evolve away.
13. Kimmel, *Manhood in America,* 81, 119–20 (quotation); Bederman, *Manliness and Civilization,* 16–20.
14. H. W. Gibson, *Boyology,* 38.
15. DeLuzio, *Female Adolescence,* 99.
16. Bederman, *Manliness and Civilization,* 87–88.
17. Kidd, *Making American Boys,* 2.
18. Testi, "Gender of Reform Politics," 1509.
19. Bederman, *Manliness and Civilization,* 184.
20. Roosevelt, "American Boy," 155, 163. *Little Lord Fauntleroy,* by Frances Hodgson Burnett, serialized in *St. Nicholas Magazine* in 1885–86 and released in book form in 1886, was enormously popular and sparked a major fashion trend in boys' suits with velvet jackets and big floppy bows. In her foreword to a 2004 reprint of the novel, Polly Horvath contends that he was as popular in his time as Harry Potter in the late twentieth century (xi). He seems to have been the tinder to light the fire under the boyologists, who uniformly regarded the character as everything emasculating about Victorian society.
21. Roosevelt, "American Boy," 163; Merrill, *Winning the Boy,* 36. Roosevelt particularly emphasized football for character-building—a game that, with few rules and little protective equipment, was seen as a particularly dangerous sport even at the time.
22. "Manliness: Echoes of Roosevelt's Speeches Heard on Common," *Boston Journal,* July 7, 1902, 8.
23. Lovett, *Conceiving the Future,* 78, 91.
24. Roosevelt, "Before the Mothers' Congress," 576–77.
25. Roosevelt, "American Boy," 155–56; "Before the Mothers' Congress," 579 (quotation).
26. For examples of Roosevelt's viewpoints, see Bederman, *Manliness and Civilization,* 179, 184; Lovett, *Conceiving the Future,* 113; Roosevelt, "The Strenuous Life" and "Before the Mothers' Congress." Roosevelt considered Americans of British stock to be descended from Germans, with infusions from the Celts, Norse, Dutch, Danish, and Norman French.
27. Testi, "Gender of Reform Politics," 1518.
28. There are multiple testimonies to girls' love for boys' books. My personal favorite is a widely published article in which the Duchess of Sutherland claims, "I spent my pocket money on boys' papers from the age of six." See "Girls' Manliness Is Duchess' Plea," *Philadelphia Inquirer,* April 14, 1902, 2.
29. Bederman, *Manliness and Civilization,* 171, 6–7.
30. Smith-Rosenberg, "Discourses of Sexuality and Subjectivity," 265.
31. Roosevelt, "Before the Mothers' Congress," 577.
32. "Manliness: Echoes of Roosevelt's Speeches Heard on Common," *Boston Journal,* July 7, 1902, 8.

33. R. K. Anderson, *Frank Merriwell*, 20.
34. Kidd, *Making American Boys*, 2.
35. For a theoretical discussion of the "liminal" period (in this case, adolescence) as a universal center of rites of passage, see V. Turner, *The Ritual Process*, 94–97.
36. H. W. Gibson, *Boyology*, 3.
37. Forbush, *The Boy Problem*, 10.
38. H. W. Gibson, *Boyology*, 82.
39. Chamberlain, *The Child*, 2.
40. DeLuzio, *Female Adolescence*, 6–7.
41. See Mintz, *Huck's Raft*, 186–90.
42. "G. Stanley Hall on 'Boyhood': Report of His Views on the Best Way to Educate Boys of Various Ages," *Springfield (MA) Republican*, February 21, 1901, 3.
43. Lesko, *Act Your Age!*, 46.
44. Chamberlain, *The Child*, 35.
45. Driscoll, *Girls*, 53. Driscoll posits "adult (genital) sexuality" because she continues to the present, but I would argue that popular texts assert childhood asexuality until Freud comes along and makes sexuality integral to selfhood.
46. Merrill, *Winning the Boy*, 113, 41–42, 11, 80.
47. Rotundo, *American Manhood*, 55; R. K. Anderson, *Frank Merriwell*, 6.
48. Rotundo, *American Manhood*, 35.
49. A. S. Blackwell, *Growing Up in Boston's Gilded Age*, 24.
50. Ruskay, *Horsecars and Cobblestones*, 38.
51. Formanek-Brunell, *Made to Play House*, 4–6.
52. "Candidates for First Young Lady of the Land," *Boston Sunday Herald*, May 19, 1912, 29.
53. Roosevelt, "Before the Mothers' Congress," 576.
54. Hunter, *How Young Ladies Became Girls*, 3–5; Driscoll, *Girls*, 29, 38.
55. Odem, *Delinquent Daughters*, 33; S. A. Miller, *Growing Girls*, 1–2; Hunter, *How Young Ladies Became Girls*, 11–13; Kline, *Building a Better Race*, 16–19, 26–28.
56. Cahn, *Coming On Strong*,19–20.
57. The ages at which boys were breeched depended greatly on local custom, but the general period appears to be from roughly ages five to nine. It also depended on the purpose of dress. Boys who wore pants for playing might expect to wear "dresses" on more formal occasions. See Paoletti, *Pink and Blue*, 20–21.
58. Ehrenpreis, "The Figure of the Backfisch," 479–83; de Ras, *Body, Femininity and Nationalism*, 3, 19.
59. G. Stanley Hall, "The Budding Girl," *Appleton's Magazine* 13 (January 1909): 47.
60. G. S. Hall, *Adolescence*, xiv.
61. Hall quoted from "The Ideal School as Based on Child Study" (1901) in Vertinsky, *Eternally Wounded Woman*, 183–91, 193.
62. DeLuzio, *Female Adolescence*, 90.
63. A. Miller, "Boyhood for Girls," 13–14.
64. Kline, *Building a Better Race*, 2; "What Is the Matter with Jane," *New York Times*, November 3, 1920, 10, quoted in S. A. Miller, *Growing Girls*, 1.
65. Kitch, *Girl on the Magazine Cover*, 30–31.
66. F. J. Turner, "Significance of the Frontier," 61.
67. Ernest Thompson Seton, "Ernest Thompson Seton's Boys," *Ladies Home Journal*, May 1902, 15.
68. Morris, "Ernest Thompson Seton," 185.
69. Cordery, *Juliette Gordon Low*, 211; S. A. Miller, *Growing Girls*, 29–30.
70. S. A. Miller, *Growing Girls*, 4.
71. Ibid., 3; Revzin, "American Girlhood," 268; Rothschild, "To Scout or to Guide?," 115, 117.

72. Deloria, *Playing Indian,* chap. 4.

73. Quoted ibid., 112–13.

74. Quoted in Rogers, *Sebago-Wohelo Camp Fire Girls,* 17.

75. S. A. Miller, *Growing Girls,* 5.

76. On Pocahontas see, for example, "Great Girls: Pocahontas, the Little Tomboy of the 'Long Houses,'" *New Orleans Times-Picayune,* December 7, 1913, 36; Sentilles, *Performing Menken,* 130–31.

77. Jacobs, *Engendered Encounters,* 180.

78. Deloria's *Playing Indian* recounts the long history of "Indian play"—the appropriation of Native dress and acting out of "Indian" roles by white Americans.

79. From Gulick's introduction to Rogers, *Sebago-Wohelo Camp Fire Girls,* 32.

80. Cordery, *Juliette Gordon Low,* 221–23.

81. Rothschild, "To Scout or to Guide?," 118.

82. S. A. Miller, *Growing Girls,* 46.

83. Quoted in Inness, "Girl Scouts," 94.

84. S. A. Miller, *Growing Girls,* 45–47, quotation on 45–46; on Roosevelt's support for the Girls Scouts see Stacy A. Cordery, "The Roosevelts and the Girls Scouts: My Two Research Worlds" (blog post), January 7, 2011, www.stacycordery.com.

85. G. S. Hall, *Adolescence,* chap. 17.

86. Frances Pass Diary, July 15, 1922, Schlesinger Library, Radcliffe Institute, Cambridge, MA.

87. Marion Taylor Diary, June 23, 1915, Marion Taylor Papers, Schlesinger Library. "Marion Taylor" was a pseudonym for Dorothy Sherman Pencharz; a Harvard psychologist, Gordon Willard Allport, had obtained Pencharz's diaries and intended to analyze them for his work on the psychological development of adolescents.

88. Mildred M. Cornish Diary, November 7, 1907, Schlesinger Library.

89. Helen Scheetz of De Soto, Iowa, quoted in Riney-Kehrberg, *Nature of American Childhood,* 42.

90. S. A. Miller, *Growing Girls,* 142.

91. Low, *Handbook for Girl Scouts,* 9, 16, 146.

92. "Tomboy Delia," *Cleveland Plain Dealer,* March 27, 1904, 40; "The Way of Hetty the Tomboy: One of Six Queer Daughters," *Springfield (MA) American,* March 31, 1905, 13.

6. The American Girl

1. "Passing of the Tomboy: Girls Are Healthy and Happier Because of Outdoor Life," *Evening Star* (Washington, DC), August 27, 1898, 17, with attribution to *Harper's Bazaar.* The story was reprinted around the country.

2. Banta, *Imaging American Women,* 89.

3. Patterson, *American New Woman Revisited,* 3.

4. Banta, *Imaging American Women,* 2, 89. Banta contends that three major female types were used to represent American culture from 1890 to the 1910s: the Charmer, who charms; the New England Woman, who thinks; and the Outdoors Girl—derived, of course, from earlier tomboy imagery—who cavorts (46).

5. Morrison, *Girls of Central High in Camp,* 147.

6. Morrison, *Girls of Central High on the Stage,* 130, quoted in Singleton, "The Girls of Central High," 225.

7. See Habegger, *Gender, Fantasy, and Realism,* 119.

8. Billman, *Secret of the Stratemeyer Syndicate,* 21.

9. D. Johnson, *Edward Stratemeyer,* 165.

10. Honey, "From Spiritual Guides to Eager Consumers," 54–72; Jones and Jones, *Boys' and Girls' Book Series,* 6–7.

11. "Biographical/Historical Information," online finding aid for the Stratemeyer Syndicate records (MssCol 2903), Manuscripts and Archives Division, New York Public Library (NYPL), archives.nypl.org; Inness, "Girl Scouts, Camp Fire Girls, and Woodcraft Girls," 92.

12. "Biographical/Historical Information," NYPL, 2.

13. Billman, *Secret of the Stratemeyer Syndicate,* 23.

14. Honey, "From Spiritual Guides to Eager Consumers," 129, quoting Mathiews's article "Blowing Out the Boy's Brains" (1914).

15. Penrose, *Motor Girls; or, the Mystery of the Road.*

16. Penrose, *Motor Girls on a Tour,* 3.

17. Romalov, "Mobile and Modern Heroines," 76.

18. There are many *Camp Fire* novels. For a good tale on the woes of a lone young woman, see Vandercook, *Camp Fire Girls in the Outside World.* Camp Fire girls save a mining town in Benson, *Camp Fire Girls Mountaineering.*

19. Inness, "Girl Scouts, Camp Fire Girls, and Woodcraft Girls," 92.

20. The *Camp Fire* series had various authors over the years, as well as various publishers; among them are Amy Blanchard (Wilde, 1915), Hildegarde Frey (Burt, 1916–20); Isabel Hornibrook (Lothrop, Lee & Shepard, 1916–1919), Margaret Sanderson (Reilly & Lee, 1913–1917), Margaret Vandercook (Winston, 1915), Elizabeth M. Duffield (Sully & Kleinteich, 1915–1918), Irene Elliott Benson (Donohue, 1912–1918), Margaret Penrose (Goldsmith, 1930), and Jane Stewart (Saalfield, 1914).

21. Stewart, *A Camp Fire Girl's First Council Fire,* 48.

22. Ibid., 49.

23. Ibid., 55.

24. Stewart, *A Camp Fire Girl in Summer Camp,* 239.

25. Sicherman, *Well-Read Lives,* 2.

26. Romalov, "Unearthing the Historical Reader," 93.

27. Hope, *Outdoor Girls on Pine Island,* 121–22.

28. Honey, "From Spiritual Guides to Eager Consumers," 179–80.

29. Morrison, *Girls of Central High; or, Rivals for All Honors,* 16.

30. Morrison, *Girls of Central High at Basketball,* 54.

31. Christine Terhune Herrick, "Women in Athletics," *Outing, an Illustrated Monthly Magazine of Recreation,* September 1902, 6.

32. Morrison, *Girls of Central High; or, Rivals for All Honors,* 75.

33. Morrison, *Girls of Central High at Basketball,* 19.

34. Morrison, *Girls of Central High; or, Rivals for All Honors,* chaps. 1–2.

35. Emerson, *Ruth Fielding and the Gypsies* (1915) and *Ruth Fielding on the St. Lawrence* (1922), quoted in Jennifer White, "The Ruth Fielding Series by Alice B. Emerson," www.series-books.com/ruthfielding/ruthfielding.html.

36. Benson, *Camp Fire Girls Mountaineering,* 10.

37. Romalov, "Mobile and Modern Heroines," 86.

38. Kitch, *Girl on the Magazine Cover,* 30–31; she quotes Edward Bok, "Breaking Down Fences," *Ladies' Home Journal,* August 1897, 14.

39. Beard, *On the Trail,* 187.

40. Barthes, *Camera Lucida,* 15.

41. Kitch, *Girl on the Magazine Cover,* 29.

42. Various scholars discuss the power of submission, notably Nancy Cott in *The Bonds of Womanhood.* The best examples come from the Beecher sisters: see Catherine Beecher, *Treatise on Domestic Economy,* and Harriet Beecher Stowe, *Uncle Tom's Cabin; or, Life among the Lowly* (1851).

43. Stoneley, *Consumerism and American Girls' Literature,* 5.

44. Kitch, *Girl on the Magazine Cover,* 31.

45. "Passing of the Tomboy: Girls Are Healthier and Happier Because of Outdoor Life."

46. Ibid.

47. "The Tomboy: A Kind of Girl Who Became Extinct in the Last Century," *Oregonian* (Portland), November 9, 1901, 10.

48. For examples see "Inspiration for Mary Pickford Tomboy Roles," *Cleveland Plain Dealer,* May 21, 1916, 71; "Tomboy Jackie Saunders at the Clyne Today," *Pueblo (CO) Chieftain,* August 25, 1917, 4; "Tomboy Girl of the Screen Is Glad She Is Not a Real Girl," *Baltimore American,* December 1, 1918, 24; "A Brave Little Tomboy," *Cleveland Plain Dealer,* December 12, 1914, 13.

49. See "Tilly the Tomboy" at www.moviemoviesite.com.

50. See, for example, "Tomboy Taylor," *Seattle Daily Times,* January 14, 1920.

51. "My Tomboy Girl" is from the musical of the same name, starring Lottie Williams, which was a stage sensation beginning in 1905. "Daddy's Little Tomboy Girl" pops up frequently in advertisements for sheet music in 1908; see, for example, *Watertown (NY) Daily Times,* June 25, 1908, 3.

52. "Favors the Tomboy Girl: All Healthy Children Like Rough Play, Says Joseph Lee," *Idaho Register,* July 20, 1915, 7; "Training the Child: Shall You Raise Your Girl to Be a Tomboy," *Boston Journal,* July 16, 1917, 7.

53. A. Miller, "Boyhood for Girls," iii.

54. "Passing of the Tomboy," *Aberdeen (SD) Daily News,* May 18, 1917, 2.

7. Tomboys as Retrospective

1. In *The Power and Passion of M. Carey Thomas,* Helen Lefkowitz Horowitz uses Thomas's personal papers to argue that in many ways her involvement with other women was a pragmatic choice. It was not that Thomas was not attracted to men (indeed, she believed herself in love with particular men in earlier stages of her life), but rather that she recognized that she would not fulfill her own potential if she chose to marry (172–74).

2. M. Carey Thomas diary, November 25–26, 1870, pp. 22–27, vol. 8, reel 1, frames 392–94, *The Papers of M. Carey Thomas in the Bryn Mawr College Archives* (hereafter *PMCT*), ed. Lucy Fisher West (217 reels; Woodbridge, CT: Research Publications International, 1982).

3. M. Carey Thomas diary, Oct. 1, 1871, vol. 10, reel 1, frame 469, *PMCT.*

4. "Oration spoken before the Scholars of Marble Hall," 1871, folder "Intellectual Development," reel 74, *PMCT,* quoted in H. L. Horowitz, *Power and Passion,* 27.

5. Until girls were in their middle teens, they tended to record days filled with outdoor activities and pranks. Anya Jabour gives some of the most succinct examples in *Scarlett's Sisters.*

6. Hunter, "Inscribing the Self in the Heart of the Family," 52–54.

7. For example, Louisa May Alcott's parents responded to her within her journal; see Alcott in Berger and Berger, *Small Voices,* 110–12. A good example of a journal as a site of exchange between a student and teacher is the Mary L. P. Williams diary, Manuscripts Collection M-417, Louisiana Research Collection, Howard-Tilton Memorial Library, Tulane University, New Orleans.

8. Anon., Diary of Young Woman in Mississippi, 1877–78, Manuscripts Collection M-940, Louisiana Research Collection, Tulane.

9. Newberry, *Julia Newberry's Diary,* 67; W. D. Johnson, *Antebellum American Women's Poetry,* 98.

10. A. S. Blackwell, *Growing Up in Boston's Gilded Age,* 36 (entry dated February 21, 1872).

11. Jabour, *Scarlett's Sisters,* 19–21.

12. Richard Watson Gilder to Jeannette Gilder, January 21, 1865, Jeannette Leonard Gilder Papers, 1865–1917 (A-141), Schlesinger Library, Radcliffe Institute, Cambridge, MA.

13. Marion Boyd Allen, Diary, 1875–1876, entry dated July 9, 1875, Octavo A, Manuscripts, American Antiquarian Society, Worcester, MA.

14. Annie Ware Winsor Allen diary, July 1882, Annie Ware Winsor Allen Papers (MC 322), Schlesinger Library.

15. Breckinridge, *Lucy Breckinridge*, 40.

16. Grimké, *Journals*, 96.

17. Ibid., 86; Eggleston, *Kathie's Diary*, 236.

18. Lee, *Growing Up in the 1850s*, 151.

19. Eggleston, *Kathie's Diary*, 54.

20. Breckinridge, *Lucy Breckinridge*, 29–30.

21. Annie Ware Winsor Allen diary, December 1882 and December 1883.

22. Alcott, *Journals*, 63.

23. Eggleston, *Kathie's Diary*, 60.

24. Breckinridge, *Lucy Breckinridge*, 30, 177.

25. Gifford, *Writing Out My Heart*, 132–57, 152, 157.

26. Letter from Emma B. Sonedecker of Louisville, *Ohio Farmer*, September 18, 1880, 187.

27. Lurline Hatton Warner, "An Excellent Letter," *Southern Cultivator*, February 1887, 4.

28. Lucy Larcom, "Clara Barton," in Phelps et al., *Our Famous Women*, 95.

29. Lucia Gilbert Runkle, "The Doctors Blackwell," ibid., 137, 135.

30. Laura Curtis Bullard, "Elizabeth Cady Stanton," ibid., 606.

31. Quoted in Kate Sanborn, "Frances Willard," ibid., 698–99.

32. Willard, *How I Learned to Ride the Bicycle;* Willard, *Writing Out My Heart*, 39, 41–42.

33. Edith Mayo, introduction to Willard, *How I Learned to Ride the Bicycle*, 1.

34. Parton, *Daughters of Genius*, 311.

35. For an example see "Anecdote of Harriet: The Means by Which She Secured a Day's Fishing," *Harrisburg Patriot*, July 27, 1888, 3.

36. Gilder, *Autobiography of a Tomboy*, 183.

37. Vicinus, *Intimate Friends*, 31–33.

38. Louise Chandler Moulton, "Louisa May Alcott," in Phelps et al., *Our Famous Women*, 49.

39. There were earlier biographies of women, as Daniel A. Cohen points out in the introduction to Gibson, *"Hero Strong" and Other Stories*, 35. Such early biographies tended to be on martial subjects, such as Joan of Arc, the Revolutionary War soldier Deborah Sampson, and the many women who participated in the Civil War. All of them portrayed their protagonists as masculinized young women. That narrative arc largely remained intact, but by the 1880s more women were writing their *own* stories, as autobiography or memoir, and were no longer linking tomboyism to military valor but to rather to achievement outside of the domestic space. See also D. A. Cohen, *The Female Marine*.

40. Frémont, *Souvenirs of My Time*, 317.

41. Sentilles, *Performing Menken*, 128–29. Menken gives herself a male role in one of the stories, traveling on horseback with only a male slave as her companion and falling in love with an Indian princess who dies tragically in her arms.

42. Velazquez, *The Woman in Battle*, 42.

43. Rice, *He Included Me*, 22.

44. Wilder, *Pioneer Girl*, 120.

45. Richard Watson Gilder to Jeannette Gilder, January 21, 1865, Jeannette Leonard Gilder Papers, Schlesinger Library.

46. Gilder, *Autobiography of a Tomboy*, 3–4.

47. Ibid., 230.

48. Despite her gender transgressions, Mary Walker became a national heroine to many women in 1866 when she defended her decision to wear trousers by famously stating,

"I wear this dress from high moral principle; the fashionable dress of the day is not such as any physiologist can defend, nor any economist wear; it sweeps the filth from your side-walks; it fastens the lungs as within a coffin, and encased within its iron bands no woman can venture out in a high wind, or attempt to climb a staircase, without immodest exposure of the limbs; it is an abomination, invented by the prostitutes of Paris, and as such unfit to be worn by a modest American woman." "A Woman and a Heroine," *Home Journal: For the Cultivation of the Memorable, the Progressive and the Beautiful* (New York), June 20, 1866.

49. Gilder, *Tomboy at Work,* 8–10.
50. Gilder, *Autobiography of a Tomboy,* 288.
51. Ibid., 66, 74–77.
52. Ibid., 349.
53. Pamela Smith Hill, introduction to Wilder, *Pioneer Girl,* xv, xix. According to scholars working on the Pioneer Girl project, Wilder initially wrote her memoir for private reading by her daughter and other family members. But because the Wilders had recently lost all of their savings in the stock market crash of 1929, others have suggested that she wrote the memoir to make money.
54. Wilder, *Pioneer Girl,* 120, 131.
55. Wilder, *Little Town on the Prairie,* 94.
56. Wilder, *On the Banks of Plum Creek,* 156.
57. Brink, *Caddie Woodlawn,* 240, 242. The Minnesota Uprising of 1862, led by the Santee Sioux, had barely been quelled by the opening of the novel in 1864, and the Native Americans were literally starving amid the rye fields while the government, focused on the Civil War to the east, delayed paying the promised annuities. The uprising would lead directly to the Battle of the Little Bighorn and the related Plains Indian Wars, culminating in the end of Native American autonomy by 1890.
58. Ibid., 243; Alcott, *Little Women,* 5.
59. Brink, *Caddie Woodlawn,* 244–45.

Coda

1. Hyde, Rosenberg, and Berhman, "Tomboyism."
2. Reported in Ruth Padawer, "What's So Bad about a Boy Who Wants to Wear a Dress?," *New York Times* online edition, August 8, 2012, www.nytimes.com.
3. Marisa Meltzer, "Where Have All the Tomboys Gone?," *New York Times* online edition, October 13, 2015 (a version of the article ran in the print edition under a different title on October 13); "Passing of the Tomboy," *Aberdeen (SD) Daily News,* May 18, 1917, 2.
4. Online reader comments on Meltzer, "Where Have All the Tomboys Gone?," October 14 and 15, 2015; and Valeriya Safronova, "Why Can't We Just Let Girls Be Girls? Readers on the Term 'Tomboy,'" *New York Times* online edition, October 19, 2015.
5. Klein, *You'll Grown Out of It,* 2.
6. Anonymous, June 7, 2016, Tomboy Stories website, https://tomboystories.org.
7. Lisa Selin Davis, "My Daughter Is Not Transgender. She's a Tomboy," *New York Times* online edition, April 18, 2017 (a version ran in the print edition under a different title on April 19).
8. A. Miller, "Boyhood for Girls," 4–5.
9. Landis, Landis, and Bolles, *Sex in Development,* 17–19.
10. A. Miller, "Am I Normal?," 23, 31, 33.
11. "Married Normal" interview form, p. 4, Series III B, box 1, The Carney Landis Collection (hereafter CLC), Library and Special Collections, The Kinsey Institute for Research in Sex, Gender and Reproduction, Indiana University, Bloomington.

12. Case 2N (m), interview date April 20, 1936. All interviews cited here are in box 1, folder 1, CLC.
13. Case 3N (m), interview date April 25, 1936.
14. Case 4N (m), interview date April 27, 1936.
15. A. Miller, "Am I Normal?," 24.
16. Ibid., 34.
17. Landis, Landis, and Bolles, *Sex in Development,* xi. See also Katie Callahan, "Eager for Help: Depression-Era Anxiety in Sex and Development," 2011, unpublished paper in the author's possession.
18. Hilary Mullins, "Evolution of a Tomboy," 40.
19. Ibid., 41.
20. Ibid., 43.
21. Ibid., 48.
22. Halberstam, *Female Masculinity,* 6.
23. Padawer, "What So Bad about a Boy Who Wants to Wear a Dress?"
24. McCullers, *The Member of the Wedding,* 461; Halberstam, *Female Masculinity,* 7.
25. Maysa, July 30, 2015, Tomboy Stories website, https://tomboystories.org (hereafter TS). Here and below, I have not noted or corrected grammar, punctuation, or spelling in quotations from posters to the site.
26. Sara, June 7, 2016; Lyd, January 26, 2015; Margo, October 7, 2016, TS.
27. Cody, November 3, 2014; Faith, January 26, 2015; Amber, August 5, 2015, TS.
28. Krystal, July 30, 2015, TS.
29. Simmons quoted in Meltzer, "Where Have All the Tomboys Gone?"
30. Klein, *You'll Grow Out of It,* 18.

Selected Bibliography

Abate, Michelle Ann. *Tomboys: A Literary and Cultural History.* Philadelphia: Temple University Press, 2008.

Adickes, Sandra. *To Be Young Was Very Heaven: Women in New York before the First World War.* New York: St. Martin's, 1997.

Adorno, Theodor. "Culture Industry Reconsidered." *New German Critique* 6 (Autumn 1975): 12–19.

Alcott, Louisa May. *Hospital Sketches.* 1863. New York: Dover Editions, 2006.

———. *Jo's Boys, and How They Turned Out: A Sequel to Little Men.* 1886. New York: Bantam Classics, 1995.

———. *The Journals of Louisa May Alcott.* Edited by Joel Merson and Danile Sheely. Boston: Little, Brown, 1989.

———. *Little Men.* 1871. New York: Hatchett, 2009.

———. *Little Women.* 1868–1869. New York: Penguin, 2004.

———. *Moods.* 1864. Edited by Sarah Elbert. Brunswick, NJ: Rutgers University Press, 1996.

———. *Work: A Story of Experience.* 1873. Edited by Sarah Elbert. New York: Schocken, 1977.

Aldrich, Thomas Bailey. *The Story of a Bad Boy.* 1870. New York: Jefferson Press, 1913.

Alexander, Ruth M. *The "Girl Problem": Female Sexual Delinquency in New York, 1900–1930.* Ithaca: Cornell University Press, 1995.

Alger, Horatio. *Tattered Tom; or, The Adventures of a Street Arab.* Boston: A. K. Loring, 1871.

Allen, Robert C. *Horrible Prettiness: Burlesque and American Culture.* Chapel Hill: University of North Carolina Press, 1991.

Amory, Hugh, and David D. Hall, eds. *The Colonial Book in the Atlantic World.* Vol. 1 of *A History of the Book in America,* edited by David D. Hall. Chapel Hill: University of North Carolina Press, 2000.

Anderson, Ryan K. *Frank Merriwell and the Fiction of All-American Boyhood: The Progressive Era Creation of the Schoolboy Sports Story.* Fayetteville: University of Arkansas Press, 2015.

Anderson, Vicki. *The Dime Novel in Children's Literature.* Jefferson, NC: McFarland, 2005.

Anon. "The Tom-Boy Who Was Changed into a Real Boy." In *Aunt Oddama-dodd: Little Miss Consequence.* New York: McLoughlin Brothers, 1859.

Ansley, Laura. "'Girls-in-Breeches': The Gendering of Female Heroines in American Western Dime Novels." Senior honors thesis, Case Western Reserve University, 2009. In the author's possession.

Ardis, Ann L. *New Women, New Novels: Feminism and Early Modernism.* New Brunswick, NJ: Rutgers University Press, 1990.

Aunt Sally; or, The Cross the Way of Freedom. A Narrative of the Slave-life and Purchase of the Mother of Rev. Isaac Williams, of Detroit, Michigan. Cincinnati: American Reform Tract and Book Society,1858.

Avery, Gillian. *Behold the Child: American Children and Their Books, 1621–1922.* Baltimore: Johns Hopkins University Press, 1994.

———. *Childhood's Pattern: A Study of the Heroes and Heroines of Children's Fiction, 1770–1950.* London: Hodder & Stoughton, 1975.

Babb, Valerie Melissa. *Whiteness Visible: The Meaning of Whiteness in American Literature and Culture.* New York: New York University Press, 1998.

Badger, Joseph Edward. *The Black Princess.* New York: Beadle & Adams, 1871.

———. *The Girl Cowboy Captain; or, The Skinners of the Carolina Swamps. 1871.* New York: Beadle & Adams, 1889.

———. *The Girl Rider; or, Nimble Ned's Surprise.* New York: Beadle & Adams, April 3, 1889.

Bailey, Beth. *From Front Porch to Back Seat: Courtship in the Twentieth Century.* Baltimore: Johns Hopkins University Press, 1988.

Bailey, J. Michael, Kathleen T. Bechtold, and Sheri A. Berenbaum. "Who Are Tomboys and Why Should We Study Them?" *Archives of Sexual Behavior* 31.4 (August 2002): 333–41.

Baker, George M. *Running to Waste: The Story of a Tomboy.* Boston: Lee & Shepard, 1875.

Banta, Martha. *Imaging American Women: Idea and Ideals in Cultural History.* New York: Columbia University Press, 1987.

Barrett, C. Waller. "*Little Women* Forever." In Stern, *Critical Essays on Louisa May Alcott,* 89–93.

Barthes, Roland. *Camera Lucida: Reflections on Photography.* Translated by Richard Howard. New York: Hill & Wang, 1980.

Baym, Nina. Introduction to Southworth, *The Hidden Hand,* ix–xxi.

———. *Novels, Readers, and Reviewers: Responses to Fiction in Antebellum America.* Ithaca: Cornell University Press, 1984.

———. "Portrayal of Women in American Literature, 1790–1870." In *What Manner of Woman: Essays on English and American Life and Literature,* edited by Marlene Springer, 211–34. New York: New York University Press, 1977.

————. *Woman's Fiction: A Guide to Novels by and about Women in America, 1820–1870*. Ithaca: Cornell University Press, 1978.

————. *Women Writers of the American West, 1833–1927*. Urbana: University of Illinois Press, 2011.

Beard, Lina, and Adelia Belle Beard. *On the Trail: An Outdoor Book for Girls.* New York: Charles Scribner's Sons, 1915.

Bederman, Gail. *Manliness and Civilization: A Cultural History of Gender and Race in the United States, 1880–1917*. Chicago: University of Chicago Press, 1995.

Benson, Irene Elliott. *Camp Fire Girls Mountaineering; or, Overcoming All Obstacles*. Chicago: M. A. Donahue, 1918.

Berenson, Senda. "The Significance of Basketball for Women." In *Line Basketball for Women,* edited by Senda Berenson, 20–27. New York: A. G. Spalding, 1901.

Berger, Josef, and Dorothy Berger, eds. *Small Voices*. New York: Paul F. Eriksson, 1966.

Bernstein, Robin. *Racial Innocence: Performing American Childhood and Race from Slavery to Civil Rights*. New York: New York University Press, 2011.

Billman, Carol. *The Secret of the Stratemeyer Syndicate: Nancy Drew, the Hardy Boys, and the Million Dollar Fiction Factory*. New York: Ungar, 1986.

Bilston, Sarah. *The Awkward Age in Women's Popular Fiction, 1850–1900: Girls and the Transition to Womanhood*. New York: Oxford University Press, 2004.

Bittel, Carla. *Mary Putnam Jacobi and the Politics of Medicine in Nineteenth-Century America*. Chapel Hill: University of North Carolina Press, 2009.

Blackwell, Alice Stone. *Growing Up in Boston's Gilded Age: The Journal of Alice Stone Blackwell, 1872–1874*. Edited by Marlene Deahl Merrill. New Haven: Yale University Press, 1990.

————. *Lucy Stone: Pioneer of Woman's Rights*. Norwood, MA: Alice Stone Blackwell Committee, 1930.

Blackwell, Antoinette Brown. *The Sexes throughout Nature*. New York: G. P. Putnam's Sons, 1875.

Blair, Amy L. *Reading Up: Middle-Class Readers and the Culture of Success in the Early Twentieth-Century United States*. Philadelphia: Temple University Press, 2012.

Blake, Mabelle Babcock. *The Education of the Modern Girl*. New York: Houghton Mifflin, 1929.

Bold, Christine, ed. *US Popular Print Culture, 1860–1920*. Vol. 6 of *The Oxford History of Popular Print Culture,* edited by Gary Kelly. Oxford: Oxford University Press, 2012.

Booth, Orrin B. *Warnings to Girls*. Cambridge, OH: The Helping Hand Society, 1906.

Bourget, Paul. *Outre-Mer Impressions of America*. London: T. Fisher, 1895.

Boyesen, Hjalmar Hjorth. *Literary and Social Silhouettes*. New York: Harper & Bros., 1894.

Brackett, Anna Callender, ed. *The Education of American Girls, Considered in a Series of Essays*. New York: G. P. Putnam's Sons, 1874.

Breckinridge, Lucy Gilmer. *Lucy Breckinridge of Grove Hill: The Journal of a Virginia Girl, 1862–1864*. Edited by Mary D. Robertson. Columbia: University of South Carolina Press, 1979.

Briggs, Caroline Clapp. *Reminiscences and Letters of Caroline C. Briggs*. Edited by George Spring Merriam. New York, Houghton, Mifflin, 1897.

Brink, Carol Ryrie. *Caddie Woodlawn: A Frontier Story*. New York: Macmillan, 1935.

Broer, Lawrence R., and John Daniel Walther, eds. *Dancing Fools and Weary Blues: The Great Escape of the Twenties*. New York: Popular Press, 1990.

Brophy, Brigid. "Sentimentality and Louisa May Alcott." In Stern, *Critical Essays on Louisa May Alcott*, 93–96.

Brown, Bill, ed. *Reading the West: An Anthology of Dime Westerns*. Boston: Bedford Books, 1997.

Brown, Brené. *Daring Greatly: How the Courage to Be Vulnerable Transforms the Way We Live, Love, Parent, and Lead*. New York: Gotham Books, 2012.

Brown, Kathleen. *Foul Bodies: Cleanliness in Early America*. New Haven: Yale University Press, 2009.

Brumberg, Joan Jacobs. *The Body Project: An Intimate History of American Girls*. New York: Random House, 1997.

Buckner, Helen, Mary F. Fielder, and Martha F. Allen. *Wo-He-Lo: The Story of the Camp Fire Girls, 1910–1960*. New York: Holt, Rinehart & Winston, 1961.

Burton, Annie L. *Memories of Childhood's Slavery Days*. Boston: Ross, 1909.

Bushman, Richard L. *The Refinement of America: Persons, Houses, Cities*. New York: Knopf, 1992.

Bushnell, Horace. *Discourses on Christian Nurture*. Boston: Massachusetts Sabbath School Society, 1847.

Butsch, Richard. *The Making of American Theater Audiences: From Stage to Television, 1750–1990*. New York: Cambridge University Press, 2000.

Buttz, Rachel Q. *A Hoosier Girlhood*. Boston: R. G. Badger, 1924.

Cahn, Susan K. *Coming On Strong: Gender and Sexuality in Twentieth-Century Women's Sport*. Cambridge: Harvard University Press, 1995.

―――. *Sexual Reckonings: Southern Girls in a Troubling Age*. Cambridge: Harvard University Press, 2007.

Calhoun, Mary. *Katie John*. New York: Harper, 1960.

Calvert, Karin. *Children in the House: The Material Culture of Early Childhood, 1600–1900*. Boston: Northeastern University Press, 1994.

Camhi, Jane Jerome. *Women against Women: American Anti-Suffragism, 1880–1920*. New York: Carlson, 1994.

Campbell, James T., Matthew Pratt Guterl, and Robert G. Lee, eds. *Race, Nation, and Empire in American History*. Chapel Hill: University of North Carolina Press, 2007.

Carr, C. Lynn. "Tomboy Resistance and Conformity: Agency in Social Psychological Gender Theory." *Gender and Society* 12.5 (October 1998): 528–53.

Castañeda, Claudia. *Figurations: Child, Bodies, Worlds*. Durham, NC: Duke University Press, 2002.

Cayleff, Susan E. "The 'Texas Tomboy': The Life and Legend of Babe Didrikson Zaharias." *OAH Magazine of History* 7.1 (Summer 1992): 28–33.

Chamberlain, Alexander Francis. *The Child: A Study in the Evolution of Man*. New York: Charles Scribner's Sons, 1902.

Chambers-Schiller, Lee. "The Single Woman: Family and Vocation among Nineteenth-Century Reformers." In Kelley, *Woman's Being, Woman's Place*, 334–50.

Chatelain, Marcia. *Southside Girls: Growing Up in the Great Migration*. Durham, NC: Duke University Press, 2015.

Cherland, Meredith Rogers. *Private Practices: Girls Reading Fiction and Constructing Identity*. London: Taylor & Francis, 1994.

Chudacoff, Howard P. *How Old Are You? Age Consciousness in American Culture*. Princeton: Princeton University Press, 1989.

Clark, Anna. *The Struggle for the Breeches: Gender and the Making of the British Working Class*. Berkeley: University of California Press, 1995.

Clark, Beverly Lyon. *Kiddie Lit: The Cultural Construction of Children's Literature in America*. Baltimore: Johns Hopkins University Press, 2003.

Clarke, Edward H. *Sex in Education*. 1873. Rockville, MD: Wildside Press, 2006.

Clary, Anna Lathrop. *Reminiscences of Anna Lathrop Clary, Written for Her Children*. 1937. Whitefish, MT: Kessinger, 2006.

Clement, Priscilla Ferguson. *Growing Pains: Children in the Industrial Age, 1850–1890*. New York: Twayne, 1997.

Clinton, Catherine. *The Columbia Guide to American Women in the Nineteenth Century*. New York: Columbia University Press, 2000.

Closz, Harriet M. Bonebright, and Sarah Brewer Bonebright. *Reminiscences of Newcastle, Iowa, 1848: A History of the Founding of Webster City, Iowa*. Des Moines: Historical Department of Iowa, 1921.

Coffin, Elizabeth W. *A Girl's Life in Germantown*. Boston: Sherman, French, 1916.

Cogan, Frances B. *All-American Girl: The Ideal of Real Womanhood in Mid-Nineteenth-Century America*. Athens: University of Georgia Press, 1989.

Cohen, Daniel A. *The Female Marine and Related Works: Narratives of Cross-Dressing and Urban Vice in America's Early Republic.* Amherst: University of Massachusetts Press, 1997.

———. "Making Hero Strong: Teenage Ambition, Story-Paper Fiction, and the Generational Recasting of American Women's Authorship." *Journal of the Early Republic* 30.1 (Spring 2010): 85–138.

———. Preface and introduction in Gibson, *"Hero Strong" and Other Stories,* vii–xviii and 1–61.

———. "Winnie Woodfern Comes Out in Print: Story-Paper Authorship and Protolesbian Self-Representation in Antebellum America." *Journal of the History of Sexuality* 21.3 (September 2012): 367–408.

Cohen, Margaret, and Christopher Prendergast, eds. *Spectacles of Realism: Body, Gender, and Genre.* Minneapolis: University of Minnesota Press, 1995.

Cohen, Ronald D. "Child-Saving and Progressivism, 1885–1915." In Hawes and Hiner, *American Childhood,* 273–309.

Colman, Penny. *Girls! A History of Growing Up Female in America.* New York: Scholastic, 2000.

Connell, R. W. *Masculinities.* Berkeley: University of California Press, 1995.

Cook, Sylvia Jenkins. *Working Women, Literary Ladies: The Industrial Revolution and Female Aspiration.* New York: Oxford University Press, 2008.

Coolidge, Susan. *What Katy Did: A Story.* 1872. Boston: Roberts Brothers, 1876.

Corbett, Ken. "Homosexual Boyhood: Notes on Girlyboys." In Rottnek, *Sissies and Tomboys,* 107–39.

Cordery, Stacey A. *Juliette Gordon Low: The Remarkable Founder of the Girl Scouts.* New York: Viking, 2012.

Cott, Nancy F. *The Bonds of Womanhood: "Woman's Sphere" in New England, 1780–1835.* New Haven: Yale University Press, 1977.

Cox, J. Randolph. *The Dime Novel Companion: A Source Book.* Westport, CT: Greenwood Press, 2000.

Creevey, Caroline A. Stickney. *A Daughter of the Puritans: An Autobiography.* New York: G. P. Putnam's Sons, 1916.

Cremin, Lawrence A. *The Transformation of the School: Progressivism in American Education, 1876–1957.* New York: Knopf, 1961.

Curd, Sam. *Sam Curd's Diary: The Diary of a True Woman.* Athens: Ohio University Press, 1984.

Dall, Carolyn Wells Healey. *"Alongside": Being Notes Suggested by "A New England Boyhood" of Doctor Edward Everett Hale.* 1900. New York: Arno Press, 1980.

Dalsimer, Katherine. *Female Adolescence: Psychoanalytic Reflections on Works of Literature.* New Haven: Yale University Press, 1986.

Damon-Moore, Helen. *Magazines for the Millions: Gender and Commerce in the Ladies' Home Journal and the Saturday Evening Post, 1880–1910*. Albany: State University of New York Press, 1994.

Davidson, Cathy N., ed. *Reading in America: Literature and Social History*. Baltimore: Johns Hopkins University Press, 1989.

Degler, Carl N. *At Odds: Women and the Family in America from the Revolution to the Present*. New York: Oxford University Press, 1980.

Deloria, Philip Joseph. *Playing Indian*. New Haven: Yale University Press, 1998.

DeLuzio, Crista. *Female Adolescence in American Scientific Thought, 1830–1930*. Baltimore: Johns Hopkins University Press, 2007.

Denning, Michael. "Cheap Stories: Notes on Popular Fiction and Working-Class Culture in Nineteenth-Century America." *History Workshop Journal* 22 (Autumn 1986): 1–17.

———. "The Fire of the Dime Novel in American Culture." In *Popular Culture in American History*, edited by Jim Cullen, 80–88. Malden, MA: Blackwell, 2001.

De Puy, Frank A. *The New Century Home Book*. New York: Eaton & Mains, 1900.

de Ras, Marion E. P. *Body, Femininity and Nationalism: Girls in the German Youth Movement, 1900–1934*. New York: Routledge, 2008.

Devlin, Athena. *Between Profits and Primitivism: Shaping White Middle-Class Masculinity in the United States, 1880–1917*. New York: Routledge, 2005.

"Diary of John Magill Steel and Sarah Eliza Steel." *Winchester-Frederick County (VA) Historical Society Papers* 3 (1955): 61–94.

Diedrich, Maria. *Cornelia James Cannon and the Future American Race*. Amherst: University of Massachusetts Press, 2010.

Dippel, John Van Houten. *Race to the Frontier: "White Flight" and Westward Expansion*. New York: Algora, 2005.

Douglas, Susan J. *Where the Girls Are: Growing Up Female with the Mass Media*. New York: Three Rivers Press, 1994.

Driscoll, Catherine. *Girls: Feminine Adolescence in Popular Culture and Cultural Theory*. New York: Columbia University Press, 2002.

Duberman, Martin, Martha Vicinus, and George Chauncey Jr., eds. *Hidden from History: Reclaiming the Gay and Lesbian Past*. New York: New American Library, 1989.

Dudden, Faye. *Women in American Theatre: Actresses and Audiences, 1790–1870*. New Haven: Yale University Press, 1994.

Dudley, Gertrude, and Frances A. Kellor. *Athletic Games in the Education of Women*. New York: Henry Holt, 1909.

Duffey, Mrs. E[liza]. B[isbee]. *What Women Should Know: A Woman's Book about Women, Containing Practical Information for Wives and Mothers*. Philadelphia: J. M. Stoddart, 1873.

おそら

Dyer, Richard. *White*. London: Routledge, 1997.

Dyhouse, Carol. *Girls Growing Up in Late Victorian and Edwardian England*. London: Routledge, 1981.

Earle, Alice Morse, ed. *Diary of Anna Green Winslow, a Boston School Girl of 1771*. Boston, Houghton, Mifflin, 1894.

Eastman, Elaine Goodale. *Sister to the Sioux: The Memoirs of Elaine Goodale Eastman, 1885–91*. Lincoln: University of Nebraska Press, 2004.

Eddy, Daniel C. *The Young Woman's Friend; or, The Duties, Trials, Loves and Hopes of Woman. Designed for the Young Woman, the Young Wife, and the Mother*. Boston: Locke & Bubier, 1873.

Eggleston, Margaret W., ed. *Kathie's Diary: Leaves from an Old, Old Diary, Written by Kathie*. New York: George H. Doran, 1926.

Ehrenpreis, David. "The Figure of the Backfisch: Representing Puberty in Wilhelmine Germany." *Zeitschrift für Kunstgeschichte* 67.4 (2004): 479–508.

Eisenstein, Sarah. *Give Us Bread but Give Us Roses: Working Women's Consciousness in the United States, 1890 to the First World War*. London: Routledge, 1983.

Elbert, Sarah. Introduction to Alcott, *Moods*, xi–xlii.

———. Introduction to Alcott, *Work*, ix–xliv.

Elise, Dianne. "Tomboys and Cowgirls: The Girl's Disidentification from the Mother." In Rottneck, *Sissies and Tomboys*, 140–52.

Elliott, Mary. "Tomboys." In Forman-Brunell, *Girlhood in America*, 669–75.

———. "When Girls Will Be Boys: 'Bad' Endings and Subversive Middles in Nineteenth-Century Tomboy Narratives and Twentieth-Century Lesbian Pulp Novels." *Legacy* 15.1 (Spring 1998): 92–97.

Ellis, Havelock. *Man and Woman: A Study of Human Secondary Sexual Characters*. New York: Scribner, 1897.

———. *Sexual Inversion: A Critical Edition*. New York: Palgrave Macmillan, 2008.

Emerson, Alice B. *Ruth Fielding and the Gypsies*. New York: Cupples & Leon, 1915.

———. *Ruth Fielding on the St. Lawrence*. New York: Cupples & Leon, 1922.

Endres, Kathleen L., and Therese L. Lueck, eds. *Women's Periodicals in the United States*. Westport, CT: Greenwood Press, 1995.

Erisman, Fred. *From Birdwomen to Skygirls: American Girls' Aviation Stories*. Fort Worth: Texas Christian University Press, 2009.

Esman, Aaron H. *Adolescence and Culture*. New York: Columbia University Press, 1990.

Etulain, Richard. *The Life and Legends of Calamity Jane*. Norman: University of Oklahoma Press, 2014.

Faderman, Lillian. *Odd Girls and Twilight Lovers: A History of Lesbian Life in Twentieth-Century America*. New York: Columbia University Press, 1991.

Fahs, Alice. *The Imagined Civil War: Popular Literature of the North and South, 1861–65*. Chapel Hill: University of North Carolina Press, 2003.

Farnham, Christie Ann. *The Education of the Southern Belle: Higher Education and Student Socialization in the Antebellum South*. New York: New York University Press, 1994.

Fass, Paula S. *Children of a New World: Society, Culture, and Globalization*. New York: New York University Press, 2007.

———. *The Damned and the Beautiful: American Youth in the 1920's*. New York: Oxford University Press, 1977.

Fass, Paula S., and Mary Ann Mason, eds. *Childhood in America*. New York: New York University Press, 2000.

Fetterley, Judith. "Alcott's Civil War." *Feminist Studies* 5.2 (Summer 1979): 369–83.

Fiedler, Leslie A. "Come Back to the Raft Ag'in, Huck Honey!" 1948. In *An End to Innocence: Essays on Culture and Politics*, 142–51. Boston: Beacon Press, 1955.

Field, Corrine T. *The Struggle for Equal Adulthood: Gender, Race, Age and the Fight for Citizenship in the Antebellum United States*. Chapel Hill: University of North Carolina Press, 2014.

Field, Corrine T., and Nicholas L. Syrett, eds. *Age in America: The Colonial Era to the Present*. New York: New York University Press, 2015.

Finley, Martha. *Elsie Dinsmore*. 1867. New York: Arno Press, 1974.

Fleissner, Jennifer. *Women, Compulsion, Modernity: The Moment of American Naturalism*. Chicago: University of Chicago Press, 2004.

Floyd, Silas X. *Floyd's Flowers; or, Duty and Beauty for Colored Children*. 1905. New York: AMS Press, 1975.

Forbush, William Byron. *The Boy Problem: A Study in Social Pedagogy*. Boston: The Pilgrim Press, 1902.

Forman-Brunell, Miriam, ed. *Girlhood in America: An Encyclopedia*. 2 vols. Santa Barbara: ABC Clio, 2001.

Forman-Brunell, Miriam, and Leslie Paris, eds. *The Girls' History and Cultural Reader: The Nineteenth Century*. Urbana: University of Illinois Press, 2011.

Formanek-Brunell, Miriam. *Made to Play House: Dolls and the Commercialization of American Girlhood, 1830–1930*. Baltimore: Johns Hopkins University Press, 1998.

———. "Sugar and Spite: The Politics of Doll Play in Nineteenth-Century America." In West and Petrik, *Small Worlds*, 107–24.

Foster, Shirley, and Judy Simons. *What Katy Read: Feminist Re-Readings of "Classic" Stories for Girls*. Iowa City: University of Iowa Press, 1995.

Freeman, Susan Kathleen. *Sex Goes to School: Girls and Sex Education before the 1960s*. Urbana: University of Illinois Press, 2008.

Frémont, Jessie Benton. *Souvenirs of My Time*. Boston: D. Lothrop, 1887.

Furness, Clifton Joseph, ed. *The Genteel Female: An Anthology.* New York: Knopf, 1931.

Gardner, Eric. "'This Attempt of Their Sister': Harriet Wilson's *Our Nig* from Printer to Reader." *New England Quarterly* 66.2 (June 1993): 226–46.

Garvey, Ellen Gruber. *The Adman in the Parlor: Magazines and the Gendering of Consumer Culture, 1880s–1910s.* New York: Oxford University Press, 1996.

Gibson, Henry William. *Boyology; or, Boy Analysis.* New York: Association Press, 1922.

Gibson, Mary. *"Hero Strong" and Other Stories: Tales of Girlhood Ambition, Female Masculinity, and Women's Worldly Achievement in Antebellum America.* Edited by Daniel A. Cohen. Knoxville: University of Tennessee Press, 2014.

Giddings, Paula. *When and Where I Enter: The Impact of Black Women on Race and Sex in America.* New York: William Morrow, 1984.

Gifford, Carolyn De Swarte, ed. *Writing Out My Heart: Selections from the Journal of Frances E. Willard, 1855–96.* Urbana: University of Illinois Press, 1995.

Gilder, Jeannette L. *The Autobiography of a Tomboy.* 1901. New York: Doubleday, Page, 1905.

———. *The Tomboy at Work.* New York: Doubleday, Page, 1904.

Ginzberg, Lori D. *Women and the Work of Benevolence: Morality, Politics, and Class in the Nineteenth-Century United States.* New Haven: Yale University Press, 1990.

Gleason, George. *Wistah, the Child Spy.* New York: Beadle & Adams, 1892.

Goetzmann, William H. *The West of the Imagination.* 2nd ed. Norman: University of Oklahoma Press, 2009.

Goldin, Claudia, and Lawrence F. Katz. "Putting the Co in Education: Timing, Reasons, and Consequences of College Coeducation from 1835 to the Present." National Bureau of Economic Research, working paper 16281, August 2010. Available at nber.org/papers/w16281.

Gorn, Elliott. *The Manly Art: Bare-Knuckle Prize Fighting in America.* Ithaca: Cornell University Press, 1986.

Graff, Harvey J. *Conflicting Paths: Growing Up in America.* Cambridge: Harvard University Press, 1995.

Grande, Sarah. *The Heavenly Twins.* 1893. Introduction by Carol A. Senf. Ann Arbor: University of Michigan Press, 1992.

Green, Elna C. *Southern Strategies: Southern Women and the Woman Suffrage Question.* Chapel Hill: University of North Carolina Press, 1997.

Greenberg, Amy S. *Manifest Manhood and the Antebellum American Empire.* New York: Cambridge University Press, 2005.

Greene, Lida L., ed. "Diary of a Young Girl: Grundy County to Correctionville, 1862." *Annals of Iowa* 36 (Fall 1962): 437–57.

Grimké, Charlotte Forten. *The Journals of Charlotte Forten Grimké.* Edited by Brenda Stevenson. New York: Oxford University Press, 1988.

Grinspan, Jon. "A Birthday Like None Other: Turning Twenty-One in the Age of Popular Politics." In Field and Syrett, *Age in America,* 86–102.

Gross, Robert A., and Mary Kelley, eds. *An Extensive Republic: Print, Culture, and Society in the New Nation, 1790–1840.* Vol. 2 of *A History of the Book in America,* edited by David D. Hall. Chapel Hill: University of North Carolina Press, 2010.

Grundy, Pamela, and Susan Shackelford. *Shattering the Glass: The Remarkable History of Women's Basketball.* New York: New Press, 2005.

Habegger, Alfred. *Gender, Fantasy, and Realism in American Literature.* New York: Columbia University Press, 1982.

Hackley, Emma Azalia. *The Colored Girl Beautiful.* Kansas City, MO: Burton, 1916.

Halberstam, Judith. *Female Masculinity.* Durham, NC: Duke University Press, 1998.

Hall, David D. *Cultures of Print: Essays in the History of the Book.* Amherst: University of Massachusetts Press, 1996.

Hall, G. Stanley. *Adolescence: Its Psychology and Its Relations to Physiology, Anthropology, Sociology, Sex, Crime, Religion and Education.* 2 vols. New York: D. Appleton, 1904.

———. "The Awkward Age." *Appleton's Magazine* 12.2 (August 1908): 149–56.

———. "Eugenics: Its Ideals and What It Is Going to Do." *Religious Education* 6.2 (June 1911): 152–59.

Hamilton, Gail. *A New Atmosphere.* Boston: Ticknor & Fields, 1865.

Hamilton-Honey, Emily. *Turning the Pages of American Girlhood: The Evolution of Girls' Series Fiction, 1865–1930.* Jefferson, NC: McFarland, 2013.

Hamlin, Kimberly A. *From Eve to Evolution: Darwin, Science, and Women's Rights in Gilded Age America.* Chicago: University of Chicago Press, 2014.

Harbaugh, Thomas Chalmers. *Kit, the Girl Detective; or, Dandy Dash in California.* New York: Beadle & Adams, March 27, 1889.

Harland, Marion (Mary Virginia Hawes Terhune), and Virginia Van de Water. *Everyday Etiquette.* Indianapolis: Bobbs-Merrill, 1905.

Harris, Sharon M., and Ellen Gruber Garvey, eds. *Blue Pencils and Hidden Hands: Women Editing Periodicals, 1830–1910.* Boston: Northeastern University Press, 2004.

Hart, Gary. "Black Codes: Uncovering the Evolution of Legal Slavery." *OAH Magazine of History* 17.3 (April 2003): 34–36.

Havens, Catherine Elizabeth. *Diary of a Little Girl in Old New York.* New York: Henry Collins Brown, 1919.

Hawes, Joseph M., and N. Ray Hiner, eds. *American Childhood: A Research Guide and Historical Handbook*. Westport, CT: Greenwood Press, 1985.

Heilbrun, Carolyn. "Jo March: Male Model—Female Person." In Stern, *Critical Essays on Louisa May Alcott*, 143–45.

Helgren, Jennifer, and Colleen A. Vasconcellos, eds. *Girlhood: A Global History*. New Brunswick, NJ: Rutgers University Press, 2010.

Henderson, Julia. *A Child's Story of Dunbar*. New York: Crisis Publishing, 1913.

Hendler, Glenn. *Public Sentiments: Structures of Feeling in Nineteenth-Century American Literature*. Chapel Hill: University of North Carolina Press, 2001.

Henley, Ann, ed. *Southern Souvenirs: Selected Stories and Essays of Sara Haardt*. Tuscaloosa: University of Alabama Press, 1999.

Hibbard, Angus Smith. *Hello, Goodbye: My Story of Telephone Pioneering*. Chicago: A. C. McClurg, 1941.

Higginbotham, Evelyn Brooks. *Righteous Discontent: The Women's Movement in the Black Baptist Church, 1880–1920*. Cambridge: Harvard University Press, 1993.

Hilgenkamp, Kathryn D., and Mary Margaret Livingston. "Tomboys, Masculine Characteristics, and Self-Ratings of Confidence in Career Success." *Psychological Reports* 90.3 (June 2002): 743–49.

Hill, Mary Armfield. *Charlotte Perkins Gilman: The Making of a Radical Feminist, 1860–1896*. Philadelphia: Temple University Press, 1980.

Hobbs, Catherine, ed. *Nineteenth-Century Women Learn to Write*. Charlottesville: University Press of Virginia, 1995.

Hofstadter, Richard. *Turner and the Sociology of the Frontier*. New York: Basic Books, 1968.

Hoganson, Kristin L. *Fighting for American Manhood: How Gender Politics Provoked the Spanish-American and Philippine-American Wars*. New Haven: Yale University Press, 1998.

Holt, Marilyn Irvin. *Linoleum, Better Babies, and the Modern Farm Woman, 1890–1930*. Albuquerque: University of New Mexico Press, 1995.

Honey, Emily A. "From Spiritual Guides to Eager Consumers: American Girls' Series Fiction, 1865–1930." PhD diss., University of Massachusetts Amherst, 2010.

Hope, Laura Lee. *The Outdoor Girls on Pine Island; or, A Cave and What It Contained*. New York: Grosset & Dunlap, 1916.

Horowitz, Daniel. *The Morality of Spending: Attitudes toward the Consumer Society in America, 1875–1940*. Baltimore: Johns Hopkins University Press, 1985.

Horowitz, Helen Lefkowitz. *Alma Mater: Design and Experience in the Women's Colleges from Their Nineteenth-Century Beginnings to the 1930s*. New York: Knopf, 1984.

———. *The Power and Passion of M. Carey Thomas.* New York: Knopf, 1994.

———. *Wild Unrest: Charlotte Perkins Gilman and the Making of "The Yellow Wallpaper."* New York: Oxford University Press, 2010.

Horsman, Reginald. *Race and Manifest Destiny: The Origins of American Racial Anglo-Saxonism.* Cambridge: Harvard University Press, 1981.

Horvath, Polly. Foreword to *Little Lord Fauntleroy,* by Frances Hodgson Burnett, xi–xviii. New York: Simon and Schuster, 2004.

Houghton, Walter R., et al. *American Etiquette and Rules of Politeness.* Chicago: Rand, McNally, 1890.

Howitt, William. *The Boy's Country Book; or, Amusements, Pleasures and Pursuits.* New York: Edward Kearny, 1843.

Hubbard, Dolan, ed. *Recovered Writers/Recovered Texts: Race, Class and Gender in Black Women's Literature.* Knoxville: University of Tennessee Press, 1997.

Huhndorf, Shari M. *Going Native: Indians in the American Cultural Imagination.* Ithaca: Cornell University Press, 2001.

Hulbert, Ann. *Raising America: Experts, Parents, and a Century of Advice about Children.* New York: Knopf, 2003.

Hult, Joan S., and Marianna Trekell, eds. *A Century of Women's Basketball: From Frailty to Final Four.* Reston, VA: National Association for Girls and Women in Sport, 1991.

Hunt, Una (Una Hunt Clarke Drage). *Una Mary: The Inner Life of a Child.* New York: Charles Scribner's Sons, 1915.

Hunter, Jane. *How Young Ladies Became Girls: The Victorian Origins of American Girlhood.* New Haven: Yale University Press, 2002.

———. "Inscribing the Self in the Heart of the Family: Diaries and Girlhood in Late-Victorian America." *American Quarterly* 44.1 (March 1992): 51–81.

Hyde, Janet S., B. G. Rosenberg, and Jo Ann Behrman. "Tomboyism." *Psychology of Women Quarterly* 2.1 (September 1977): 73–75.

Ignatiev, Noel. *How the Irish Became White.* London: Routledge, 1995.

Illick, Joseph. *American Childhoods.* Philadelphia: University of Pennsylvania Press, 2002.

Inness, Sherrie A., ed. *Delinquents and Debutantes: Twentieth-Century American Girls' Cultures.* New York: New York University Press, 1998.

———. "Girls Scouts, Camp Fire Girls, and Woodcraft Girls: The Ideology of Girls' Scouting Novels, 1910–1935." In Inness, *Nancy Drew and Company,* 89–100.

———, ed. *Nancy Drew and Company: Culture, Gender, and Girls' Series.* Bowling Green, OH: Bowling Green State University Popular Press, 1997.

Jabour, Anya. *Scarlett's Sisters: Young Women in the Old South.* Chapel Hill: University of North Carolina Press, 2007.

Jacobi, Mary Putnam. "Mental Action and Physical Health." In Brackett, *The Education of American Girls*, 255–306.

Jacobs, Margaret. *Engendered Encounters: Feminism and Pueblo Cultures, 1879–1934.* Lincoln: University of Nebraska Press, 1999.

Jacobson, Lisa. *Raising Consumers: Children and the American Mass Market in the Early Twentieth Century.* New York: Columbia University Press, 2004.

Jacobson, Marcia Ann. *Being a Boy Again: Autobiography and the American Boy Book.* Tuscaloosa: University of Alabama Press, 1994.

Jacobson, Matthew Frye. *Whiteness of a Different Color: European Immigrants and the Alchemy of Race.* Cambridge: Harvard University Press, 1998.

James, Allison, Chris Jenks, and Alan Prout. *Theorizing Childhood.* New York: Teachers College Press, Columbia University, 1998.

James, Edward T., Janet Wilson James, and Paul Boyer, eds. *Notable American Women: A Biographical Dictionary.* 3 vols. Cambridge: Belknap Press of Harvard University Press, 1971.

Jiménez, Tomás R. *Replenished Ethnicity: Mexican Americans, Immigration, and Identity.* Berkeley: University of California Press, 2010.

Johannsen, Albert. *The House of Beadle and Adams and Its Dime and Nickel Novels: The Story of a Vanished Literature.* Vol. 2. Norman: University of Oklahoma Press, 1950.

Johnson, Deidre. *Edward Stratemeyer and the Stratemeyer Syndicate.* New York: Twayne, 1993.

Johnson, Wendy Dasler. *Antebellum American Women's Poetry: A Rhetoric of Sentiment.* Carbondale: University of Southern Illinois Press, 2016.

Johnson-Feelings, Dianne. *Telling Tales: The Pedagogy and Promise of African American Literature for Youth.* New York: Greenwood Press, 1990.

Jones, Diane McClure, and Rosemary Jones. *Boys' and Girls' Book Series: Real World Adventures.* Paducah, KY: Collector Books, 2002.

Kaestle, Carl F. *Pillars of the Republic: Common Schools and American Society, 1780–1860.* New York: Hill & Wang, 1983.

Kaestle, Carl F., and Janice Radway. "A Framework for the History of Publishing and Reading in the United States." In Kaestle and Radway, *Print in Motion*, 7–21.

Kaestle, Carl F., and Janice Radway, eds. *Print in Motion: The Expansion of Publishing and Reading in the United States, 1880–1940.* Vol. 4 of *A History of the Book in America*, edited by David D. Hall. Chapel Hill: University of North Carolina Press, 2009.

Kaplan, Amy. *The Anarchy of Empire in the Making of U.S. Culture.* Cambridge: Harvard University Press, 2002.

Kasson, Joy S. *Buffalo Bill's Wild West: Celebrity, Memory, and Popular History.* New York: Hill & Wang, 2000.

————. *Marble Queens and Captives: Women in Nineteenth-Century American Sculpture.* New Haven: Yale University Press, 1990.

Katz, William Loren. *The Black West: A Documentary and Pictorial History of the African American Role in the Westward Expansion of the United States.* New York: Touchstone, 1996.

Keith, Lois. *Take Up Thy Bed and Walk: Death, Disability, and Cure in Classic Fiction for Girls.* New York: Routledge, 2001.

Kelley, Mary, ed. *Woman's Being, Woman's Place: Female Identity and Vocation in American History.* Boston: G. K. Hall, 1979.

Kent, Kathryn R. *Making Girls into Women: American Women's Writing and the Rise of Lesbian Identity.* Durham, NC: Duke University Press, 2003.

Kidd, Kenneth B. *Making American Boys: Boyology and the Feral Tale.* Minneapolis: University of Minnesota Press, 2004.

Kimmel, Michael. *Manhood in America: A Cultural History.* New York: Free Press, 1996.

Kitch, Carolyn L. *The Girl on the Magazine Cover: The Origins of Visual Stereotypes in American Mass Media.* Chapel Hill: University of North Carolina Press, 2001.

————. *Pages from the Past: History and Memory in American Magazines.* Chapel Hill: University of North Carolina Press, 2005.

Klapper, Melissa R. *Jewish Girls Coming of Age in America, 1860–1920.* New York: New York University Press, 2005.

Klein, Jessi. *You'll Grow Out of It.* New York: Grand Central Publishing, 2016.

Kline, Wendy. *Building a Better Race: Gender, Sexuality, and Eugenics from the Turn of the Century to the Baby Boom.* Berkeley: University of California Press, 2001.

Kraus, Natasha Kirsten. *A New Type of Womanhood: Discursive Politics and Social Change in Antebellum America.* Durham, NC: Duke University Press, 2008.

The Ladies' Book of Etiquette, and Manual of Politeness. Boston: G. W. Cottrell, 1860.

The Ladies' Vase; or, Polite Manual for Young Ladies. Boston: Lewis & Sampson, 1843.

Lamb, Sharon. *The Secret Lives of Girls: What Good Girls Really Do—Sex Play, Aggression, and Their Guilt.* New York: Free Press, 2001.

Landis, Carney, Agnes T. Landis, and M. Marjorie Bolles. *Sex in Development: A Study of the Growth and Development of the Emotional and Sexual Aspects of Personality, Together with Physiological, Anatomical, and Medical Information on a Group of 153 Normal Women and 142 Female Psychiatric Patients.* New York: Paul B. Hoeber, 1940.

LaPlante, Eve. *Marmee and Louisa: The Untold Story of Louisa May Alcott and Her Mother.* New York: Simon & Schuster, 2013.

Larrabee, Lisa. "Women and Cycling: The Early Years." In Willard, *How I Learned to Ride the Bicycle*, 81–97.

Lears, T. J. Jackson. *Rebirth of a Nation: The Making of a Modern America, 1877–1920*. New York: Harper, 2009.

Leavitt, Judith Walzer. *Brought to Bed: Childbearing in America, 1750–1950*. New York: Oxford University Press, 1986.

Ledger, Sally. *The New Woman: Fiction and Feminism at the Fin de Siècle*. Manchester, UK: Manchester University Press, 1997.

Lee, [Eleanor] Agnes. *Growing Up in the 1850s: The Journal of Agnes Lee*. Edited by Mary Custis Lee. Chapel Hill: University of North Carolina Press for the Robert E. Lee Memorial Association, 1984.

Lehr, Susan S., ed. *Beauty, Brains, and Brawn: The Construction of Gender in Children's Literature*. Portsmouth, NH: Heinemann, 2001.

Leloudis, James L. *Schooling the New South: Pedagogy, Self, and Society in North Carolina, 1880–1920*. Chapel Hill: University of North Carolina Press, 1996.

L'Engle, Madeleine. *A Wrinkle in Time*. New York: Farrar, Straus & Giroux, 1962.

Lesko, Nancy. *Act Your Age! A Cultural Construction of Adolescence*. New York: Routledge/Falmer, 2001.

Leslie, Eliza. "Billy Bedlow, or The Girl-Boy." *Juvenile Miscellany* 1.3 (February 1832): 397–98.

———. "Lucy Nelson, or The Boy Girl." *Juvenile Miscellany* 1.2 (December 1831): 149–59.

Levander, Caroline F., and Carol J. Singley. *The American Child: A Cultural Studies Reader*. New Brunswick, NJ: Rutgers University Press, 2003.

Linton, Eliza Lynn. "The Girl of the Period." 1868. In *The Girl of the Period and Other Social Essays*, vol. 1, 1–9. London: Richard Bentley & Son, 1883.

Lloyd, T. A. *The Romp: A Musical Entertainment. As Altered from Love in the City. By Isaac Bickerstaff. Taken from the Manager's Book at the Theatre Royal, Drury-Lane*. London: R. Butters, 1795. Reprint, n.p.: Gale ECCO Print Editions, 2010.

Love, Eric T. L. *Race over Empire: Racism and U.S. Imperialism, 1865–1900*. Chapel Hill: University of North Carolina Press, 2004.

Lovett, Laura. *Conceiving the Future: Pronatalism, Reproduction, and the Family in the United States, 1890–1938*. Chapel Hill: University of North Carolina Press, 2007.

Low, Juliette. *Handbook for Girl Scouts: How Girls Can Help Their Country*. N.p., 1917.

Lowry, E. B. *Herself: Talks with Women concerning Themselves*. Chicago: Forbes, 1920.

———. *Preparing for Motherhood*. Chicago: Forbes, 1918.

Lystra, Karen. *Searching the Heart: Women, Men, and Romantic Love in Nineteenth-Century America.* New York: Oxford University Press, 1989.

MacCann, Donnarae. *White Supremacy in Children's Literature: Characterizations of African Americans, 1830–1900.* New York: Garland, 1998.

Machor, James, ed. *Readers in History: Nineteenth-Century American Literature and the Contexts of Response.* Baltimore: Johns Hopkins University Press, 1993.

MacLeod, Anne Scott. *American Girlhood: Essays on Children's Literature of the Nineteenth and Twentieth Centuries.* Athens: University of Georgia Press, 1994.

Macleod, David I. *The Age of the Child: Children in America, 1890–1920.* New York: Twayne, 1998.

———. *Building Character in the American Boy: The Boy Scouts, YMCA, and Their Forerunners, 1870–1920.* Madison: University of Wisconsin Press, 1983.

Mafly-Kipp, Laurie F., and Kathryn Lofton, eds. *Women's Work: An Anthology of African-American Women's Historical Writings from Antebellum America to the Harlem Renaissance.* New York: Oxford University Press, 2010.

Mangan, J. A., and Roberta J. Park, eds. *From "Fair Sex" to Feminism: Sport and the Socialization of Women in the Industrial and Post-Industrial Eras.* London: Routledge, 1987.

Mann, Dorothea Lawrance. "When the Alcott Books Were New." In Stern, *Critical Essays on Louisa May Alcott,* 85.

Marks, Patricia. *Bicycles, Bangs, and Bloomers: The New Woman in the Popular Press.* Lexington: University Press of Kentucky, 1990.

Matthews, Jean V. *The Rise of the New Woman: The Women's Movement in America, 1875–1930.* Chicago: Ivan R. Dee, 2003.

McArthur, Judith N. *Creating the New Woman: The Rise of Southern Women's Progressive Culture in Texas, 1893–1918.* Urbana: University of Illinois Press, 1998.

McCabe, Lida Rose. *The American Girl at College.* New York: Dodd, Mead, 1893.

McClelland, Averil Evans. *The Education of Women in the United States: A Guide to Theory, Teaching, and Research.* New York: Garland, 1992.

McCrone, Kathleen E. "Play Up! Play Up! and Play the Game: Sport at the Late Victorian Girls' Public School." *Journal of British Studies* 23.2 (Spring 1984): 106–34.

McCullers, Carson. *The Member of the Wedding.* In *Carson McCullers: Complete Novels.* New York: Library of America, 2001.

McEwen, Christian, ed. *Jo's Girls: Tomboy Tales of High Adventure, True Grit, and Real Life.* Boston: Beacon Press, 1997.

McGovern, James R. "The American Woman's Pre–World War I Freedom in Manners and Morals." *Journal of American History* 55.2 (1968): 315–33.

McHenry, Elizabeth. *Forgotten Readers: Recovering the Lost History of African-American Literary Societies.* Durham, NC: Duke University Press, 2002.

McLaird, James D. *Calamity Jane: The Woman and the Legend.* Norman: University of Oklahoma Press, 2005.

McRobbie, Angela, and Mica Nava, eds. *Gender and Generation.* Basingstoke, UK: Macmillan, 1984.

Mead, Margaret. *Male and Female: A Study of the Sexes in a Changing World.* New York: William Morrow, 1949.

Merish, Lori. "Story Papers." In Bold, *US Popular Print Culture, 1860–1920,* 43–62.

Merrill, Lilburn. *Winning the Boy.* New York: Fleming H. Revell, 1907.

Mettler, Lizzie Garrett. *Tomboy Style: Beyond the Boundaries of Fashion.* New York: Rizzoli, 2012.

Meyerowitz, Joanne J. *How Sex Changed: A History of Transsexuality in the United States.* Cambridge: Harvard University Press, 2002.

———. *Women Adrift: Independent Wage Earners in Chicago, 1880–1930.* Chicago: University of Chicago Press, 1988.

Miller, Allison. "Am I Normal? American Vernacular Psychology and the Tomboy Body, 1900–1940." *Representations* 122 (Spring 2013): 23–50.

———. "Boyhood for Girls: American Tomboys and the Transformation of Eroticism, 1900–1940." PhD diss., Rutgers University, 2014.

Miller, Susan A. *Growing Girls: The Natural Origins of Girls' Organizations in America.* New Brunswick, NJ: Rutgers University Press, 2007.

Mintz, Steven. *Huck's Raft: A History of American Childhood.* Cambridge: Belknap Press of Harvard University Press, 2004.

———. *A Prison of Expectations: The Family in Victorian Culture.* New York: New York University Press, 1983.

Mitchell, Sally. *The New Girl: Girls' Culture in England, 1880–1915.* New York: Columbia University Press, 1995.

Mordecai, Ellen. *Gleanings from Long Ago.* Raleigh, NC: Raleigh Historic Properties Commission, 1933.

Morgan, Ruth, and Saskia Wieringa, eds. *Tommy Boys, Lesbian Men, and Ancestral Wives: Female Same-Sex Practices in Africa.* Aukland, South Africa: Jacana Media, 2006.

Morris, Brian. "Ernest Thompson Seton and the Origins of the Woodcraft Movement." *Journal of Contemporary History* 5.2 (1970): 183–94.

Morrison, Gertrude. *The Girls of Central High; or, Rivals for All Honors.* New York: Grosset & Dunlap, 1914.

————. *The Girls of Central High at Basketball; or, The Great Gymnasium Mystery.* New York: Grosset & Dunlap, 1914.

————. *The Girls of Central High in Camp: The Old Professor's Secret.* Akron, OH: Saalfield, 1915.

————. *The Girls of Central High on the Stage; or, The Play That Took the Prize.* New York: Grossett & Dunlap, 1914.

Mott, Frank Luther. *A History of American Magazines.* Vol. 2, *1850–1865.* Cambridge: Harvard University Press, 1938.

Mullins, Hilary. "Evolution of a Tomboy." In Yamaguchi and Barber, *Tomboys!,* 40–49.

Mumford, Mary E. *Hila Dart: A Born Romp.* Philadelphia: Wm. B. Evans, 1871.

Murphy, Peter F. *Feminism and Masculinities.* New York: Oxford University Press, 2004.

Murray, Gail Schmunk. *American Children's Literature and the Construction of Childhood.* New York: Twayne, 1998.

Nagadya, Maria, with Ruth Morgan. "'Some Say I Am a Hermaphrodite Just Because I Put on Trousers': Lesbians and Tommy Boys in Kampala, Uganda." In Morgan and Wieringa, *Tommy Boys, Lesbian Men, and Ancestral Wives,* 65–75.

Nash, Margaret A. *Women's Education in the United States, 1780–1840.* New York: Palgrave Macmillan, 2005.

Nash, Roderick. "The American Cult of the Primitive." *American Quarterly* 18.3 (Autumn 1966): 517–37.

————. *Wilderness and the American Mind.* New Haven: Yale University Press, 1967.

Nelson, Claudia, and Lynne Vallone, eds. *The Girl's Own: Cultural Histories of the Anglo-American Girl, 1830–1915.* Athens: University of Georgia Press, 1994.

Nelson, Mariah Burton. "Introduction: Who We Might Become." In Smith, *Nike Is a Goddess,* ix–xix.

Newberry, Julia Rose. *Julia Newberry's Diary.* Edited by Margaret Ayer Barnes and Janet Ayer Fairbank. New York: Norton, 1933.

Newcomb, Dan. *When and How; or, A Collection of the More Recent Facts and Ideas upon Raising Healthy Children.* Chicago: Arthur W. Penny, 1872.

Newcomb, Harvey. *How to Be a Man: A Book for Boys, Containing Useful Hints on the Formation of Character.* Boston: Gould & Lincoln, 1855.

Newman, Louise Michele. *White Women's Rights: The Racial Origins of Feminism in the United States.* New York: Oxford University Press, 1999.

Newsome, Effie Lee. "Child Literature and Negro Childhood." *Crisis,* October 1927, 260.

Nidiffer, Jana. "Crumbs from the Boy's Table: The First Century of Coeduca-
    tion." In *Women Administrators in Higher Education: Historical and Con-
    temporary Perspectives,* edited by Jana Nidiffer and Carolyn Terry Bashaw,
    13–36. Albany: State University of New York Press, 2001.
Nutt, Amy Ellis. "Swinging for the Fences." In Smith, *Nike Is a Goddess,* 33–54.
O'Brien, Sharon. "Tomboyism and Adolescent Conflict: Three Nineteenth-
    Century Case Studies." In Kelley, *Woman's Being, Woman's Place,* 351–72.
Odem, Mary E. *Delinquent Daughters: Protecting and Policing Adolescent Female
    Sexuality in the United States, 1885–1920.* Chapel Hill: University of North
    Carolina Press, 1995.
O'Keefe, Deborah. *Good Girl Messages: How Young Women Were Misled by Their
    Favorite Books.* New York: Continuum, 2000.
"Old Scout." *Young Wild West: An Original Western Melodrama.* In *Young Wild
    West Series: Wild West Weekly: A Magazine containing Stories, Sketches Etc. of
    Western Life* (New York: Frank Tousey; hereafter *YWWS*), no. 1 (October
    24, 1902).
———. *Young Wild West and the 'Mixed Up' Mine; or, Arietta a Winner. YWWS,*
    no. 143 (July 14, 1905).
———. *Young Wild West, The Prince of the Saddle. YWWS,* no. 1 (October 24,
    1902).
———. *Young Wild West's Deadly Aim; or, Arietta's Greatest Danger. YWWS,* no.
    131 (June 30, 1905).
———. *Young Wild West's Even Chance, or, Arietta's Presence of Mind. YWWS,* no.
    153 (September 22, 1905).
———. *Young Wild West's Luck; or, Striking It Rich at the Hills. YWWS,* no. 2
    (October 31, 1902).
Ovington, Mary White. *Hazel.* New York: Crisis Publishing, 1913.
Painter, Nell Irvin. *A History of White People.* New York: Norton, 2010.
Paoletti, Jo B. *Pink and Blue: Telling the Boys from the Girls in America.* Bloom-
    ington: University of Indiana Press, 2012.
Paris, Leslie. *Children's Nature: The Rise of the American Summer Camp.* New
    York: New York University Press, 2008.
Park, Roberta J. "Sport, Gender and Society in a Transatlantic Victorian Perspec-
    tive." In Mangan and Park, *From "Fair Sex" to Feminism,* 58–93.
Parton, James. *Daughters of Genius: A Series of Sketches of Authors, Artists, Reform-
    ers, and Heroines.* Philadelphia: Hubbard Brothers, 1888.
Patterson, Martha, ed. *The American New Woman Revisited: A Reader, 1894–1930.*
    New Brunswick, NJ: Rutgers University Press, 2008.
Pawley, Christine. *Reading on the Middle Border: The Culture of Print in Late
    Nineteenth-Century Osage, Iowa.* Amherst: University of Massachusetts
    Press, 2001.

Pearson, Edmund Lester. *Dime Novels; or, Following an Old Trail in Popular Literature.* Boston: Little, Brown, 1929.

Peiss, Kathy Lee. *Cheap Amusements: Working Women and Leisure in Turn-of-the-Century New York.* Philadelphia: Temple University Press, 1986.

Penrose, Margaret. *The Campfire Girls of Roselawn; or, A Strange Message from the Air.* New York: Goldsmith, n.d.

———. *Motor Girls; or, the Mystery of the Road.* New York: Cupples & Leon, 1910.

———. *The Motor Girls on a Tour; or, Keeping a Strange Promise.* New York: Cupples & Leon, 1911.

Perry, Claire. *Young America: Childhood in 19th-Century Art and Culture.* New Haven: Yale University Press, 2006.

Phelps, Elizabeth Stuart. *Gypsy Breynton.* 1866. New York: Dodd, Mead, [1895].

Phelps, Elizabeth Stuart, et al. *Our Famous Women: An Authorized Record of the Lives and Deeds of Distinguished American Women of Our Time.* Hartford, CT: A. D. Worthington, 1886.

Pickens, Donald K. *Eugenics and the Progressives.* Nashville: Vanderbilt University Press, 1968.

Piott, Steven L. *Daily Life in the Progressive Era.* Santa Barbara, CA: Greenwood, 2011.

Plumb, Pat, and Gloria Cowan. "A Developmental Study of Destereotyping and Androgynous Activity Preferences of Tomboys, Nontomboys, and Males." *Sex Roles: A Journal of Research* 10.9–10 (May 1984): 703–12.

Porter, Rev. James. *The Operative's Friend, and Defence; or, Hints to Young Ladies, Who are Dependent on Their Own Exertions.* Boston: Charles H. Peirce, 1850.

Powers, Mrs. S. D. *Behaving; or, Papers on Children's Etiquette.* Boston: D. Lathrop, 1877.

Proehl, Kristen Beth. "Battling Girlhood: Sympathy, Race and the Tomboy Narrative in American Literature." PhD diss., College of William and Mary, 2011.

Qualey, Elizabeth Cummings. *When I Was a Little Girl.* Ossippee, NH: privately printed, 1981.

Radke-Moss, Andrea G. *Bright Epoch: Women and Coeducation in the American West.* Lincoln: University of Nebraska Press, 2008.

Rayne, Mrs. M. L. *Gems of Deportment and Hints of Etiquette: A Manual of Instruction for the Home.* Detroit: Tyler & R. D. S. Tyler, 1881.

Reinier, Jacqueline S. *From Virtue to Character: American Childhood, 1775–1850.* New York: Twayne, 1996.

Reisen, Harriet. *Louisa May Alcott: The Woman behind "Little Women."* New York: Henry Holt, 2009.

Revzin, Rebekah E. "American Girlhood in the Early Twentieth Century: The Ideology of Girl Scout Literature, 1913–1930." *Library Quarterly: Information, Community, Policy* 68.3 (July 1998): 262–75.

Rice, Sarah. *He Included Me: The Autobiography of Sarah Rice.* Edited by Louise Westling. Athens: University of Georgia Press, 1989.

Richardson, Angelique, and Chris Willis, eds. *The New Woman in Fiction and in Fact: Fin-de-Siècle Feminisms.* Basingstoke, UK: Palgrave Macmillan in association with the Institute for English Studies, University of London, 2001.

Riis, Jacob. *How the Other Half Lives.* 1890. Cambridge: Harvard University Press, 1970.

Riley, Glenda. *The Life and Legacy of Annie Oakley.* Norman: University of Oklahoma Press, 1994.

Riney-Kehrberg, Pamela. *The Nature of Childhood: An Environmental History of Growing Up in American since 1865.* Lawrence: University Press of Kansas, 2014.

Roberts, Mary Louise. *Civilization without Sexes: Reconstructing Gender in Postwar France, 1917–1927.* Chicago: University of Chicago Press, 1994.

Rogers, Ethel. *Sebago-Wohelo Camp Fire Girls.* With an introduction by Mrs. Luther Halsey Gulick. Battle Creek, MI: Good Health Publishing, 1915.

Romalov, Nancy Tillman. "Mobile and Modern Heroines: Early Twentieth-Century Girls' Automobile Series." In Inness, *Nancy Drew and Company,* 75–88.

———. "Unearthing the Historical Reader, or, Reading Girls' Reading." In Sullivan and Schurman, *Pioneers, Passionate Ladies, and Private Eyes,* 93–101.

Romesburg, Don. "The Tightrope of Normalcy: Homosexuality, Developmental Citizenship, and American Adolescence, 1890–1940." *Journal of Historical Sociology* 21.4 (December 2008): 417–42.

Roosevelt, Theodore. "The American Boy." In *The Strenuous Life: Essays and Addresses,* 155–64. New York: The Century Co., 1903. Originally published in *St. Nicholas,* May 1900.

———. "Before the Mothers' Congress, Washington, D.C., March 13, 1905." In *A Compilation of the Messages and Speeches of Theodore Roosevelt, 1901–1905,* edited by Alfred Henry Lewis, 576–81. N.p.: Bureau of National Literature and Art, 1906.

———. "The Strenuous Life." In *The Strenuous Life: Essays and Addresses,* 1–22.

Rose, Sonya O. *Limited Livelihoods: Gender and Class in Nineteenth-Century England.* Berkeley: University of California Press, 1992.

Rosenberg, Rosalind. *Beyond Separate Spheres: The Intellectual Roots of Modern Feminism.* New Haven: Yale University Press, 1982.

Rosenthal, Michael. *The Character Factory: Baden-Powell and the Origins of the Boy Scout Movement.* New York: Pantheon, 1986.

Rosenthal, Naomi Braun. *Spinster Tales and Womanly Possibilities.* Albany: State University of New York Press, 2002.

Rosenzweig, Linda W. *The Anchor of My Life: Middle-Class American Mothers and Daughters, 1880–1920.* New York: New York University Press, 1993.

Ross, Dorothy. *G. Stanley Hall: The Psychologist as Prophet.* Chicago: University of Chicago Press, 1972.

Rothschild, Mary Aickin. "To Scout or to Guide? The Girl Scout–Boy Scout Controversy, 1912–1941." *Frontiers: A Journal of Women Studies* 6.3 (Autumn 1981): 115–21.

Rottnek, Matthew, ed. *Sissies and Tomboys: Gender Nonconformity and Homosexual Childhood.* New York: New York University Press, 1999.

Rotundo, E. Anthony. *American Manhood: Transformations in Masculinity from the Revolution to the Modern Era.* New York: Basic Books, 1993.

———. "Boy Culture." In *The Children's Culture Reader,* edited by Henry Jenkins, 337–62. New York: New York University Press, 1998.

Rourke, Constance. *Troupers of the Gold Coast; or, The Rise of Lotta Crabtree.* New York: Harcourt Brace, 1928.

Ruskay, Sophie. *Horsecars and Cobblestones.* New York: Beechhurst Press, 1948.

Russ, Lavinia. "Not to Be Read on Sunday." In Stern, *Critical Essays on Louisa May Alcott,* 99–102.

Rutter, Michael. *Changing Youth in a Changing Society: Patterns of Adolescent Development and Disorder.* Cambridge: Harvard University Press, 1980.

Ryan, Cary, ed. *Louisa May Alcott: Her Girlhood Diary.* Mahwah, NJ: Bridgewater Books, 1993.

Ryan, Mary. *Cradle of the Middle Class: The Family in Oneida County, New York, 1790–1865.* New York: Cambridge University Press, 1981.

Sánchez-Eppler, Karen. *Dependent States: The Child's Part in Nineteenth-Century American Culture.* Chicago: University of Chicago Press, 2005.

Saxton, Martha. *Being Good: Women's Moral Values in Early America.* New York: Hill & Wang, 2003.

Scanlon, Jennifer. *Inarticulate Longings: The Ladies' Home Journal, Gender, and the Promises of Consumer Culture.* New York: Routledge, 1995.

Schmidt, James D. "'Rendered More Useful': Child Labor and Age Consciousness in the Long Nineteenth Century." In Field and Syrett, *Age in America,* 148–65.

Schrum, Kelly. *Some Wore Bobby Sox: The Emergence of Teenage Girls' Culture, 1920–1945.* New York: Palgrave Macmillan, 2004.

Scott, Anne Firor. *Making the Invisible Woman Visible*. Urbana: University of Illinois Press, 1984.

———. *The Southern Lady: From Pedestal to Politics, 1830–1930*. Chicago: University of Chicago Press, 1970.

Scott, Joan Wallach. *The Fantasy of Feminist History*. Durham, NC: Duke University Press, 2011.

Sentilles, Renée M. *Performing Menken: Adah Isaacs Menken and the Birth of American Celebrity*. New York: Cambridge University Press, 2003.

Shackelford, Otis. *Seeking the Best: Dedicated to Negro Youth*. Kansas City, MO: Franklin Hudson, 1909.

Shamir, Milette, and Jennifer Travis, eds. *Boys Don't Cry? Rethinking Narratives of Masculinity and Emotion in the U.S.* New York: Columbia University Press, 2002.

Shi, David E. *The Simple Life: Plain Living and High Thinking in American Culture*. New York: Oxford University Press, 1985.

Sicherman, Barbara. *Well-Read Lives: How Books Inspired a Generation of American Women*. Chapel Hill: University of North Carolina Press, 2010.

Simmons, LaKisha Michelle. *Crescent City Girls: The Lives of Young Black Women in Segregated New Orleans*. Chapel Hill: University of North Carolina Press, 2015.

Simmons, Rachel. *The Curse of the Good Girl: Raising Authentic Girls with Courage and Confidence*. New York: Penguin, 2009.

Sims, Sue, and Hilary Claire. *The Encyclopaedia of Girls' School Stories*. Aldershot, UK: Ashgate, 2000.

Singleton, Ellen. "*The Girls of Central High:* How a Progressive Era Book Series for Girls Furthered the Cause of Female Interschool Sport." *Children's Literature in Education* 37.3 (September 2006): 211–27.

Skemp, Sheila. *Judith Sargent Murray: A Brief Biography with Documents*. Boston: Bedford/St. Martin's, 1998.

Slotkin, Richard. *The Fatal Environment: The Myth of the Frontier in the Age of Industrialization, 1800–1890*. New York: Atheneum, 1985.

Smith, Fanny R. *Manners and Conduct in School and Out, by the Deans of Girls in Chicago High Schools*. Boston: Allyn & Bacon, 1921.

Smith, Lissa, ed. *Nike Is a Goddess: The History of Women in Sports*. New York: Atlantic Monthly Press, 1998.

Smith, Michelle J. *Empire in British Girls' Literature and Culture: Imperial Girls, 1880–1915*. New York: Palgrave Macmillan, 2011.

Smith-Rosenberg, Carroll. "Discourses of Sexuality and Subjectivity: The New Woman, 1870–1936." In Duberman, Vicinus, and Chauncey, *Hidden from History*, 264–80.

———. *Disorderly Conduct: Visions of Gender in Victorian America.* New York: Knopf, 1985.

Sneider, Allison L. *Suffragists in an Imperial Age: U.S. Expansion and the Woman Question, 1870–1929.* New York: Oxford University Press, 2008.

Sochen, June. *The New Woman: Feminism in Greenwich Village, 1910–1920.* New York: Quadrangle, 1972.

Solomon, Barbara Miller. *In the Company of Educated Women: A History of Women and Higher Education in America.* New Haven: Yale University Press, 1985.

Southworth, E. D. E. N. *The Hidden Hand.* 1888. With an introduction by Nina Baym. New York: Oxford University Press, 1997.

Stamp, Shelley. *Movie-Struck Girls: Women and Motion Picture Culture after the Nickelodeon.* Princeton: Princeton University Press, 2000.

Stanley, Autumn. *Raising More Hell and Fewer Dahlias: The Public Life of Charlotte Smith, 1840–1917.* Bethlehem, PA: Lehigh University Press, 2009.

Stavney, Anne. "'Mothers of Tomorrow': The New Negro Renaissance and the Politics of Maternal Representation." *African American Review* 32.4 (Winter 1998): 533–61.

Stern, Madeleine B. *Louisa May Alcott: From Blood and Thunder to Hearth and Home.* Boston: Northeastern University Press, 1998.

———, ed. *Critical Essays on Louisa May Alcott.* Boston: G. K. Hall, 1984.

Stevenson, Michael R., ed. *Gender Roles through the Life Span: A Multidisciplinary Perspective.* Muncie, IN: Ball State University, 1994.

Stewart, Janet. *A Camp Fire Girl's First Council Fire.* Akron, OH: Saalfield, 1914.

———. *A Camp Fire Girl in Summer Camp.* Akron, OH: Saalfield, 1914.

Stockton, Kathryn Bond. *The Queer Child, or Growing Sideways in the Twentieth Century.* Durham, NC: Duke University Press, 2009.

Stoneley, Peter. *Consumerism and American Girls' Literature, 1860–1940.* Cambridge: Cambridge University Press, 2003.

Sullivan, Larry E., and Lydia Cushman Schurman, eds. *Pioneers, Passionate Ladies, and Private Eyes: Dime Novels, Series Books, and Paperbacks.* New York: Haworth Press, 1996.

Susman, Warren. *Culture as History: The Transformation of American Society in the Twentieth Century.* New York: Pantheon, 1984.

Sutherland, Abby A. *Talks with Girls.* Philadelphia: privately printed, 1915.

Swanwick, H. M. *The Future of the Women's Movement.* London: G. Bell, 1913.

Syrett, Nicholas. *American Child Bride: A History of Minors and Marriage in the United States.* Chapel Hill: University of North Carolina Press, 2016.

———. "Statutory Marriage Ages and the Gendered Construction of Adulthood in the Nineteenth Century." In Field and Syrett, *Age in America*, 103–23.

Tebbel, John, and Mary Ellen Zuckerman. *The Magazine in America, 1741–1990.* New York: Oxford University Press, 1991.

Tedesco, Laureen. "Making a Girl into a Scout: Americanizing Scouting for Girls." In Inness, *Delinquents and Debutantes,* 19–39.

Testi, Arnaldo. "The Gender of Reform Politics: Theodore Roosevelt and the Culture of Masculinity." *Journal of American History* 81.4 (March 1995): 1509–33.

Theobald, Marjorie R. *Knowing Women: Origins of Women's Education in Nineteenth-Century Australia.* New York: Cambridge University Press, 1996.

Thomas, Mary Martha. *The New Woman in Alabama: Social Reforms and Suffrage, 1890–1920.* Tuscaloosa: University of Alabama Press, 1992.

Titcomb, Timothy, Esq. [Josiah G. Holland]. *Titcomb's Letters to Young People, Single and Married.* New York: Charles Scribner, 1860.

Tocqueville, Alexis de. *Democracy in America.* Translated by Gerald E. Bevin. New York: Penguin Classics, 2003.

Tompkins, Jane. *West of Everything: The Inner Life of Westerns.* New York: Oxford University Press, 1992.

Townsend, John Rowe. *Written for Children: An Outline of English Children's Literature.* New York: Lothrop, Lee & Shepard, 1967.

Trites, Roberta Seelinger. "'Queer Performances': Lesbian Politics in *Little Women.*" In *"Little Women" and the Feminist Imagination: Criticism, Controversy, Personal Essays,* edited by Janice M. Alberghene and Beverly Lyon Clark, 139–60. New York: Garland, 1999.

———. *Twain, Alcott, and the Birth of the Adolescent Reform Novel.* Iowa City: University of Iowa Press, 2007.

Turner, Frederick Jackson. "The Significance of the Frontier in American History." 1893. In *History, Frontier, and Section: Three Essays,* 59–92. Albuquerque: University of New Mexico Press, 1993.

Turner, Victor. *The Ritual Process: Structure and Anti-Structure.* Ithaca: Cornell University Press, 1969.

Twain, Mark. *The Adventures of Tom Sawyer.* 1876. New York: Oxford University Press, 1996.

Vacca, Carolyn S. *A Reform against Nature: Woman Suffrage and the Rethinking of American Citizenship, 1840–1920.* New York: Peter Lang, 2004.

Vallone, Lynne. *Disciplines of Virtue: Girls' Culture in the Eighteenth and Nineteenth Centuries.* New Haven: Yale University Press, 1995.

Vandercook, Margaret. *The Camp Fire Girls in the Outside World.* Philadelphia: John C. Winston, 1914.

Velazquez, Loreta Janeta. *The Woman in Battle: The Civil War Narrative of Loreta Janeta Velazquez, Cuban Woman and Confederate Soldier.* 1876. Madison: University of Wisconsin Press, 2003.

Vertinsky, Patricia A. *The Eternally Wounded Woman: Women, Doctors, and Exercise in the Late Nineteenth Century.* Urbana: University of Illinois Press, 1989.

Vicinus, Martha. *Independent Women: Work and Community for Single Women, 1850–1920.* Chicago: University of Chicago Press, 1985.

———. *Intimate Friends: Women Who Loved Women, 1778–1928.* Chicago: University of Chicago Press, 2006.

Yonge, Charlotte M. *Womankind.* London: Mozley & Smith, 1876.

Wadsworth, Sarah. *In the Company of Books: Literature and Its "Classes" in Nineteenth-Century America.* Amherst: University of Massachusetts Press, 2006.

Wald, Priscilla. *Constituting Americans: Cultural Anxiety and Narrative Form.* Durham, NC: Duke University Press, 1995.

Warner, Patricia Campbell. *When the Girls Came Out to Play: The Birth of American Sportswear.* Amherst: University of Massachusetts Press, 2006.

Warren, Joyce W. *The American Narcissus: Individualism and Women in Nineteenth-Century American Fiction.* New Brunswick, NJ: Rutgers University Press, 1984.

West, Elliott. "Reconstructing Race." *Western Historical Quarterly* 34.1 (Spring 2003): 6–26.

West, Elliott, and Paula Petrik, eds. *Small Worlds: Children and Adolescents in America, 1850–1950.* Lawrence: University Press of Kansas, 1992.

Westerhoff, John H. *McGuffey and His Readers: Piety, Morality, and Education in Nineteenth-Century America.* Nashville: Abingdon, 1978.

Wheeler, Edward L. *Apollo Bill, the Trail Tornado; or, Rowdy Kate from Right Bower.* New York: Beadle's Half-Dime Library, January 31, 1882.

———. *Bob Woolf, the Border Ruffian; or, The Girl Dead-Shot.* New York: Beadle & Adams, August 6, 1884. Originally published as Woolf, *Hurricane Nell.*

———. *Bonanza Bill, Miner; or, Madam Mystery, the Female Forger: A Tale of the City of San Francisco.* New York: Beadle's Half-Dime Library, December 16, 1879.

———. *Captain Crack-Shot, the Girl Brigand; or, Gipsy Jack from Jimtown.* New York: Beadle's Half-Dime Library, September 20, 1881.

———. *Deadwood Dick on Deck; or, Calamity Jane, the Heroine of Whoop-Up.* New York: Beadle's Half-Dime Library, 1885; June 21, 1899.

———. *Deadwood Dick's Doom; or, Calamity Jane's Last Adventure.* New York: Beadle's Half-Dime Library, June 1881; December 6, 1899.

———. *The Girl Sport.* New York: Beadle & Adams, October 3, 1888.

———. *Hurricane Nell, the Girl Dead-Shot; or, The Queen of the Saddle and Lasso.* New York: Frank Starr's Ten Cent Pocket Library, May 4, 1877.

Wheeler, Marjorie Spruill. *New Women of the New South: The Leaders of the Woman Suffrage Movement in the Southern States.* New York: Oxford University Press, 1993.

Whetham, Catherine Durning. *The Upbringing of Daughters.* London: Longmans, Green: 1917.

White, Barbara A. *Growing Up Female: Adolescent Girlhood in American Fiction.* Westport, CT: Greenwood Press, 1985.

———. "'Our Nig' and the She-Devil: New Information about Harriet Wilson and the 'Bellmont' Family." *American Literature* 65.1 (March 1993): 19–52.

Wiebe, Robert H. *The Search for Order, 1877–1920.* New York: Hill & Wang, 1967.

Wilder, Laura Ingalls. *By the Banks of Plum Creek.* 1937. New York: Harper Collins, 1971.

———. *Little House in the Big Woods.* New York: Harper & Brothers, 1932.

———. *Little Town on the Prairie.* 1941. New York: Harper Collins, 1971.

———. *Pioneer Girl: The Annotated Autobiography.* Edited by Pamela Smith Hill. Pierre: South Dakota Historical Society, 2014.

Willard, Frances Elizabeth. *Glimpses of Fifty Years; The Autobiography of an American Woman.* Chicago: Woman's Temperance Publication Association, 1889.

———. *How I Learned to Ride the Bicycle: Reflections of an Influential 19th Century Woman.* Edited by Carol O'Hare; introduction by Edith Mayo. Sunnyvale, CA: Fair Oaks, 1991.

———. *A Wheel within a Wheel: How I Learned to Ride the Bicycle, with Some Reflections by the Way.* 1895. Bedford, MA: Applewood Books, 1997.

Williams, Fannie Barrier. *The New Woman of Color: The Collected Writings of Fannie Barrier Williams, 1893–1918.* DeKalb: Northern Illinois University Press, 2002.

Willis, Chris. "'Heaven Defend Me from Political or Highly Educated Women!': Packaging the New Woman for Mass Consumption." In Richardson and Willis, *The New Woman in Fiction and in Fact,* 53–65.

Winch, Gil. "What Are Tomboys? Sex Roles, Preferences, Popularity and Self Esteem in Preadolescent Tomboy Girls." PhD diss., Tel Aviv University, 1989.

Woollacott, Angela. *To Try Her Fortune in London: Australian Women, Colonialism, and Modernity.* New York: Oxford University Press, 2001.

Worden, Daniel. *Masculine Style: The American West and Literary Modernism.* New York: Palgrave Macmillan, 2011.

Worster, Donald. *Nature's Economy: A History of Ecological Ideas.* New York: Cambridge University Press, 1994.

————. "New West, True West: Interpreting the Region's History." *Western Historical Quarterly* 18.2 (April 1987): 141–56.

Wright, Nazera Sadiq. *Black Girlhood in the Nineteenth Century.* Urbana: University of Illinois Press, 2016.

Yamaguchi, Lynne, and Karen Barber, eds. *Tomboys! Tales of Dyke Derring-do.* Los Angeles: Alyson, 1995.

Zboray, Ronald J. *A Fictive People: Antebellum Economic Development and the American Reading Public.* New York: Oxford University Press, 1993.

Zelizer, Viviana A. *Pricing the Priceless Child: The Changing Social Value of Children.* Princeton: Princeton University Press, 1985.

Ziff, Larzer. *All-American Boy.* Austin: University of Texas Press, 2012.

Index

Page numbers in *italics* refer to figures.